In the Time of Oil

In the Time of Oil

Piety, Memory, and Social Life in an Omani Town

Mandana E. Limbert

Stanford University Press
Stanford, California

Stanford University Press
Stanford, California

Printed in the United States of America on acid-free, archival-quality paper

Library of Congress Cataloging-in-Publication Data

Limbert, Mandana E.
 In the time of oil : piety, memory, and social life in an Omani town / Mandana E. Limbert.
    p. cm.
 Includes bibliographical references and index.
 ISBN 978-0-8047-5626-6 (cloth : alk. paper) -- ISBN 978-0-8047-5627-3 (pbk. : alk. paper)
 1. Bahla' (Oman)--Social life and customs. 2. Collective memory--Oman--Bahla'. 3. Islam--Oman--Bahla'. 4. Social change--Oman--Bahla'. 5. Petroleum industry and trade--Social aspects--Oman--Bahla'. I. Title. DS247.4.B32L46 2010
 953.53--dc22
                                    201000817

Typeset by Bruce Lundquist in 10/14 Minion Pro

For Dorothy Limbert

Contents

Illustrations

Acknowledgments

This book could never have been written without the generous support of numerous institutions and friends. An IIE Fulbright fellowship as well as a number of fellowships from the University of Michigan (including a Radcliffe-Ramsdale fellowship and a George and Celeste Hourani fellowship) supported the initial research in Oman and London. The City University of New York also supported the research of this book with generous faculty grants for return trips to Oman and London and for my first visits to Zanzibar. The initial writing was made possible by support from the Rackham Graduate School as well as the scholars program at the Institute for Research on Women and Gender at the University of Michigan. A year at the Hagop Kevorkian Center for Near Eastern Studies at New York University, funded by the Ford Foundation, as well as a semester in the Sultan Program at the Center for Middle Eastern studies at the University of California, Berkeley, provided additional and exceptional support for its writing. And, finally, the American Council of Learned Societies—and kindly allowed time away from teaching at CUNY—enabled me to finish the manuscript.

I owe my deepest thanks to the friends and colleagues who encouraged me over the many years it has taken to write this book. In Ann Arbor, Müge Göçek, Alexander Knysh, Bruce Mannheim, and especially Brinkley Messick guided me as I attempted to combine a commitment to Near Eastern studies with my excitement about anthropology. Conversations with Marty Baker, Laurent Dubois, Paul Eiss, Riyad Koya, Esra Özyürek, Penelope Papailias, David Pedersen, and Steven Pierce always encouraged me to think about this project in novel ways. In Florence, I benefited greatly from Ugo Fabietti's expansive knowledge of anthropological theory and history. I owe special gratitude to Setrak Manoukian whose own commitment to critical inquiry challenged me through some of the most trying moments of this project. At New York University, Khaled Fahmy, Michael Gilsenan, and Bernard Haykel welcomed me into their department, allowing me to learn from their experience and subtle questions. At The City University of New York, I feel especially thankful for the support of Beth Baron, who provided the most wonderful example of dedicated scholar, mentor, and friend. Talal Asad, Kevin Birth, John Collins, and Louise Lennihan helped create an inspiring academic setting, both at Queens College and the Graduate Center. And, most recently, at North Carolina State University I have been deeply fortunate to be welcomed and encouraged by the most rigorous community of scholars.

I hope that my gracious and patient hosts in Bahla and Muscat see in these words my most humble gratitude. They, and all the women in the Bahla neighborhood where I lived, not only allowed me into their already full households and busy lives, but also patiently saw that I learn about and enjoy their beautiful town. I must especially thank Sulayman bin Ali al-Harthi, Ahmad bin Sa'id al-Qassabi, Fatima bint Ali al-Qassabi, Gamal bin Nassir al-Qassabi, Nassir bin Ali al-Qassabi, Rayya bint Sa'ad al-Qassabi, Shaykh Sa'id bin Ali al-Qassabi, Shamsa bint Nassir al-Qassabi, and Gaukha bint Muhammad al-Shakayli for their extraordinary kindness and generous help with this project. I feel honored to have met them and hope that I have done some justice to what they tried to teach me. In Muscat, Shaykh Abdulrahman bin Sulayman al-Salimi, Shaykh Zaher bin Abdullah al-Abri, Shaykh Sa'id bin Abdullah al-Harthi, and Shaykh Muhammad bin Sa'id al-Wahaybi continually encouraged my interests in Oman. John Peterson welcomed me into his home where I learned about Omani political history and where I especially enjoyed the respite of his balcony overlooking the beautiful sea. At Sultan Qaboos University, I would like to thank Harrith al-Ghassani and Moosa N. al-Mufraji at the library. The Ministry of Information, the Ministry of Justice, Awqaf and Islamic Affairs (now divided into the Ministry of Justice and Ministry of Awqaf and Religious Affairs), and the Ministry of National Heritage and Culture provided institutional support for my extended stay in Bahla and Muscat.

This book would not have been possible without the help and encouragement of numerous friends who I came to know in Ann Arbor and with whom I was exceedingly lucky to continue sharing my life in New York. Elizabeth Ferry, Laura Kunreuther, Anupama Rao, Lucine Taminian, and David Wood's commitment to intellectual endeavors is always an inspiration. The writing group of Pamila Gupta, Ilana Feldman, Rachel Heiman, Brian Mooney, and Karen Strassler provided not only invaluable feedback, but also the friendship for which I feel I could never adequately thank them. Our weekly meetings on Grand Street, with their intellectual intensity and moral support, remain etched in my memory as an example of the best of academic life. While I have mentioned Laura Kunreuther, Anupama Rao, and Karen Strassler already, my most profound gratitude for their repeated (not to mention brilliant and careful) readings as well as discussions of particular sentences, arrangements, and rewritings warrants repetition. They are, of course, in no way responsible for any mistakes or misrepresentations in this book.

I wish to thank my brother Shervin and my parents, John and Parvaneh Limbert, not only for providing the highest example of respect and analytic honesty, but also for having so kindly refrained from asking too many questions about the completion of the book. I want to express my greatest appreciation for Thomas Ort. This book would never have been finished without him and his diligent readings and suggestions. But, my appreciation for him goes far beyond his help and support for this book. I could have hardly imagined, years ago, when I first went to Bahla, that as I was sending off this manuscript, I would do so with him and with our children. Otto and Sonya deserve their own special acknowledgement as they have thankfully forced me to turn off the computer at the end of their naps and share in their ever-changing joys. As I send off this manuscript, Otto is learning to ride a tricycle and Sonya has begun to screech with delight at playing peek-a-boo. Elizabeth Ferry once told me about her children that she loves them so much, it hurts. I could not fully understand at the time; I do now.

And, finally, I wish to thank the two anonymous reviewers, who provided the most insightful and careful readings that an author could hope for, and of course, my editors at Stanford, Kate Wahl and Joa Suorez, who ever so kindly provided the prodding that I needed.

Notes on Names
and Transliteration

In consultation with the people with whom I worked in Bahla, I have—except for scholars and political leaders—changed most people's names, as well as a few aspects of their personal lives not crucial to the analysis. I have transcribed Arabic terms using standards established by the *International Journal of Middle East Studies*. When transcribing from written texts, I have maintained the spellings and pronunciations of Modern Standard Arabic and, for Arabic words common in English, I have used common English spellings. I have not transliterated people's names or most place names, except neighborhoods and areas in Bahla. When transcribing words and phrases from speech I have used my discretion in suggesting Bahlawi dialect. With the exception of the epigraph in Chapter 1 (which is from an official English translation), all translations from Arabic to English throughout this book are my own.

In the Time of Oil

1 In the Dreamtime of Oil

Wealth and Development in an Anomalous Time

THERE WAS A FURIOUS KNOCK at the door of my room one afternoon. I had been in Bahla, the beautiful walled oasis town in the interior region (*al-Dakhiliya*) of the Sultanate of Oman for just two months, but I already knew that this was highly unusual. I threw on the headscarf that my hosts had asked me to wear while I lived in their home and cautiously opened the door. To my surprise, it was one of my landlord's grown sons. We were both suddenly uncomfortable; until then only my landlady or the young children of the family had come to my door, mostly to let me know that a meal was ready, that visitors had come, or to ask whether I would like to join my landlady as she went to a neighbor's house for a coffee gathering. After an awkward pause, Majid suddenly announced: "Come quickly, there has been a coup d'état!" "What?" I asked, even more surprised. "Yes, a change in government, come downstairs. It's on television," he said urgently. We ran downstairs and joined the rest of the family as they stood silently and solemnly in front of the large television perched on the bookcase of the otherwise furniture-less family room. Indeed, the usual afternoon cartoon programming on Omani national television had been interrupted and a stern-faced newswoman was declaring that the government was about to make an important announcement. But soon it became clear that there had been no coup; rather, the government was issuing a constitution.

I could not stop thinking about Majid's actions. Why had he expected or assumed that there would be a coup? What had motivated him to leave his home in one of the new suburbs of Bahla, jump in his car, and speed over rutted dirt roads to his father's house in the interior of the walled town? There had been no sign of high-level political instability and the Sultan remained, despite

some whispered discontent here and there, immensely popular. And, yet, Majid
was convinced that the interruption that day of state-run television could mean
only one thing: a coup.

Several months later, I gained a better understanding of the anxieties that
had motivated Majid's actions from an unlikely source. A popular Omani soap
opera (*halqa*) aired on state-run television. The soap opera seemed to transfix
the nation, as it did Bahla. Every evening, after dinner and after the evening
prayers, my host family and I would sit on the floor of their family room and
watch the program. Whereas the television often served as a source of background noise rather than the focus of the family's or guests' social activities,
during the airing of this program, as on the day the constitution was proclaimed, it commanded everyone's undivided attention. Even the ubiquitous
tray of coffee and dates, or, my favorite, an evening round of diluted fresh milk
mixed with thyme and finely crushed red peppers, would wait until the program was over. The plot of the soap opera was simple, even pat. But, it clearly
drew on, tapped into, and encapsulated people's deep-seated anxieties about
Oman's unexpected oil wealth, the massive infrastructural, bureaucratic, and
social transformations that this wealth produced, and the anticipation of its
equally sudden decline.

The elevator in a building where a wealthy businessman works breaks down
one day as he enters it. The elevator falls several floors, and the man inside
is seriously injured. He is rushed to a hospital and for several days remains
in a coma while we, the viewers of the soap opera, follow the turmoil of his
family as they grapple with the prospect of losing him, with tensions over his
estate, and with anxiety over a lost briefcase full of money that mysteriously
disappeared from the elevator during the accident. Several days later, the man
awakes from the coma. He has made a complete recovery but for one thing: he
cannot remember anything that has happened in the previous thirty years. In
the episodes that follow, viewers share in the businessman's awe at the incred-
ible buildings and infrastructure that have become modern Oman: highways,
luxury cars, "modern" (non-Qur'anic) schools, the gold doors of a bank, enor-
mous new mosques. Everything is a shock to this man, who has just woken up
and cannot believe that what he sees is real.

As the soap opera made explicit, Bahlawis also described Oman's dramatic
and sudden transformation from isolation and poverty since 1970, the year Sultan Qaboos bin Sa'id al-Bu Sa'id ousted his father in a palace coup d'état, as a
"reawakening." They also called it "hard to believe" (*ṣaʿb al-taṣdīq*). Are all the

changes since oil began to be commercially exported in 1967 and since Qaboos
bin Saʻid al-Bu Saʻid became Sultan real? Or is it a dream? Will all the apparent
wealth and infrastructural glamour disappear, like the briefcase, just as mysteriously and suddenly as it appeared? After all, Oman's oil supplies are, as the
state continually reminds its citizens, limited. Indeed, could the entire structure
of everyday life, including the government, suddenly change again as well? By
anticipating a coup and pre-empting the future, Majid had merely drawn a les-
son from the past and linked Oman's political fate to that of its oil. And, by
standing at that crucial moment shoulder-to-shoulder with his father, a man
distinctly of an older generation, Majid was affirming his relationship to locality and to the past of interior Oman.

Over the year and a half between 1996 and 1997 that I spent in Bahla participating in everyday neighborly life, I came to see that Oman's post-1970 era
of political stability, oil wealth, prosperity, and modernity—no matter how
tenuous, unevenly distributed, or experienced as successful or failed—was
also often understood as *anomalous*. It was thought of as a time "in between"
times of political instability and poverty, of the past and quite possibly of the
future too. This book explores how Bahlawis inhabited and understood Oman's
dramatic oil-produced transformations. It examines how the past was evoked,
experienced, and managed in the present, and how the present was haunted
by the future.[1] The book focuses on key institutions, infrastructures, and social practices that Bahlawis described to me as having changed since the early
1970s: the systems of governance and order in Bahla, the availability of leisure time and women's practices of sociality, the implementation of mass state
schooling, the introduction of piped water, and, finally, the breaking of connections with East Africa. Tensions about sociality and community more broadly, I
argue, were products not only of displeasure with current social and economic
conditions, but also of contested understandings of the past and uncertain expectations of the future.

Citizens, development policies, and states often produce and assume
multiple and at times contradictory temporalities, sometimes tied to the exploitation of natural resources, often linked to shifts in rule, and, of course,
frequently presumed to follow teleologies of progress and modernization.
However, while most states, and especially authoritarian ones, presume to
hold the keys to a deferred utopian future (Eiss 2002), other states and their
development discourses seem to encourage mysteries, miracles, surprises, and
deferred dystopias. This is the case of Oman. In part because the state has

encouraged such discourses, many Omanis also wonder if they might "wake up" one day only to discover that the years of prosperity since the 1970 coup have been a dream.

The Sultanate of Oman and the Miracle of the Renaissance

> *The success that has been achieved in Oman during the years of the renaissance amounts to a miracle. It is the achievement of the leader, and his people guided by the wisdom and determination of His Majesty Sultan Qaboos bin Said.*
> Introduction, Royal Speeches of H.M. Sultan Qaboos bin Said, 1970–1995

Located on the southeastern edge of the Arabian Peninsula, Oman lies between Saudi Arabia to its west, Yemen to its south, the United Arab Emirates to its northwest, and the Arabian Sea to its east.

Today, this territory is known as the Sultanate of Oman, but it only came to be known as such after the 1970 coup d'état that brought Sultan Qaboos bin Sa'id al-Bu Sa'id to power.[2] Until the mid-1950s, what is now known as the "interior region" (al-Dakhiliya), where the town of Bahla is located, was a quasi-independent theocratic state, the Imamate of Oman, based on Ibadi doctrine, a third branch of Islam after Sunnism and Shi'ism.[3] The coastal regions, in contrast, were collectively known as the Sultanate of Muscat.[4] In the 1950s, when Sultan Sa'id bin Taymur al-Bu Sa'id (r. 1932–1970), with support from the British military, gained control of Imamate villages and towns in the interior, including Bahla, the newly unified territory came to be known as the Sultanate of Muscat *and* Oman.[5] Then, in 1970, when Sultan Qaboos bin Sa'id al-Bu Sa'id overthrew his father, Sultan Sa'id bin Taymur, in a nearly bloodless coup d'état, the name of the unified territory changed again, this time to the Sultanate of Oman.[6]

Despite the change in name suggesting a fully unified state, the sense that the historic Imamate territory is unique and distinct from the coast continues to have significant social and political import. Indeed, various modes of the state's self-representation (such as textbooks, monuments, and national histories) have encouraged the view that the interior region is unique for being the site of the nation's special religious heritage, solidifying for those in al-Dakhiliya and beyond a sense that theocratic traditions remain particularly important there. Many elderly people I knew in Bahla even continued to refer to the interior region of al-Dakhiliya as Oman and to the coastal region surrounding the capital as Muscat.

The name of the territory is by no means the only thing that changed in the years immediately following the 1970 coup d'état. The infrastructural transformation in the first decade after the coup was especially dramatic. The new state constructed schools, hospitals, roads, and a modern state bureaucracy, first in the capital area and then in the outlying regions.[7] According to commonly cited statistics, while in 1970 there were three "Western" (that is, non-Qur'anic) schools in Oman, by 1980 there were 363 such schools; while in 1970 there was

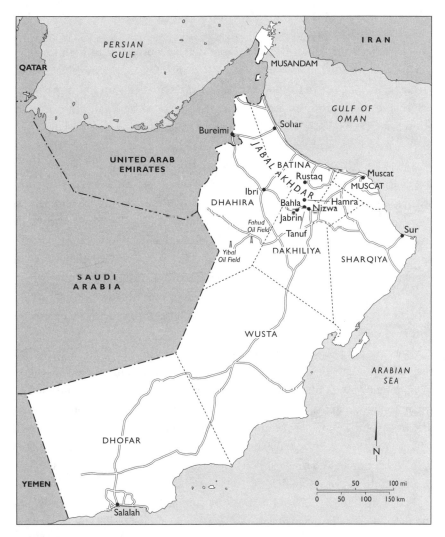

Figure 1.1 Map of Oman

one hospital, by 1980 there were 28; and while in 1970 there were six kilometers of asphalt roads, by 1980 there were 12,000.[8] Within ten years, Oman went from being one of the most isolated states in the world (in league with Albania, Nepal, or North Korea at various moments in the twentieth century) to being an internationally recognized and economically interconnected petro-state. By 1980, Oman ceased to be described by most European and American journalists or visitors as "medieval," where such amenities as radios and sunglasses were banned, where the "state" was comprised primarily of individual advisors rather than a bureaucracy, and where basic modern infrastructure was all but nonexistent. All that had changed.

The time from Sultan Qaboos's coup d'état in July 1970 to the present is officially known as the *al-nahḍa*,[9] translated into English as "renaissance" or "awakening." The use of the notion of *al-nahḍa* to mark a shift in history is not original to the Qaboos era or to Oman.[10] Influenced by Salafiya movements elsewhere in the Middle East,[11] the notion of an "awakening" was also deployed in the nineteenth century by Ibadis in Oman, as well as in North Africa and Zanzibar (Hoffman 2004; Wilkinson 1987: 152–153). The Ibadi awakening of the nineteenth century, however, unlike that of the late twentieth century, was specifically one of religious revival aimed at synthesizing and explaining features of Ibadism for both Ibadis and non-Ibadis (Wilkinson 1987).[12] And, while in other places in the Arab world in the second half of the twentieth century eras referred to as *al-nahḍa* tend to be associated with literary and intellectual revival, the contemporary Omani renaissance tends to be linked to industriousness, cosmopolitanism, piety, and seriousness of purpose, an association that nicely overlaps with development discourses that emphasize private enterprise and hard work.

But *how* did Oman awake? By what cause and to what effect? Oman's late twentieth-century renaissance, its literal rebirth or awakening from the "coma" of its recent past, is often officially said to have been spurred, as indicated in the introduction to the Royal Speeches, almost miraculously, by Sultan Qaboos. The magic of the Omani state is manifest not simply in the production of wealth without the labor required to extract oil from the earth (as in Fernando Coronil's description of Venezuela [1997]), but also in that wealth seems to have been produced almost without oil itself. The "anti-politics of development discourse" (J. Ferguson 1990) in Oman functions by emphasizing the miraculous rule of the Sultan and a reawakened spirit of industriousness as well as by de-emphasizing the history of oil and oil-related war in the creation of the unified state.

Downplaying the role of oil in the most recent "renaissance" belies its centrality in the establishment of modern Oman.[13] Indeed, the unified state that is now known as Oman experienced three wars between the mid-1950s and 1970s, all of which were instigated by oil exploration. These determined the territorial boundaries of the contemporary state and shaped the nature of the new political regime.[14] The first war (1952–1954) was a border conflict with Saudi Arabia over the oasis town of Bureimi. Whereas Saudi Arabia was supported by the American oil company Aramco, the Sultanate of Muscat (in alliance with the Emirate of Abu Dhabi) drew support from Britain. Despite well-known, deep theological tensions between Ibadis and Wahhabis (the particular approach to Islam propagated by the Saudi state), Saudi Arabia was able to motivate Imamate subjects, including those from Bahla, to fight against the Sultanate in this conflict.

The second war (1954–1959) affected Bahla most directly, pitting the coastal Sultanate against the Imamate territories as the Sultan and oil companies aimed to gain access to potential oil fields in what is now al-Dakhiliya. Many Bahlawis fought in support of the Imamate against the British-backed army of the Sultan, which had been sent to "protect" oil exploration teams. When the fighting abated after 1955 and then shifted to a guerilla war in the Jebel Akhdar mountains in 1957, many Bahlawis joined that movement as well.[15] British planes bombed the Bahla fort in 1957 as Imamate forces had retaken the town before moving to the mountains. Guerilla fighting continued until 1959, when the Imamate was finally defeated.

The third war began in 1963 as a Marxist rebellion in the southern Dhofar region (touched off by the assassination of the guard of a British oil engineer) but by 1970 had spread north to the more established oil regions. It was during this conflict, on July 23, 1970, that a young Qaboos bin Sa'id al-Bu Sa'id overthrew his father as Sultan of Muscat and Oman.[16] The war officially ended in 1975 with the defeat of the insurgency.

Downplaying oil as a source of the modern Omani state's establishment also produces a paradox. While oil is conspicuously, though not surprisingly, tangential to narratives about the founding and development of the nation, oil (and, in particular a preoccupation with its limits) is central to expectations of Oman's future. Over and over during my time in Oman, people would tell me that the country had twenty years of oil reserves remaining, a time frame, as I illustrate in Chapter 7, that the official press has also projected. Such projections have been made since the early 1970s, but crucially, the horizon of the exhaustion of the country's oil supply keeps extending into the future. Even the US Department of Energy in 2005 predicted that Oman had about twenty years of oil remaining (US Energy Information Administration 2005).

To be sure, the uncertainty surrounding Oman's future is shaped not only by national proclamations about limited oil supplies, but also by concern about rule. It is generally presumed that Sultan Qaboos has no heir, although, as I also discuss in Chapter 7, rumors about mysterious sons persist. After a nearly fatal car accident in 1995, discussions about possible successors became particularly urgent. It was in the following year that the state issued its constitution, which directly addressed the question of succession. Rather than quelling uncertainty, however, the constitution spawned additional questions and mysteries. Although the document declares that the Sultan has selected a successor, his name is written and sealed in a secret envelope to be opened only upon His Majesty's demise.

Questions about Oman's future, furthermore, are inflected by religion, perhaps nowhere more strongly than in the interior region. Interior Oman's past form of theocratic government, based on Ibadism, remains an imagined and, in some cases, hoped for and redemptive, future. Unlike in Shi'ism and Sunnism, in Ibadi political philosophy, the leader of the Muslim community need not be either a direct descendant or a member of the tribe (the Quraysh) of the Prophet Muhammad, opening the way to a more profane and accessible form of religious governance. Similarly, in Ibadism the theocratic state is understood to exist in one of four "ways of religion" (*masālik al-dīn*) and can, depending on particular political and religious contexts, shift from one to the other, making transition into and out of theocratic rule relatively more available than in most interpretations of Shi'ism and Sunnism.[17] Therefore, while recent revivalist discourses in Oman intersect with transnational Islamist movements that demand social piety and call for the establishment of an Islamic state, the language of theocratic revival in Oman more often draws from people's memories and understandings of local history and political philosophy. Given that the last Ibadi Imamate lasted from 1913 to 1955, it remains part of the living memory of older Omanis. At the beginning of 2005, thirty-one Omanis were arrested, convicted, and then pardoned for plotting to reinstall the Ibadi Imamate state.[18]

The era of Oman's "renaissance," defined by dramatic infrastructural development, oil wealth, and modern modes of governance has indeed been remarkable. It has also been, however, an uncertain time, marked by miraculous beginnings and a preoccupation with a future that may look very different from the present. The exploration of everyday understandings and experiences of these dramatic changes is the subject of this book.

The Problem of Time

In an interview with the Associated Press in 1985 about the then current state of affairs in Oman, the minister of education, Yahya bin Mahfoudh al-Mantheri, repeated what I often heard while I was in Oman over ten years later: "The problem is a problem of time" (*al-mas'ala mas'alat al-waqt*). For al-Mantheri, as for many others, this "problem of time" referred both to the fast pace of Oman's transformation since 1970 and to the eventual end of oil. The minister continued: "Oman in 1970 was nothing. As we say in Oman, we are running, not walking, to get our infrastructure built."[19] The hurry for al-Mantheri and others was not only that Oman needed "to catch up" with the rest of the world, but also that at some point in the relatively near future oil reserves would be depleted. Indeed, the title of the article was: "Oman Rushing into Modern Times before Oil Money Runs Out." The nation's basic infrastructure therefore needed to be built before this could happen. The present for al-Mantheri was thus sandwiched between the rapidity of change from the past and the threat of the depletion of oil in the future. The future, moreover, was expected both to be an end—to the availability of capital that enabled massive infrastructural projects—and to be unknowable—what life might be like under such conditions was impossible to predict. The present was therefore an anomalous time, set between eras of no oil, and, thus, probable poverty, when the infrastructure of contemporary Oman either did not exist or could no longer be built. As such, Oman's present was not a step along a trajectory of infinite progress, but an interlude, surprisingly and perhaps miraculously prosperous.

Considering the present to be an interlude (and a surprising one at that) in history rather than a step along a trajectory of progress revises some generally accepted understandings of development discourses and developmentalist states. Literature on development discourses has highlighted the "myth of permanence" associated with urbanization, modernization theory, and development models in general (J. Ferguson 1999), as well as the ways life-cycle stages—birth and maturity—have served as metonyms for national development, both relegating the developing world to the status of the "immature" (Gupta 1998) and setting the world along a linear teleology (Ludden 1992; Manzo 1991). While the problem of time is clearly tied to development discourses in Oman too, Oman presents a case in which there is no myth of permanence—and no linear teleology—in the first place. The case of Oman likewise suggests that if life-cycle stages serve as metonyms for national trajectories, then the workings not only of birth and maturation but also of death need to be considered. It is precisely the impermanence of oil—its finiteness—that emerges as central to both official declarations about Oman's future and to personal expectations about it. Thus, in contrast to the optimism of most nationalist and developmentalist discourses, apprehension and the unknowable mark expectations of Oman's future.[20]

How then do we understand the effects and implications of a future-oriented sensibility that is pessimistic, redemptive (in the sense of a possible return to theocratic rule), or accepting of the unknowability of the future? And, what is at stake in the perpetual twenty-year temporal deferral and the fixation on this figure?[21] The expectation of an oil (and Sultan)-less future could be interpreted as apocalyptic (Baudrillard 1994; Harding and Stewart 1999), as producing a "state of emergency" (Berlant 1996), as entangled in disciplinary technologies and economic conditions that tame chance (Hacking 1990) and manage risk (Mason 2007), or as a future-oriented antonym of the experiential and psychological conditions of "hope" (Crapanzano 2003; Miyazaki 2003, 2006). But it can also be a distinct form of development temporality, one in which "modernity" becomes less an irrevocable and final stage in a teleology of development than a contingent, surprising, and bounded era.

The importance of miracles, surprises, and uncertainties renders the Omani form of development temporality, distinct from other forms of "modern" temporality. Reinhart Koselleck, for one, has emphasized a shift, especially since the eighteenth century, in historical consciousness from a kind of messianic temporality to a linear and progressive one. For Koselleck, messianic history involves a certainty: salvation. Messianic time differs from "modern time" in that with modern time the future "is thought to be open and without boundaries. The vision of last things or the theory of the return of all things has been radically pushed aside by the venture of opening up a new future: a future which, in the emphatic sense of the notion, is totally different from all that passed before" (2002: 120). Koselleck further associates this sense of a "new future" with the notion of progress, whereby the "horizon of sameness" becomes open and whereby progress can happen, when there is planning. Planning makes the openness of the future appear controllable by humans, but also teleological in the developmentalist sense.

This does not fully describe the processes at work in Oman. Or, rather, these processes are intertwined with other temporal (and political) sensibilities, those shaped by an oil industry that predicts limited oil reserves, by questions about hereditary rule, by memories of local history that recognize the possibility of the establishment of a theocratic state, and by understandings of God whose powers include his unique hold on the future. Instead of being set within a myth of permanence or conceived as a step in an "open" teleology of progress, Oman's present can be thought of as a "dreamtime,"[22] a time in between the "realities" of poverty. It is a time of great possibility, when surprise and surreal transformation are the rule rather than the exception. Dreams may be expressions of unconscious desires and fears, as the psychoanalytic tradition emphasizes, but they are also transitory and fleeting, unstable and always about to end. One eventually wakes up from a dream and the surreal qualities of the dream are replaced by the (harsh) realities of life.

To be sure, for some philosophers of modernity such as Walter Benjamin (1969, 1983, 1986), the post-dream awakened state is a revolutionary moment where the truths of inequality are finally laid bare. In the Omani dreamtime there is no Marxian revolutionary teleology, though the future establishment of a theocracy serves, for some, as a form of redemption. Awakening from the dream of unexpected prosperity is an entrance into "reality," but not one in which revolution ushers in an era of hoped-for equality. It should also be noted, however, that a reestablished theocratic state, in the Omani context, is a far cry from the notion of "messianic time" as described by Koselleck, not to mention Benjamin. A theocracy in the Omani context would be a much more mundane affair, headed by a scholar with purely human qualities who would be elected by a council of male elders.

While the future and its uncertainties haunt Oman's present, producing an uncanny and disquieting sense of potential return, the past, in multiple forms, is omnipresent too. The businessman in the television soap opera, for example, not only had to adapt to a suddenly changed world, but he also continued to embody the past in ways that were anachronistic in the present, making for both some light comedy and criticism of contemporary values. Indeed, as Bahlawis grappled with and quickly made banal the novelties of oil-enabled development, the past seemed everywhere, and often flattened into a uniform pre-1970 time: "the past."

In Bahla, "the past" was evident in official monuments and histories, in bodily habits that no longer seemed necessary and yet were practiced as if they were, in conscious attempts to invigorate an idealized theocratic religiosity, in nostalgic actions and comments about a simpler and more respectful age, in the management of objects that retained their symbolic significance despite a vastly altered social and economic environment, and in attempts to skirt (past) social inequalities in a new social world where the same distinctions and hierarchies were supposed to not matter, or at least not be acknowledged. Such memories and views of the past were clearly "moral practices" (Lambek 1996; vom Bruck 2005) and often tied to material culture (Serematakis 1994). The past was evident too in family genealogies, in ghosts, in the names of property and documents of inheritance, as well as in the genealogical histories of practices and objects.

While the modern Omani state, like most modern nation-states, has a vested interest in promoting particular representations of the past that support its national image, Bahlawis drew in numerous ways on local histories and memories (as well as these national representations) to understand past events, chronologies, and activities in their town and newly formed country. Sometimes personal pasts disrupted official (national or local) narratives; other times they were clearly shaped by them.[23] This book begins with the premise that multiple processes of interpreting and enacting the past were at work in Bahla, and were also influenced by the context as well as the form or genre (Papailias 2005) through which such remembering happened. Indeed, to limit the analysis to one perspective would hardly do justice to the rich details of the past or to the forms—discursive, embodied, and material—through which Bahlawis experienced their dramatically transformed world.

Of Ties and Time

How, then, did Bahlawis experience Oman's rapid transformation? How did they make sense of the dramatic changes in their town? And, how did their views about the past shape their social relationships and senses of belonging? Not surprisingly, Bahlawis often explicitly compared, for better or worse depending on their religio-political views, their current lives with the past.[24] At the heart of these comparisons were concerns about proper personal behavior and proper society: How should people embody and practice pious community or social life? Majid's return to the home of his father, a highly respected shaykhly man who (like most Bahlawis) had supported the Imamate in the 1950s, signaled his desire to stand with the previous generation and possibly to be part of the decision-making process for the community should it have become necessary. Similarly, much of the plot of the television soap opera re-volved around the degraded values of contemporary life; the good of the family had been forsaken by individual greed. But such loyalties to locality and explicit moral comparisons were not the only ways that the past revealed itself.

Almost every aspect of everyday life was affected by this temporal con-sciousness and the material conditions of oil wealth. Not long after I arrived in Bahla to live with the wonderful family who, most generously, agreed to rent me a room in their home and to allow me to spend the next year and a half participating in their everyday lives, I began to get a sense of the complexities of Oman's dramatic transformation. Indeed, on the morning after I arrived, once I had unpacked my suitcase, set up my computer on the desk in my room, and shared my first meals with my landlady Zaynab (it would take another month before I would join the rest of the family for meals, because, I later learned, my landlord believed that I—as a "respectable" woman—would feel more comfort-able eating separately), Zaynab asked whether I would be interested in joining her to visit her neighbors. Not exactly sure what I was supposed to do on my first official day of fieldwork, I happily agreed.

Zaynab picked up a thermos of coffee and a container of dates and I fol-lowed her out of the house. We opened the metal gate in front of her home, stepped over the irrigation canal that ran outside, and turned left down the dirt road. Though the palm trees gave the road some shade, the beating sun made the short walk excruciatingly hot. When we arrived at a neighbor's house, four other women were already there. I soon learned that the women were proxi-mate neighbors and some were relatives. After I introduced myself and after Zaynab explained that I was "American," the women began what I soon learned was their daily routine of sharing coffee and dates.

My first thought was that I was participating in an old social custom. It was the content of the conversations of these gatherings that I thought would be interesting and, indeed, it often was. The women discussed issues and events in town as far-ranging as the price of goods, someone's impending marriage, their own health, rumors of sorcery (sihr), new infrastructure projects, and govern-ment policies pertaining to education and property. However, it soon became clear to me that even more than the content, it was the form of the gathering itself (the exchange of coffee and dates, the walks through town), as well as the debates surrounding it, that were more revealing about the complex issues at stake in the changes in their town. What appeared at first glance to be a deeply "traditional" practice, made almost banal through its daily repetition, I soon came to understand, was considered rather new and served as a nexus around which the tensions emerging from Oman's sudden wealth often focused.[25]

I was often told that very few women enjoyed such leisure time in the past when agricultural labor was required of them. Before oil wealth shifted the town's economy away from agriculture and, as in other oil-wealthy states, towards government jobs and the local market, I was told, women spent most mornings in the fields collecting alfalfa for their livestock and firewood for cooking. It was, however, not simply the availability of "leisure" time that was new. The essential components of the visiting were new too. Until the early 1970s, coffee was scarce, thermoses nonexistent, and the most popular types of dates, now relatively common, only available to a few families. Nevertheless, as I discuss in Chapter 3, the long histories and symbolic meanings of these luxuries continued to affect how people understood and practiced their exchange, even in the transformed context.

In addition, the town's new spatial order rearranged women's visiting patterns. While quarters and neighborhoods had previously been maintained by gates and walls, by the late 1990s, neighborhood boundaries were marked by asphalt roads and clusters of homes that had become established when families moved out of the old walled neighborhoods to larger plots of land in their former fields (not to mention to the new suburbs on the outskirts of town). While some neighborly groups were composed primarily of kin, many were not, and many included women of different social and economic statuses.

Notions and assumptions about sociality, individual piety, and religiosity were shifting as well. While older Bahlawis considered neighborly sociality a condition of being a proper and pious person, I quickly learned that some younger Bahlawis considered this visiting to be an impediment to human responsibilities to God. Being social, younger Bahlawis argued, was a distraction from the constant remembering of God that was incumbent on pious individuals.[26] Thus, rather than considering this sociality to be "proper" (that is, religiously sanctioned), younger Bahlawis argued that it was useless (*ghayr nafa'a*), a waste of time, and thus a sin.[27] While visiting was the embodiment of proper behavior for older Bahlawis, some younger Bahlawis believed that women, if they must gather (individual piety at home was considered preferable), should primarily focus on the explicit discussion of what they took to be "religious" matters. In contrast, in defense of their practices and drawing from both religious and developmentalist discourses of productivity, older women, including Zaynab, would often say of their visiting, "you see, this is my work (*shughlí*)."

Thus, a social practice that appeared at first deeply "traditional" and a means for understanding other issues in town, was itself tied to historical trajectories and revealed contemporary anxieties about usefulness, productivity, homo-social intimacy, and the meaning of proper piety.

Conflicting views about sociality emerged in Bahla in part because many young people were divided in their attitudes towards the previous generations. On the one hand, those of the new era (who came of age after the 1970s) admired their parents and grandparents because these older generations had lived under and supported a theocratic regime. It goes without saying that there was no unitary post-1970 generation, just as there was no unitary pre-1970 generation. And yet, the break in Omani history represented by the year 1970 continually reinforced the sense of a generational divide and gave it ethnographic salience (Rofel 1999; Winegar 2006). On the other hand, some of the older generations' practices were deemed to be inappropriate by members of the younger generations. Indeed, while I was conducting research, some Bahlawis celebrated Oman's post-1970 modernity as "moving forward," away from improper traditional activities (Deeb 2006).

Certainly, many of these conflicts in Bahla hinged, as they do elsewhere, on gender. Views about women's "traditions" in particular, as Partha Chatterjee (1989) influentially argued for Indian nationalists, served as a way for some Bahlawis to claim authentic, spiritual values, while simultaneously enabling them to embrace technological and infrastructural modernity. In Bahla, however, not all (or even most) "women's practices" were remembered nostalgically or considered authentic and pure, as the concern about daily neighborhood visits makes clear.

This book's attention to practices of visiting and neighborliness emphasizes, therefore, the ways that sociality is historically contingent and tied to political-economic conditions as well as to notions of proper womanhood and religion.[28] The deep concern with proper sociality exposes an uneasy relationship to Oman's contemporary conditions. In Bahla, sociality was an object of political concern and economic change as well as of religious and national discourses. It was shaped by the material effects, regulatory forces, and ideological powers of shifting infrastructural conditions and bureaucratic practices as well as by beliefs about national character, bodily comportment, and religio-legal responsibilities and obligations. It was a product of concerns for an ethic of work, productivity, and piety. And, sociality in turn helped shape what it meant to be female, from the roles expected of married, divorced, or widowed women to the forms of comportment they were to embody. Zaynab's daily visits with her neighbors were thus hardly the simple acts of social custom that I first believed them to be.

And, indeed, conflicting views about Zaynab's sociality underscored other concerns about what constituted proper community, whether it be a community of believers, a community of the nation of "Omanis" (within the nation-state or beyond), or a community of the town or neighborhood. This book therefore explores these layers of community—the ties—as they are shaped by the temporal uncertainties—the time—of the Omani oil-state.

Chapter Summaries

The chapters of this book examine the administrative, infrastructural, and social features that Bahlawis told me had most changed since the early 1970s: its built environment and related system of rule, social life, education, water, and connections with East Africa. In each, I explore how different generations of Bahlawis understood and experienced these changes, from nostalgia and gratitude to less conscious habits that persisted, somewhat anachronistically, into the present. I also explore their complex and varied relations to "the past." The past in Oman assumed particular salience not simply because of the obvious differences from the present or because of questions surrounding the state's development policies, but also because many people considered the present to be an interlude, an anomalous time between a past of poverty and theocratic rule and a future that might look similar. These tensions animate the social relations as well as understandings of built environment and political order examined in the text. The book is divided into six ethnographic chapters.

Chapter 2 introduces the town of Bahla through its changing built environment and system of rule. By transforming the fort into a national heritage museum, allowing the outer walls to become ruins, remaking the spatial division of the town, and attempting to reorganize the neighborhoods into coherent administrative units, the new political order helped shape conflicting perceptions and experiences of the town. Such perceptions were not only fraught with tensions about the town's moral bearings, but also illustrated shifting understandings of history and expectations of proper governance as they transformed from the personal to the grandiose and from the intimate to the bureaucratic.

Chapter 3 analyzes everyday sociality and especially women's highly organized visiting practices. Though often described as a key component of good personhood, sociality also became the focus of debate about proper and pious activity, particularly among those who argued that it was a new practice available only with the advent of the oil economy and the demise of subsistence agriculture. Such views about sociality were evident in everyday comments as well as in the poetic associations and histories of the objects exchanged during visits: coffee, dates, and words. As Bahlawis compared the past and the present through such tropes as luxury and leisure, life and survival, human connection and unnecessary verbosity, everyday sociality (and women's sociality in particular) came to represent both the ease and the excesses of the oil era.

The relationship of sociality and proper piety is explored more fully in Chapter 4. Through an examination of a young women's study group, this chapter focuses on the introduction of modern mass education in Oman, growing concerns about religious knowledge, and the emergence of new forms of sociality and religiosity. Criticizing the new school system and harkening back to what they believed to be traditions of Ibadi scholarly life, the study group aimed to teach and discuss the Qur'an, prophetic traditions, and Ibadi doctrine. The young women also opposed their mothers' and grandmothers' visiting practices, complaining that older women engaged in idle talk rather than the pursuit of knowledge. In their critique of everyday sociality, the young women were fundamentally redefining both what it meant to be good women and religion itself. For them, in contrast to their mothers' generation, religion meant consistent and individualized focus on God.

While Chapters 2, 3, and 4 focus on the changing structures of rule, sociality, and education, Chapter 5 examines the effects of shifts at the level of basic infrastructure. The introduction of piped water, along with new systems of water ownership and distribution, also generated concerns and conflicts about history, community, and piety. Just as the forms, methods, and content of modern schools shaped the critique of them, the introduction of piped water was also accompanied by tensions over proper and pious access and distribution as well as nostalgia for local engineering and technology. The chapter analyzes one man's quest to rebuild an old-style well, a family's generational disagreements over how to share drinking water with neighbors, and a college-aged woman's distress at her realization that older women used to bathe together. The parallels and differences between oil and water were certainly not lost on Bahlawis either, as people's concern about the value and potential limits of these natural resources made evident.

Chapter 6 traces the history of Oman's long-standing ties to East Africa (Zanzibar in particular) as well as the severing of these connections in the twentieth century and Oman's subsequent reorientation as an Arab state. Through a comparison of two women's personal memories, this chapter explores both how the shift towards emphasizing Oman's Arabness has affected forms of hierarchy in Bahla from "caste" to "race" and how the women's personal memories are punctuated by accounts of sociality and neighborliness. Both women also shared the view that Zanzibar, and East Africa more generally, was a place of wealth when they were young, unlike Bahla. Indeed, to one woman, the strange twist of fate that made Oman and Bahla wealthy (and East Africa poor) was evidence of the unpredictability of time and history.

The final chapter expands this discussion of the uncertainty of Oman's future through an examination of official oil projections since 1970 and the constant anticipation of oil's depletion in twenty years—an ever-deferred horizon. It addresses Bahlawi reluctance to make claims about the future ("for only God knows") and the ways that such reluctance has become more prominent in light of predictions about Oman's oil supply and concerns about succession. Limited oil supplies, a mortal Sultan, and an understanding that the future is unknowable to humans combine to create a view of the future that is not linear and a sense of the present as profoundly anomalous.

2 Now, the Police Only Drive

Remembering Rule and Disorder in Bahla

ON HIS TRIP TO BAHLA IN 1885, the British political agent to Muscat, Lieutenant-Colonel Samuel Miles records:

> The first view [of Bahla] presents a long white wall with bastions at intervals enclosing a large extent of cultivated ground with a huge white fort and lofty tower standing on an eminence in the centre, picturesquely overlooking and commanding the town beneath. Its appearance indeed is more striking than that of any other town I have seen in Oman. (IOR, R/15/6/18)

The spectacular whiteness of Bahla's twelve kilometer wall and dramatic fort have long since disappeared,[1] but while I was in Bahla, the fort was being rebuilt with hand-molded mud bricks and covered in beige plaster. The beige plaster, and the reconstructions more generally, although not as striking as the gypsum-covered walls and fort that Miles described and photographed, nevertheless convey, to a vastly different audience of foreign tourists and Omani school children, a sense of Oman's austere and grand past.[2] For many Bahlawis, the fort no longer "overlooked" or "commanded" the town beneath, or, at least, not as it once did. Rather, it was in the process of being transformed from political and military center to national heritage museum.

This chapter examines the ways that different generations of Bahlawis understood, remembered, and experienced the main features of Bahla's built environment: the fort, the wall, the upper and lower division of the town, and its neighborhoods. In particular, I explore how Bahlawis understood these structures as integral to the town's mechanisms and practices of governance, order, and sociality. No longer inhabited by governors and their entourages, the fort came to be seen as either "empty" or as emblematic of Oman's grand, "ancient" history, depending on generational perspective. Bahla's twelve-kilometer wall was, until the late twentieth century, the town's most important self-defining structural feature. By the late 1990s, however, sections had either been left to ruin or had been destroyed to make way for a highway that cut through the middle of town. Nevertheless, for some mostly older Bahlawis, the wall still evoked the sense of a protective boundary beyond which only marginal activity took place and chaos might rein. The division of the town into upper and lower halves and its neighborhood organization were also in the process of being re-configured, giving rise to new forms of local management and new expectations about proper social conduct. People's comparisons with previous systems of rule, order, and governance pervaded their understandings of the current, and possibly future, conditions of the town.

If the relationship between the built environment, order, and piety has long been the subject of historical research in Middle East Studies, then the notion of "the Islamic city" has been one of its key features.[3] Although these debates no longer have the academic purchase they once did, the connections between the built environment, order, and piety mattered intensely for most people I knew in Bahla. Still, Bahla can hardly be compared to the "great" Islamic cities described either in the classic Orientalist texts or even in later works, such as Janet Abu-Lughod's pioneering revision (1987).

Bahla is by no means a large cosmopolitan city like Cairo, Fez, or Damascus. Until the early 1970s, when the population was about eight thousand, the only non-Ibadis living in Bahla were Sunnis, mostly women who had married Bahlawi men. The main social division was not between Muslims and people of other religions, but between "Arabs" and "servants" (akhdām), a hierarchical social and economic division between patrilineal descendants of "free" Arabs and patrilineal descendants of clients and slaves. The economy of the town, through the 1970s, was based on subsistence farming, though there was some trade in crafts and produce, especially in dates. Otherwise, in the early twentieth century, cash was accumulated by remittances from Bahlawis living in East Africa or in the other Persian Gulf states. Despite these differences with the great Islamic cities described in the classic literature, one could argue that the town, with the presence of a market and spectacularly ascetic Friday mosque (the primary structures taken to define "the Islamic city"), could be interpreted as a smaller version of the larger cities of the Arab North and Iranian East.

At the same time, while the market and mosque were critical to the life of the town, to many Bahlawis, especially the women with whom I spent most of my time, they were not the most important elements of its built environment. On the contrary, the town's fort, the twelve-kilometer wall, the division of the town into two halves, and the approximately eighteen walled neighborhoods within the larger wall, more so than the main mosque and market, shaped their understandings and perceptions of the town's changing spatial order and its system of rule.

By way of introduction to the beautiful town of Bahla, therefore, this chapter describes what many people noted to me were the most significant features of its built environment. The description of "place" is thus not a static backdrop for anthropological research, but part of the changing process I examine. Not only had the new Omani state (and the social, political, and economic conditions of the renaissance) altered the function of these features, but Bahlawis experienced, remembered, and related to them differently as well.

Forts

In 1987 the Bahla fort was "inscribed" as a UNESCO world heritage site, the first such site in the Arabian Peninsula. In line with an already existing policy of maintaining national heritage and culture through the reconstruction and restoration of forts,[4] the honor bestowed on the Bahla fort further confirmed and supported government policy. Not only were forts chosen to become one of the primary symbols of Oman's glorious history, but the interior region and Bahla were also confirmed as bearers of tradition.

Indeed, while the tradition industry touches all parts of Oman, the Dakhiliya region has been specifically designated for the role of the carrier of custom. This designation was made evident in 1994 when the National Day celebrations for the "Year of Omani Heritage" were held in Nizwa, the capital of the Dakhiliya region. Unlike the "anywhere" quality of Japanese rural nostalgia (Ivy 1995), Oman's religious and traditional values have been placed specifically within the interior region.

The Omani government, with technical support from Moroccan architects, began its restoration efforts in Bahla in the early 1990s, and work was still continuing while I was conducting fieldwork in the late 1990s. As of 2010, it had not yet been completed. In Oman, fort reconstruction takes precedence over any other type of national conservation work.

Figure 2.1 Bahla fort. Photo courtesy of the author.

The centrality of forts and fort imagery in Oman cannot be overemphasized: the Omani government has not only supported the reconstruction of forts, but has also built and encouraged fort imagery and fort characteristics to appear as features of office buildings, private homes, mosques, bus stops, telephone booths, and even water tanks. As visual evidence of Oman's strength and historic grandeur, the crenellations associated with forts have provided a proud theme in contemporary Omani architecture.

According to most people in Bahla, the fort, which is called Ḥiṣn Ṭammāḥ, was named after the Iranian ruler of the town in pre-Islamic (probably Sassanid (226–651 CE)) times. Others, instead, explained to me that the name refers to the fort's lofty position on a hill in the middle of the town; *Ṭammāḥ* means covetous in Arabic. Although the fort has a single name, it is not one building. Rather, it is a complex of buildings, towers, a mosque, and wells. As one young man explained, it is "like a neighborhood in itself." And, while the fort's origins might be pre-Islamic, Bahlawis often noted that different parts of the complex were built at different times, the oldest section of the fort being the tall, narrow tower (*burj*), known as Burg al-Rīḥ, in the southern part of the fort complex.

While Bahlawis I knew reported that sections of al-Ṭammāḥ were built in pre-Islamic times, according to the main written histories of Oman, the Bahla fort was completely destroyed at the beginning of the seventeenth century,[5] near the end of the Nabhani dynasty.[6] The destruction is important to Omani history because it marks the end of the Nabhani dynasty and the rise of the Ya'ariba dynasty, the dynasty that preceded that of the al-Bu Sa'idi, the present ruling family of Oman. Whether it was completely destroyed and then built again in sections or whether parts of the older structure remained and further sections were rebuilt or added on, is not critical here.[7] What is important is that for Bahlawis (and for Oman in general) the Bahla fort is proof of the town's antiquity.

By the 1990s, forts had become some of the main tourist sites in Oman. No longer inhabited by governors (*wālis*) and their entourages, by prisoners or by spirits, the forts had become museums. This transformation from sites of local political-military control to emblems of past Omani grandeur is recent. In 1960, as part of its long-term plans for Muscat and Oman, the British military recommended the reconstruction of the forts after its own bombing campaign during the re-ignited Imamate rebellion in 1957. It was then that British Royal Air Force jets stationed in Sharjah bombed forts throughout Oman, including Bahla.[8] Upon seeing these British recommendations, Sultan Sa'id bin Taymur told the British consul general that he wished to take care of the forts himself (Foreign Office records [FO], archive number 371/149018, confidential letter from Consul General Monteith in Muscat to Consul General Bullock in Bahrain). The British subsequently dropped the reconstruction project from their plans and, in the end, the Sultan did not invest in a program of reconstruction either. This reconstruction program was proposed under the rubric of a defense program for Oman. For the Sultan's army and *wālis* to be able to administer the towns of Oman, they had to have a seat of power—and, clearly, the forts served this purpose.

Although the RAF bombed many of the forts in Oman in July and August 1957, some, like Bahla, were not completely destroyed, and the governors continued to use them as their residences, offices, and town jails through the middle of the 1970s. By the mid-1990s, *wālis* and the police were housed in cement, air-conditioned buildings outside the walls of the town. No one, it seems, considered rebuilding the forts to be used for direct political or military control. But it would be naïve to say that the forts had ceased to be symbols of state power in Oman: most of the major forts, whether renovated or not, have large Omani flags flying above them.[9] Still, the forts were, in the 1990s, hardly sites of local control, "commanding the town beneath."

Visiting Jabrin

The transformation of the forts from seats of military and political power into emblems of Oman's glorious past had not gone unnoticed in Bahla. This shift was of interest to several older women I knew in Bahla and to one woman in particular, Ghania, who asked whether we could organize a trip to the nearby palace of Jabrin, also a newly restored emblem of Oman's past grandeur.[10] She wanted to see for herself what the great palace of Jabrin was like. She had heard about it and its residents her entire life and now she could go inside and explore.

Although not within the walls of Bahla, Jabrin was an integral part of the town. From the middle of the nineteenth century, at least, the Bahla fort and Jabrin palace were connected; whoever controlled one tended to control the other. The Jabrin palace was built in the late seventeenth century by the Sultan Bal'arab bin Sultan al-Ya'ariba, who ruled as Sultan of Oman from Jabrin.[11] By 1842, it had fallen into the hands of the increasingly prominent Shaykh Rashid bin Humayd al-Ghafri, who shortly afterwards took the Bahla fort as well (Wilkinson 1987: 126). Jabrin and Bahla remained under the control of Rashid bin Humayd and his grandsons until the early twentieth century. When Rashid bin Humayd died in 1863, his eldest grandson Barghash bin Humayd, under the guardianship of a servant, became *amīr* of Jabrin and Bahla (M. A. al-Salimi n.d.: 282).[12] During the short-lived Imamate of Azzan bin Qays (1869–1871), Barghash was expelled from Bahla and returned to Jabrin, and the famous scholar Majid bin Khamis al-Abri became *wāli* of Bahla. However, when Azzan bin Qays's Imamate fell and Majid bin Khamis al-Abri fled to Rustaq and then to Hamra (Wilkinson 1987: 356 n. 5), Barghash bin Humayd returned to control Bahla (M. A. al-Salimi n.d.: 282).

This close relationship between Jabrin and Bahla continued after Barghash's death in 1883. Barghash's brothers, Rashid and Nassir bin Humayd al-Ghafiri, organized Barghash's assassination and then installed Rashid, the next eldest of the three brothers, as *amīr*. However, soon after, in 1884, Nassir killed his second brother Rashid as well. Nassir bin Humayd then remained *amīr* of Jabrin and Bahla until 1915–1916, when supporters of the newly elected Imam, Salim bin Rashid al-Kharusi, took Bahla and exiled Nassir and his family to Jabrin. Several years later, the new *wāli* of Bahla, the famous Shaykh Abdullah bin Muhammad al-Riyami, better known as Shaykh Abu Zayd, expelled Nassir bin Humayd and his family from the Jabrin palace, though they were allowed to continue living in the nearby village also known as Jabrin. Abu Zayd, who was the *wāli* of Bahla from 1916 until his death in 1945, controlled the palace. Under the new, post-1970 Qaboos regime, the village of Jabrin became part of the "county," or *wilāya*, of Bahla.

For many older Bahlawis, the Jabrin palace was associated with Nassir bin Humayd, rather than its original founder, Sultan Bal'arab bin Sultan al-Ya'ariba. The thirty-year rule of Nassir bin Humayd and then the thirty-year rule of Abu Zayd have marked Bahla's late nineteenth and early twentieth century history. Key actors in Bahlawi history, the former was often described to me as evil and unjust while the latter was described as righteous, hard-working, humble, and able to perform miracles (*kārīmāt*).

Abu Zayd's reputation, however, was not completely untarnished. Non-Bahlawis suggested his "improprieties" with women he was curing. A local biography of Abu Zayd describes his reprimand by the older Majid bin Khamis al-Abri for his severe punishments (al-Bimani 1990). And finally, elder Bahlawis described their fear of Abu Zayd's wrath.

Nevertheless, Abu Zayd—as opposed to Nassir bin Humayd—was regarded, in many ways, as the savior of Bahla's economy and soul, a view most evident in a two-day conference in Bahla in 1997 dedicated entirely to Abu Zayd's life and career. Ghania remembered when Abu Zayd was the *wāli* of Bahla and Jabrin and knew many stories of the evil Nassir bin Humayd of Jabrin. Her relationship with the Jabrin palace was formed through her memories of these two key figures.

Ghania and I, along with two of her grandchildren, borrowed a car one day at the beginning of April 1997 and drove the thirty minutes to visit the Jabrin palace. On the way there Ghania asked: "Will there be a guard at the gate? Will they require us to identify ourselves? Are you sure it is open to the public?" "Yes, yes," the grandchildren insisted, "we've gone to Jabrin on school trips, it's open." Ghania's first reaction upon entering was to note that it was a shame that no one was actually living in the palace: "This place is so large. It could house a lot of people. Are you sure it's empty?" For Ghania, the palace of Jabrin was still a living place. It could or, rather, should be inhabited. Ghania thought of it as a house that was occupied by Nassir bin Humayd and later controlled by Abu Zayd.

As we toured the rooms, Ghania's grandchildren were interested in the secret passages and "tricks" of battle: one of the planks of the staircase could be removed and hot oil or honey thrown down on unsuspecting attackers below. They were curious about aspects of battle that seemed too distant to be real, parts of the fort that were strange and fascinating. Ghania, instead, was interested in the implements of the kitchen: the objects of quotidian life, a past that she knew and recognized.

Actually, the implements mounted on a wall were, she pointed out, objects she used when she lived in Zanzibar in the 1950s. They would most likely not have been found in this palace. For foreign tourists or young Omanis, this lack of authenticity, apparently, would not matter. The implements were there because they were old and would signify a past they did not recognize or remember.

The Jabrin palace, like the other fort museums of Oman, was not didactic. It did not have written guides explaining its history or plaques transcribing or translating inscriptions. Only the names of some of the rooms and the carefully placed props signaled the function of different rooms and areas of the forts. The props included rifles on the walls, Ministry of National Heritage books in the libraries, carpets or mats on the floors of sitting rooms (*majālis*), and a few kitchen implements in cooking areas. None of these props, however, was dated, and like the names of the rooms, they were there simply to suggest what might have taken place in specific parts of the forts, in some generic past. The props were "traditional," and it did not matter whether they were used during the time of the founders or later, whether they were used in 1660 or 1960.

As we continued our tour of Jabrin, Ghania became more reticent while her grandchildren became more animated. The children ran from one room to the next, repeating the basic stories of Sultan Bal'arab bin Sultan that they had heard on their school trips and had read in their textbooks or calling out the names of the rooms they could read from the signs on the walls. This is where Sultan Bal'arab established his famous library and school, these were the women's quarters, the children pointed out. Ghania instead entered the rooms with care, taking her sandals off in rooms with carpets or mats. She had entered someone's house and had to act accordingly.

After a short time, though, Ghania got bored and wanted to return to Bahla. It seemed as though there was nothing to be interested in since there was nothing left in the house that could be connected to either Nassir bin Humayd or Shaykh Abu Zayd. In fact, this was no longer a house. Ghania had been interested in seeing the house that she had heard about so much growing up: maybe she could have learned something about the occupants she had known about, occupants who had directly influenced the management and governance of Bahla. Instead, there was a museum, almost empty, rebuilt, and completely unreal. When we returned to Bahla, her daughter asked about her impressions of the fort. Ghania's only response was that it was "big, big and empty, there was no one there."

I expect reactions to be the same to the reconstructed Bahla fort. No longer part of the daily workings of the town, no longer connected to the local ruler who could be considered either an unjust or righteous governor, it will be "empty," its significance geared towards its origins. A few facts and a general atmosphere of ascetic grandeur should suffice for the visitors, mostly foreign tourists and school groups. This is not to say that people no longer spoke of the Bahla fort (they actually spoke a lot about how long the reconstruction was taking) but that the fort, as a working institution and neighborhood, was now part of their memories, which were becoming less about daily happenings and intrigues and more about the great founders and the generic past.

The growing "emptiness" of the rebuilt fort for the inhabitants of the town was already noticeable in the mid-1990s, since it had been closed to visitors for almost ten years and few of the men working on the fort were Bahlawis. The clearest indication of people's expectations came from a comment one man made to me when I asked him about the fort: "Oh, the fort, yes, I hear they're going to tear down al-'Aqur [the old neighborhood near the fort] and turn it into a parking lot for buses." The rebuilding of the fort was also expected to mark the destruction of the old neighborhood; room for tourist buses would take precedence over maintaining and supporting life in al-'Aqur.

This expectation was not far-fetched: the village next to the Jabrin palace had been razed when the palace was "restored." And, a newspaper article on Bahla in 1996 already laid the groundwork for the leveling of al-'Aqur: it stated that the neighborhood was already completely abandoned and in ruins (*Oman Daily Observer*, October 5, 1996, 16). Although there was, to be sure, steady migration away from the old neighborhood to other areas within the walls of the town and to the new suburbs outside the walls, the neighborhood was hardly abandoned. Elderly couples, migrant laborers from the Indian subcontinent, poorer families, and single women whose husbands worked (or lived) elsewhere inhabited old al-'Aqur. Another man just laughed at the suggestion that the fort meant something for the people of Bahla any longer: "It is there for the tourists now," he said.

Walls

While the Bahla fort, like other fortlike structures in Oman, captured the attention of the government and foreign visitors, Bahlawis, both young and old,

Figure 2.2 A section of Bahla's outer wall, as seen from a hill in al-Sifāla; mosque in foreground. Photo courtesy of the author.

tended to view the walls as emblematic of the town's identity. Bahla is surrounded by a twelve-kilometer mud brick wall, which was built, according to Bahlawi accounts, by a woman named Ghaytha to protect the town from the 'ajam, or Iranians. Unlike the Bahla fort, which does not have a well-established origin myth, the wall's story was well known and often repeated.

My landlord related to me two slightly different versions of the story while I was living in his house. In the first account, which he told me during my first week in Bahla, he described how there once was an Iranian named Hamad al-Farsi, who would arrive every year and steal money and food from the people. One year Ghaytha decided that she would pay for a wall to be built in order to stop al-Farsi. She convinced the Iranian to leave them alone for one year and then the following year they would give him double the amount of money, dates, and wheat. He agreed, and during the following year townspeople built the wall. When the Iranian arrived the next year, he did not recognize the town and kept on going.

In the second account, which my landlord told me two months after I had been in Bahla, Ghaytha was said to have built the wall to protect the town from attacks from the 'ajam, who would arrive every year and pillage the town. When the Iranians arrived one year and saw the wall, they decided to try to enter the town through the water channels. The guards, who were stationed along the wall, realized what was happening and killed the *'ajam*. The blood flowed down the water channels and thus warned the townspeople of the attack.[13] Whether from Ghaytha's trick or a violent defense, the walls of the town protected the people from malevolent outsiders.

The importance of the wall to Bahla's inhabitants was evident in much more than the oft-repeated story of its construction. Written local histories also focus on the details of its use, maintenance, and restoration. And, indeed, according to a local history written by a former judge (*qāḍī*) named Ali bin Nassir al-Mufarji (but known in Bahla as Dawood), Shaykh Abu Zayd once remarked that the wall (rather than the fort) is the "emblem" of the town:

And in the first days [of Abu Zayd's governorship], the river of Bahla dried and the wells dried and Bahla closed up from fear and hunger and lack of fruit [dates] and that is what the people earned for their deeds from the wisdom and justice of God.[14] Abu Zayd got to work and prepared for everything and began with the struggles of the hostilities toward the town. He said: "the security of the town [has] priority and the sign, *'anwān*, of Bahla is this wall and [it was] not built only for beauty, but rather created [for] security and the protection of the town." And sensible [people] take examples from the past and prepare for the future and Abu Zayd began with the repairs of the wall and he chose strong workers. (al-Mufarji 1995: 7)

Dawood quotes Abu Zayd to the effect that the "sign" of Bahla, its flag, so to speak, was the wall. The twelve-kilometer wall seemed to emblemize the town's identity: closed, strong, and independent.[15]

The town's wall, as Abu Zayd's biographer noted, was not there simply for beauty, it served to protect the town from its enemies. Abu Zayd not only repaired the walls, but stationed guards all along the walls and in the towers (*burūj*). At night, he would call out the names of the guards or the names of their posts to make sure they were not sleeping. Whoever did not answer would be called to the fort the next morning and punished. The town walls, however, also enabled control of what was inside. Just as the fort stood at the center of the town, in a commanding position above the neighborhoods and fields, the wall managed the boundaries of the town. The guards along the walls were not only responsible for looking outside the walls, but were also there to control what was going on inside.

Control of the town, in terms of protection from external attacks or from internal strife, was not limited to keeping watch from the fort or from the wall. Control also came from Abu Zayd's nightly walks through the streets. I was often told that Abu Zayd would walk the length of the town every evening, accompanied by and talking to his guards ('*asākir*). And this was a clear distinction from the late twentieth century: "Now, the police (*shurṭa*), only drive." Abu Zayd's knowledge of and control over the minutiae of town life was much greater, these stories suggested, than the police's. Acccording to Bahlawis I spoke to, Abu Zayd's walks through town revealed much more about possible illicit activity and local conflicts than the police's occasional drives.

Dawood's biography goes on to describe, in detail, the process of repairing the wall, a task that Abu Zayd had assigned to a man named Muhammad bin Ghayth al-Mazahmi. The narrative begins with the old main gate to the west of the town, the gate that was torn down in the 1970s to make space for the new highway:

> . . . and he began the work with Bāb Bādī descending to Burg al-ʿAqad until reaching Maghīwa al-ʿĀlī and east until al-Budʿ and [then] north until Naqub al-Ḥazāza and from this opening to the opening Naqub al-Ḥaḍārmubiya.[16] This work was supported by Salim bin Salim bin Sarur al-Mufarji.From this opening [he moved] to the Ṣabaḥ al-Sharīgāt, the entrance to the neighborhood of al-Salt bin Khamis al-Kharusi, who was Abu Muʾthir (PBUH [Peace be Upon Him]).[17] And from this door [he went] to the door (Bāb Sīlī), the entrance to the area of al-Khaṭwa (and the path Kadam) and Muhammad bin Salih al-Yahyai helped in its repair. From this door [he went] west to Burg bin Zaydaʾ and then to Burg Sabīkhaʾ [and] Muhammad bin Salih al-Madhkur supported its repairs. From Burg Sabīkhaʾ to the door Gabiya Magra, the owners of the adjoining fields supported the repairs of the wall. Everyone who had adjoining lands and fields supported the repairs of the wall. The Shaykh would [in turn] support these people from the *bayt al-māl* funds and every day a man would come and give each hired worker ten [baisa?]. From this door to the limit of Bāb Bādī, Muhammad bin Salih al-Yahyai supported the repairs. This is what we remember of the repairs of the wall.

Dawood's local history reveals a style of history writing that emphasizes detailed documentation and lists. It also reveals the extent to which Dawood wished to illustrate that (for the respected scholar and ruler Abu Zayd at least) the wall signified the town's distinct identity. His narrative can be viewed, perhaps, as a subtle expression of discontent with the wall's more recent state of ruin, especially in contrast to the fort. The emphasis on community involvement in Dawood's description of the wall's reconstruction also contrasts with the means of the fort's restoration, where foreign architects and builders rather than Bahlawis managed and worked on its rebuilding. This focus on the walls, and the impetus to document the details of the town's history under Abu Zayd were also aimed at salvaging and documenting a local memory that he feared would soon be lost. Histories such as Dawood's, alongside widely circulating popular accounts of the wall's origins, helped in differing ways to preserve the town's protective border—and possible independence.

Within (*dākhil*) the walls was, while I was in Bahla, often described as the place of the town and its *ḥaḍar* (settlement, civilization); it was contrasted with the *barra* (outside), the place of *khaṭar* (danger). On the other side was the cemetery, known as Maqābir Bū Knānīb. The *barra* was also where some people would meet to drink cologne in an attempt to imbibe alcohol. And, it was where people would gather to perform *zār* (spirit possession). Marginal activities took place in marginal spaces. On the other side of the wall lived the Bedouin: "Sometimes they would even come into the walls and kidnap people, take them to Dubai or Saudi Arabia, sell them like *ḥuwsh* ('goats')," an elderly man explained to me. Although "outside the walls" did not have a single formal name, the names of the different areas outside the walls give an indication of what was expected there and reveal their status in the eyes of Bahlawis.

In one direction, to the north and northeast, there was the area previously called Maskhūṭa, which means "odious, hated." By the mid-1990s, this area was a new suburb of Bahla, called al-Maʿamūra, "the inhabited place." To the southwest of Bahla, there was the area of al-Mustaghfir, which means "someone who asks forgiveness." Then, to the south of walls, there were the areas of Maghīwa, al-Khurm, and al-Bidū. *Maghīwa* seems to derive from *ghawaya*, "to seduce, stray, or sin"; *al-Khurm* means "the hole" and is related to the words *kharm*, a "blank" or "gap," and *inkhirām*, a "state of unsettlement" or "disturbance." *Al-Bidū* refers to the Bedouin. Another area to the south of the town was called *Ṣīḥ*, "to cry." The hills to the east and west of Bahla are steep, barren rock, reaching in both directions to about seven hundred meters. Between them is a riverbed, along which Bahla sits. If plains to the north and south of the town were considered dangerous because of the Bedouin, the hills flanking the town were even more dangerous because, I was told they were inhabited by evil spirits that ate dogs and cannibalized humans.

The juxtaposition between inside and outside, safety and danger, order and chaos, good governance and lawlessness was both undermined and reaffirmed by the movement of people and water across this boundary. Although the outside of the walls was remembered as a place of great danger, it did not follow that people would not venture outside. Women, I was told, routinely went outside to collect wood for cooking. In addition, one of the five smaller water canals (*sāqīya*), Ray, off the main canal (*falaj*), Falag Maytha, of lower Bahla, runs outside the walls and serves the area of al-Ṣīḥ. This *sāqīya*, though outside the walls, is maintained and controlled by the *'arīf* (water-time manager) of lower Bahla. Still, the distinction between inside and outside the walls remained a central referant for Bahlawis even as the town's post-1970 transformation elided that distinction.

The placing of danger outside the walls does not mean, however, that there were no dangers within the town walls. Each of the neighborhoods of the town was also walled, with at least one gate that would, until the early 1970s, either be locked or guarded at night. Yet, these internal dangers came from within the community and, whether from people or spirits, there might be someone, also from within the town, who could do something about them. The dangers on the outside instead represented harms that could not be requited; those who caused them could not be punished.

If danger was potentially everywhere—in your neighbor's eye, in the evil spirits controlled or even befriended by some humans—the dangers outside the walls of the town were closer to a state of chaos (*fitna*), beyond the control of those inside.[18] Lawlessness was described to me as the ultimate danger, the ultimate threat to society and community. And, in Bahla, this lawlessness was placed outside the walls. *Fitna* could also occur within the walls, but when it did, it was usually described as the spreading of lawlessness from outside to inside.

The arrival of the evil Nassir bin Humayd from Jabrin represented one such moment. To emphasize how far from the "outside" he had come, I was once told that he was not even from Jabrin but from *al-Sharqiya*, the eastern region of Oman. And yet, once Nassir bin Humayd seized control of Bahla, the state was no longer really *fitna*. As I was told by an elderly man: "Yes, it was bad, he was bad, but there were those who agreed with him. Yes, in Bahla there were those in agreement (*mu'afaqīn*)." Once Nassir bin Humayd took control of the Bahla fort, chaos gave way to a more manageable hazard.

By the late 1990s, although parts of the walls were crumbling and the gates were no longer guarded, the wall still evoked the sense of a protective barrier.

This was most evident when one passed from one side to the other, especially on foot. It was less clear when traveling by car. People would rarely note the passage from inside to outside when driving on the main highway either towards Ma'amūra, Nizwa, and Muscat or towards Mustaghfir, Ibri, and the Abu Dhabi border. Occasionally, people would acknowledge driving through the various gates and expanded holes. Although the main highway through the middle of the town was the newest and most dramatic transformation of the town's structure and the one path that carried with it the most significance in terms of the changes in Bahla, it was also the least "noted" in relation to the boundaries of the town. The highway simply expanded the area of Bahla into the new suburbs.[19]

But walking from inside the walls to the outside through a hole was almost always to be noted: a held breath or a prayer marked the passage on foot from inside to outside, from the place of safety to the place of danger. In writing about New York City in his article "Walking in the City," de Certeau (1984) draws a distinction between walking and other forms of movement through cities. He argues that it is on foot that particular spatial configurations become experienced. As different as it is from New York, in Bahla too, it was through the experience of movement on foot that the spatial boundaries of the outer walls of the town were most noted. Walking, as an earlier form of mobility, was itself also a way of remembering the former boundaries and organization of space. Driving, associated with modernity and modern forms of mobility, was not subject to the former spatial structures or ethics of fear and piety. Entering the car, one entered a new spatial regime.

Upper Bahla and Lower Bahla

The highway that was built through the middle of Bahla not only partly erased the clear boundaries of inside and outside that the wall had previously maintained, but also partly reconfigured the spatial organization of the town within the walls. The new road marked a shift in people's understandings of how the town was divided. Like most towns in Oman, Bahla is divided into "upper" (al-'Ālī) and "lower" (al-Sifala) halves. For the younger generations who grew up with the highway as a clear dividing line in the town, anything north of the highway was considered al-'Ālī and anything south was considered al-Sifāla. For the older generations who grew up without the highway dividing their town, al-Sifāla included neighborhoods that became, for the younger generations, part of al-'Ālī.[20]

This generational difference became clear to me early in my stay in Bahla through two arguments I witnessed, one between a father and son and another between a grandmother and grandson. On the first occasion, I was sitting with a father and son and had asked the father to list the neighborhoods of the town for me and to tell me whether they were in al-ʿĀlī or al-Sifāla. He began listing the neighborhoods from the southernmost part of the wall. As he reached the neighborhoods near the market, north of the highway, and described them as part of al-Sifāla, the son reacted, saying that his father was wrong and that these were part of al-ʿĀlī. The father in turn responded angrily that the son did not know what he was talking about.

On the second occasion, I had gone to the neighborhood of Būstān Laḥma, which lies north of the road, near the old Bāb Bādī, with a grandmother and grandson to visit a relative of theirs. As we left the relative's house, the grand-mother said that since we had the car that day she would like to visit another family member in al-ʿĀlī. At this, the grandson laughed and said, but we're al-ready in al-ʿĀlī. No, the grandmother insisted, this is al-Sifāla.

Not only had the upper-lower division of the town changed with the new infrastructural order, but the ways of defining direction also shifted. By the late 1990s, deeds of land sale indicated the location of a plot of land according to the name of the property (or, at least, the section [qism] of a named property) and whether it was east (sharq), west (gharb), north (shumāl) or south (junūb), in relation to other people's lands or a road. In the 1970s, land deeds defined the location of a particular property according to a different set of coordinates. Instead of shumāl and junūb, the documents from the 1970s defined direction according to the north star (al-naʿashī) and the coast (al-sahilī). In contrast, in deeds dating from the 1960s, coordinates of properties were not given at all: the names of the piece of property (as properties often had names) would suf-fice. If the land being sold was not the entire named property, then the history of the acquisition of that section of land would be described. For example, a deed might say: "the share of land in the property named such-and-such that was inherited or bought from so-and-so." Land deeds from the 1920s similarly indicated the name of the property, with an explanation noting from whom it had been inherited or purchased.

Although the boundaries of pieces of property were not detailed in land deeds until the early 1970s, the coordinates of the north star and the coast were used in the 1960s for describing other points in the town. For example, in reli-gious endowment records, one finds individual palm trees that were being sold or given as religious endowments (awqāf) described in terms of the north star and the coast. This earlier local use of the north star and the coast for indicating the directions of things, people, places—even if not for describing particular properties in land deeds until the 1970s—suggests how the new bureaucratic order had shifted the semantic fields of spatial categories.

Whereas "north" replaced "the north star" and "south" replaced "the coast" in official documents, at first glance it seems that ways of indicating east and west had not changed. However, unlike north and south, in Arabic, east (*sharq*) and west (*gharb*), in addition to referring to abstract directions, also refer to specific locations: the *place* where the sun rises and the *place* where the sun sets. And, as the daily prayer schedule is regulated according to the sun, the directions of east and west are always known.[21] Thus, just as north and south were the direction of the north star and the coast, east and west were the directions of the sunrise and the sunset. In other words, the abstract directions of east, west, north, and south replaced the directions of "where the sun rises," "where the sun sets," "the north star," and "the coast." Just as the road marked the changing spatial organization of the town, the ways that directions are conveyed have also shifted. The boundaries of what constitutes upper and lower Bahla have changed not only because of the building of the road, but also because the frame of their directions has changed.

Upper and lower Bahla, however, were not simply the area towards "the north star" or the area towards "the coast," now north and south. They were "above and below," *fawq wa taht*. They were closer to the source of the irrigation water or farther away from the source. They were the areas where there were more "Arabs" or the areas where there were more former servants. While not always overt, living in upper Bahla connoted a higher status than living in lower Bahla. In other towns of Oman, Izki being the most well-known example for scholars of southern Arabia, the upper and lower division corresponded to a division between the two main tribal groupings, the Ghafri and Hinawi.[22] In Bahla, however, this has not been the case: most of the tribes of Bahla, although certainly not all, have been associated with the Ghafri grouping.

Just as the upper and lower division of Bahla carried with it assumptions about status as well as changing understandings of where town boundaries lay, this division was also managed and marked by three significant institutions, one religious, one political, and one commercial: the old Friday mosque, the fort, and the market. All situated at the border of upper and lower Bahla, these institutions stand at the midway point of the two halves of the city, making it possible for those who live in each half to share access to them and for the institutions to regulate both sections. However, because they were considered "male" institutions—that is, they were primarily (though not exclusively) fre-quented by men—it was not so much the institutions themselves as the division of the town that appeared more significant to the everyday lives of the women I knew in Bahla. This was especially true as the new road that came to mark the boundary helped shift people's expectations of what movement for men and women was appropriate.

Interestingly, the highway that ran through the middle of town lessened the authority of these structures by making them and the entire town more acces-sible to and more easily managed by non-Bahlawis—that is, by government officials. Indeed, the highway served as the primary artery from Muscat to the interior and its contruction had destroyed sections of Bahla's protective wall, the chief symbol of its coveted independence.

The significance of the main road in connecting Bahla to Muscat was made clear to me the day Sultan Qaboos drove through town. I had been asked to drive several children to the local hospital because two of them had colds. After the doctor's examination, we picked up the prescribed aspirin and then returned to the car to drive the one kilometer home. As we tried to leave the hospital parking lot, two policemen stopped us and said that the main road, onto which we needed to turn briefly, was closed because His Majesty, the Sul-tan, was going to be driving through.

Thrilled to be able to see the Sultan, the children and I went to a nearby jewelry store and waited. We waited for about forty-five minutes until the first policemen on motorcycles arrived, soon followed by armored cars and trucks and more armored cars, with soldiers holding automatic weapons pointed at the people who were lining the road. Helicopters and military planes began to fly overhead and suddenly the usually sleepy highway through the middle of town became the site of a military convoy. Eventually, the Sultan arrived in a bulletproof BMW. He was driving himself, alone in the car. It was a symbolic act of self-reliance that contrasted with the military convoy around him. After he drove through, another equally large number of armored vehicles followed him, also with soldiers perched on top aiming their automatic weapons at the cheering crowd.

The contrast between the Sultan's "everyman" image, albeit an extremely popular and wealthy everyman, and the military convoy that accompanied him was striking. Even more striking for me, however, was that in the 1950s, Bahlawis had fought, along with other pro-Imamate guerillas, against joining a

Sultanate and for an independent Imamate. The way the Sultan came through the middle of town, both applauded and threatening, brought home to me the fact that the road itself confirmed Bahla's place in the Sultan's nation. This show of force demonstrated that the crumbling walls around the town could no longer keep out the central government. The genuine affection for the Sultan that I witnessed was coupled with the sense that the road on which he was driving was his own artifact. Just as the military convoy marked the Sultan's era as one of strength and stability, the road on which he was driving marked his place in Omani history as the author of Oman's post-1970 "renaissance."

The highway that divided the town also, though, affected *how* people were to cross it. Because the new road, by cutting trees and closing old paths, made those who wished to cross it increasingly visible to "strangers," its salience as a border between upper and lower Bahla increased. Indeed, rather than walk across the raised, treeless, and highly visible road, women would try to travel by car (where they could remain somewhat anonymous) to the other side. And, whereas on the old dirt roads of the neighborhoods (many of which have now been asphalted), women walked around in control of public space, the raised road—with its "modern" visibility—became for them a space to avoid.

Neighborhoods

Although changing experiences of the upper and lower division of Bahla affected people's everyday movements and their understandings of the town's structural unity, it was local memories, practices, and hierarchies associated with "neighborhoods" (*ḥārāt*) that most clearly revealed tensions over Oman's past, its system of rule, and shifting practices of social regulation. Bahla's neighborhoods continued to serve (albeit in new forms) as the organizational backbone for the services, management, and administration of the town. In addition, they functioned as the primary means for the social regulation of everyday behavior.

When describing how much had changed since Qaboos became Sultan, many people (both those who had living memories of the pre-1970 era as well as those who did not) would say to me that now, at least, there was no fighting between the neighborhoods, that now it was perfectly safe for someone to go from one neighborhood to another. While the outer wall of the city had warded off the danger of external threats and chaos, the interior walls dividing the neighborhoods had maintained a fragile peace through separation.

But this fragile peace, people's memories suggested, had often been broken. Implicitly, then, the new political system was capable of maintaining peace and order.

On the other hand, the effects of the new regime on the maintenance of the social order were less clear. After 1970, people in Bahla were contending with a new administrative structure (and economy) with its simultaneous centrifugal and centripetal pressures, encouraging more diffuse residential patterns along-side increased bureaucratic centralization. Just as new wealth enabled many families to move out of the old neighborhoods to larger plots, the new state also attempted (not always with success) to create a uniform bureaucratic system such that each official neighborhood had one shaykh, one mosque, and one meeting room. The new bureaucratic structure, in addition to lacking the promised effectiveness, also produced new tensions over who had the greatest authority, not to mention power, locally. Politically suitable appointees with clear allegiances to the Sultanate replaced older scholars who had reputations for having supported the Imamate system. Displeasure with such appointments and nostalgia for Imamate era governance, though not common, were evident in the quiet and not-so-quiet complaints about new hierarchies and the qualifications of the appointees.

While movement away from the old neighborhoods has increased since the 1970s, people were by no means confined to their neighborhoods before then. On the contrary, the town's earlier dependence on subsistence agriculture meant that men and women were often working in the fields, moving back and forth from neighborhood to field each day. And, women's visiting practices, though less common before the oil economy, were still important to daily life. Contrary to what might be expected, there were also no restrictions on the movement of servants in the areas of the "Arabs" or vice versa, though these groups tended to live apart from each other.[23] Nevertheless, until the mid-1980s, most people in Bahla lived in the old neighborhoods, within the limits of the walls and the gates and with the knowledge that their movements could easily be controlled.

An official publication of the municipality of Bahla from 1996 lists eighteen neighborhoods of the town.[24] Officially, the term "neighborhood" was reserved for areas with a group of mostly attached houses, at least one gate or door, a meeting room, and a wall, sometimes made up from the backs of houses. Such official lists of neighborhoods became important for the town's administration in the post-1970 era. In the late 1990s, residents, including school children, who filled out almost any official document were asked to indicate the neighborhood in which they lived. And, each neighborhood was assigned a shaykh to manage its affairs. This seemingly simple arrangement was undermined and confounded by numerous other pressures.

In particular, families with enough means were increasingly moving away from the old neighborhoods.[25] The new areas to which people had moved, however, were not generally considered official neighborhoods. Therefore, many Bahlawis continued to claim on official forms that they lived in their original neighborhoods. If, however, the new area—an area delimited by people's movements rather than walls—had an established name, taken from the name of the largest or most important farm, from a landmark, or from a well-known person, then the family might also have begun to declare their residence in the new area, de facto creating a new neighborhood.[26] Yet, such new naming was not always possible (either because the name of the area was not an acceptable, established name or because it was not officially recognized), so people often resorted to declaring residence in their old neighborhoods. The bureaucratic impulse to account in a uniform way for people's residences not only ran up against increased mobility, but also against increased confusion about where people actually lived.

With the evolving bureaucratic system of the Sultanate, each official neighborhood was also assigned a shaykh, employed under the auspices of the Ministry of Interior. The shaykh was responsible for the neighborhood and would report to the town mayor and county governor (*wāli*). The shaykh of the neighborhood was charged with keeping the peace in the neighborhood, with furnishing lists of eligible voters, and with noting if there were problems to be addressed by the local government or police. He served as the most local intermediary between the apparatus of the central government—with its Muscat-appointed officials and bureaucrats—and the townspeople.

Residents would often take disputes to the shaykh, who could act as an impartial conciliator between the parties. But, as his views were not legally binding, if an agreement could not be reached, he would sometimes encourage the parties to go to the town's judge (*qāḍī*). While I was in Bahla, disputes taken to the shaykh included ones about precarious tree limbs, sorcery, and wandering and ravenous goats. Although stories of a recent murder abounded, none, fortunately, occurred while I was conducting fieldwork. Some people would bypass the shaykh and go directly to the judge as they sought an even more "impartial" venue to address their difficulties. Going to the judge, though, was not an easy feat (especially for women), not only because it was difficult to find time, but also because the government offices were far enough away from the center of town that it required a car, not to mention someone trustworthy to make the drive.

Whereas most top officials and some of the middle-ranking officials in local administration, such as the mayor, judge, religious endowment officer, and police officers, were non-Bahlawis assigned to work in the town,[27] the neighborhood shaykhs came from the individual neighborhoods and most often belonged to local "shaykhly" families. The Qaboos era bureaucracy had simply subsumed shaykhly families—especially family members who were clearly supportive of the Sultanate—into its administrative hierarchy and organization. It was clear, however, that once these particular families were officially considered to be shaykhly families by the new state, there was less chance for shifts in neighborhood hierarchies. While in previous eras, *wālis* would appoint their own neighborhood shaykhs, under the new regime, people who were shaykhs or who were considered to be from "shaykhly families" at the time of Qaboos's coup, remained shaykhs no matter who the *wāli* was.

In some neighborhoods of Bahla, the shaykh was a respected religious figure or scholar.[28] But this was not always the case, and there were other people in the neighborhood who could take on the role of scholar, healer, and advice giver. Of course, who was considered "respected" differed widely, and comparisons between the past and the present often centered on the role and reputation of the shaykhs. Nostalgia for a time of highly respected, scholarly, and yet also powerful (official) shaykhs was especially apparent when disputes flared.

The neighborhoods were not only administrative locales. They were also sources of affiliation and identity, sometimes overlapping with "tribal" (*qabalī*) association. Some of the neighborhoods were associated with a particular tribe and, occasionally, the name of the neighborhood would be evident in the name of the tribe: for example, al-Furag was the neighborhood of the Mufargi.[29] With the establishment of the new bureaucracy under Qaboos, in addition to the neighborhood shaykhs, each tribe also came to have a shaykh. Some of the neighborhood shaykhs were also the local tribal shaykhs, though this was not often the case. What constituted a "tribe" was also open to dispute. What some people might consider a tribe locally would not be recognized officially and would thus not have a shaykh. Several elderly men complained to me that their tribe was not officially recognized, and they disapproved of the double structure of having shaykhs of neighborhoods and shaykhs of tribes. Another man even pointed out that under the new regime there was an *increased* emphasis on tribal affiliation. More often, though, I heard the complaint that now there were just "too many shaykhs."

By saying that now there were too many shaykhs, the elderly men were saying that in the past, in accordance with the egalitarian principles of Ibadism, only "true" shaykhs, men with superior scholarly (and perhaps occult) knowledge, would be called shaykhs. Now, instead, against proper Ibadi views, anyone who had attained an official status within the state, as head of a neighborhood, as head of a tribe, or as an official in what was then the Ministry of Islamic Affairs and Religious Endowments, could be called a shaykh.

Just as each official neighborhood and official tribe had a person to oversee that the people under his responsibility were behaving properly, each neighborhood also had a meeting room (*sabla*). In Dawood's account of Abu Zayd's life, he reports how Abu Zayd was disturbed by the fact that men were meeting in mosques to discuss local issues and even to mourn. Abu Zayd said that the mosques should only be used for praying and for remembering God. Other topics of conversation and mourning should take place elsewhere. He therefore ordered each neighborhood to build a *sabla* where the men could meet and mourn. The relatively recent addition of the *sablas* to the life of the neighborhoods was evidenced by the fact that many of Bahla's *sablas* were not in the middle of the neighborhoods, but on the edges either directly within the gates or just beyond them. In the case of al-'Aqur, the original *sabla* was built above one of the doors to the neighborhood.

In the late 1990s, while each neighborhood had one shaykh and one *sabla*, it may have had more than one mosque. In al-Sifāla alone I counted thirty-five mosques, including the old Friday mosque.[30] Although some of these mosques were not in use because they had too few attendees or because the mud buildings had been damaged by water, there was still more than one mosque per neighborhood.[31] Alliances, friendships, and family disputes would be displayed through mosque membership and mosque attendance. Men would sometimes switch mosques when there was a dispute, making a point of displaying their differences and arguments through their unwillingness to pray together.

According to an official at the Ministry of Islamic Affairs and Religious Endowments in Nizwa with whom I spoke, the government had a new policy of not approving more than one mosque within one and a half kilometers of another one in order to "prevent competition."[32] Although older mosques that needed to be renovated or rebuilt and could prove, through petitions and letters, that they would have enough attendees, could be granted permission and funds for rebuilding, this practice was discouraged. During the time of my fieldwork, only one man, after a heroic struggle and despite his good connections with local and national officials, was able to get a mosque rebuilt. Thus, although in the late 1990s there were many more mosques than neighborhoods in Bahla, there was a clear effort to enforce the uniformity of the neighborhood organization: one shaykh, one meeting room, and one mosque. And yet, despite these efforts, the multitude of mosques continued to suggest the incompleteness of the drive for bureaucratic uniformity. Even the Friday mosque, which moved from near the fort to near the market to outside of town in the early 2000s, hardly brought a sense of unity to the town.[33]

Just as there were multiple mosques associated with each of the walled neighborhoods, there were also multiple women's bathing rooms (magāzī).[34] One woman named sixteen bathing rooms in lower Bahla, some within the courtyards of houses, but most along the canals outside private homes. Although few of the bathing rooms were in use by the late 1990s, their crumbling walls testified to their previous centrality to neighborhood life.[35] Like mosques for men, many of these magāzīs had miḥrābs (recesses in the wall indicating the correct direction of prayer) and, as many women pointed out to me, women would often pray together, like men. Although increasingly prayer and washing shifted to private houses, some of the bathing rooms continued to be frequented, especially by young girls who would use them as places to play in the water during the hot summer months.[36]

The tensions surrounding the social management of the neighborhoods were clear every day in Bahla. As described in the first chapter, Bahlawi women belonged to neighborly groups called gīrān, mostly determined by proximity, but also by social hierarchy. Each morning, the group would go to a different person's house, rotating among the women. These married, widowed, or divorced women would often also go together to visit or host other groups. Women were therefore constantly moving from one neighborhood to another in Bahla. Given that the walls of the neighborhoods no longer marked definitive boundaries, and given that people increasingly moved away from the walled neighborhoods, either to their former fields or to the new suburbs, it was, in many ways, the boundaries drawn by the movement of women that marked local limits of acceptable intimacy as well as the limits of who could "see" whom.

As these groups of women moved through town, they tended to dominate the streets through their physical presence and their voices. Men would often skirt oncoming groups of women by moving to the side of the road or taking a different path. Appropriate gendered religiosity in a town known to be particularly righteous and pious did not mean that women remained isolated in their homes. On the contrary, women were constantly walking from house to house, visiting, and gathering.

On the other hand, both men and women often expressed unease about women's movement, sometimes by questioning what women were doing and whether their actions were "useful." Were they going to visit someone for a birth? Were they going to the hospital to see a sick relative? Or, less appropriately, might they be going to the market or to visit other women (to engage in "idle talk" and "gossip")?[37] As the neighborhoods no longer provided clear boundaries to people's movement and as fewer women regularly worked in the fields, their movements seemed to generate uncertainty and unease.

Bahlawis I spoke to often compared the previous systems of neighborhood management with the current one, both, paradoxically, by complaining of the violence between the neighborhoods in the past and by praising the older systems' personal engagement and tight control. It was at the level of the neighborhood that the post-1970 regime's administrative reorganization, and people's struggles with it, became most apparent. It was here too that the practices of social life focused concerns on the nature of proper community.

Conclusions

Because of Bahla's status as one of the most important towns in al-Dakhiliya, the Omani region that has most been associated (through official state policy) with history, heritage, and religious authenticity, it is no surprise that Bahlawis consider their town to be the embodiment of these very characteristics. This is not to suggest that Bahla's link with such concepts was wholly invented. On the contrary, piety, scholarship, independence, order, as well as disruptive spirits and occult knowledge, had for a long time been central to Bahlawi history. Nor is this to suggest that Bahlawi understandings of the town were limited to or simplistically experienced through the prism of these categories. Indeed, Oman's "renaissance" so altered both the ways of thinking about the past and the structures of rule that even though the town and its main structural features continued to be associated with such notions, there were unmistakable generational rifts with respect to the experience of Bahla's built environment.

As forts were transformed from sites of political and military power to symbols of the new regime's authority in the form of national heritage museums, different generations came to relate to the past differently. Ghania's grandchildren understood the Jabrin palace through the lens of its founders and its origins (understandings that were shaped by the state schools). Ghania, on the other hand, tried to discern more about the inhabitants she had known and had heard so much about as a child. Ghania approached the museum as if it were a living house and was sorely disappointed when the visit to the palace revealed nothing of the people she had known. For her grandchildren, instead, the history of rule in interior Oman, as represented in the museum, was distant, grand, and fantastical. But, the children also understood that the museum was not in fact a house: they too would have taken off their shoes when entering the rooms had the house been "real." Thus the grand past for the grandchildren was disconnected in crucial ways from the world of living Bahla.

For those who never entered the town through the former main gates, the highway running through the middle of town erased a clear dividing line between inside and outside, between security and danger, order and chaos. The highway served to connect Bahla, literally and figuratively, with the rest of Oman, but it also made it particularly easy to enter and, perhaps, to control. Such a road, to be sure, was not absolutely essential to the control of the town (as the bombardments of 1957 indicate), but through the partial destruction of the wall, it affirmed that the town was part of and not independent from the nation. And yet, the habit of praying or holding one's breath as one walked through the wall's openings, not to mention oft-repeated stories of the wall's origins and recently published local histories, emphasized the importance of the wall to the security and independence of the town. While the forts had been given over to "tourists," the wall had been retained for its inhabitants, or at least that was what some Bahlawis hoped.

The division of the town into two halves and the administration of the neighborhoods were also undergoing profound transformation. While neither of these features was upheld as an emblem of the town's heritage or as an example of the town's independence, they both continued, albeit in new ways, to help keep order and ensure the maintenance of proper social life. And just as a generational divide existed in people's relationships to the forts, so too did one exist between older Bahlawis who experienced or remembered order to be produced through an effective personal mission and younger Bahlawis who knew order to be maintained by a governor who few people had seen and by the police who "only" drove.

At the same time, a variety of pressures were confounding and undermining attempts at maintaining the new system of order. While the bureaucratic system strove for uniformity, people's movements, multiple mosques, and bathing rooms, not to mention familial allegiances and preferences for scholars independent of state-sanctioned authorities, all worked against it. And yet, many people remembered the past as one of conflict and harsh rule and appreciated the state's success at establishing order.

If the shifting experiences and meanings of Bahla's built environment revealed conflicting understandings of history and good governance, then people's expectations of Oman's future (even as "return") were also conflicted. Would future models of proper rule and piety resemble the intimate forms as exemplified by Abu Zayd or as represented in the model of the heritage museum? Would order and property be managed by rulers cognizant of local place names or dependent on abstract organizational forms? Would walls come to maintain peace or would people regulate each other's and their own movements? Within the context of Oman's (limited) oil wealth, people's understandings of what constituted and constitutes good governance shaped not only their current politics, but their hopes, concerns, and expectations as well.

3 In the Eye of the Neighbor, There is Fire

Hazards and Histories of Sociality

ONE MORNING, rather than visiting with my neighbors (*gīrān*) as I usually did, I went instead to meet with the principal of one of Bahla's girls' schools. By the time I returned from the school, Zaynab, my landlady, had also returned from visiting our neighbors. As I took off my sandals and walked into the main family room on the ground floor, Zaynab asked if I wanted coffee, adding that she would join me: "It isn't good to drink coffee by yourself," she said. From the cabinet along the wall of the family room, I took a thermos (*midlah*) of coffee, a tray with small coffee cups (*fināgīn*), and a plastic container of dates (*ṣuh*). Zaynab sat with me, serving from the thermos. When I drank from one of the small cups, she took it back and said, "Ok, that one was mine, now (still pouring from her own thermos) here is Rayya's. Drink that and then there is Mariam's and Gaukha's." She was joking, but her teasing touched on the fact that I had been absent that morning, had missed the morning sharing, and had to make up for it by "drinking from each thermos." Zaynab made the requirement of sociality evident: not only was it not good to drink coffee alone, but I also had to drink from each neighbor's thermos.

Why was it not appropriate for me to drink coffee by myself? Was there something specific to coffee or to the act of drinking, something to do with liquids or with eating in general that underlay Zaynab's comments and actions? Claude Lévi-Strauss once asserted that "the group confusedly sees a sort of social incest in the individual accomplishment of an act which normally requires collective participation" (1969: 58). Zaynab was, in fact, concerned about the individual accomplishment of an act that normally required collective participation, and she moved to intervene. While her response might not have signified an unconscious fear of incest—reciprocity (and thus sociality) being the safeguard against incest—she was nonetheless uncomfortable enough with my individual drinking to comment, sit, and join me. Over the course of my time in Bahla, as I will examine in this chapter, it became clear that Zaynab's discomfort in that moment also related to what I was going to be ingesting: coffee.

What, then, was there about coffee that required sociality? Lévi-Strauss, again, noted that while food is for nourishment of the body and thus acceptably individual, wine is an honor and a luxury and therefore necessarily social (1969). Drinking wine in Lévi-Strauss's context of twentieth-century France could, indeed, be compared to drinking coffee in twentieth-century Oman, both in terms of its luxuriousness and its intoxicating effects. Although coffee was hardly a luxury item in the late 1990s, memories of it as such continued to inform its meaning. It was precisely coffee's former status as a luxury item that helped shape people's ideas about women's visiting as decadent and a sign of contemporary waste and leisure.[1] As coffee ceased to be a luxury item and became a common commodity—a change effected by Oman's economic transformation—people's memories and popular discourses around coffee emphasized the notion that visiting itself was decadent.

Rather than condemning its luxuriousness, Omani and other Muslim scholars who oppose the legality of coffee have focused on coffee's similarity to wine because of its "intoxicating" (sakar) effects and because of the social activities—the very activities that are meant to manage its luxuriousness, according to Lévi-Strauss—that accompany its consumption.[2] While Bahlawis (and most devout Muslims) do not accept such arguments against coffee drinking, and coffee was widely enjoyed and served in everyday gatherings and visits throughout Oman, these notions (especially those concerning sociality) also influenced its consumption in Bahla and, in turn, the social world in which it was most enjoyed. Thus, while sociality could be argued to have contained coffee's luxurious or intoxicating qualities, sociality may, in so doing, also be infected by such qualities. At the same time, for some scholars, sociality itself may have been the problem, causing an otherwise benign drink to be considered inappropriate.

Whatever the relationship between sociality and coffee, the strong connection between the two was, I realized, especially evident in language: Bahlawis would regularly turn the noun *coffee* into a verb *to coffee* and use it as a synonym for "to visit with your neighbors." *Coffee*, to borrow Mikhail Bakhtin's language, was an overpopulated word, carrying with it a host of discrepant meanings (1981: 294).

In this brief moment, Zaynab not only commented that it was not good to drink coffee by myself, but also made me reenact my participation in the neighborly group. Active participation in the neighborly group reenforced my membership in the community, and helped make me a proper woman and person. Women in Bahla worked towards becoming fully accepted women not only by marrying, serving their husbands, bearing an acceptable number of children, and fulfilling the functions appropriate of wives within the house and for the family, but also by participating in neighborly groups. In Bahla, the domain of gendered domesticity, therefore, clearly extended beyond the confines of the house and family to include the neighbors and the neighborhood.

It was in discussions about the obligation of visiting and of being social that I detected some of the greatest unease about productivity, leisure, and appropriate religiosity in the post-1970 renaissance. Most Bahlawis of the pre-1970 generation that I knew understood sociality to be a (religious) duty or obligation. For them, visiting embodied the goodness of humans to maintain and uphold social bonds and to support each other. These everyday notions were not disconnected from scholarly discussions: concepts about and practices of neighborliness and sociality, as I describe shortly, also have scholarly genealogies in Oman, often tied to notions of social obligation and responsibility. While everyday notions and older scholarly writings encouraged neighborly visiting, in the late 1990s, some younger Bahlawis saw sociality, instead, as an impediment to appropriate religiosity. In their view, people should continually and individually remember God; such visiting was a distraction from focused attention on what they took to be proper religion.

Attitudes about the recent past were also conflicted. On the one hand, women who participated regularly in this visiting sometimes told me that in the past, when coffee was a luxury, women did not have the time to visit with each other. Regular visiting was new and was a sign of the excesses of the current era. These women understood their visiting to be a social responsibility and sometimes defended it by calling it their "work." But they also undermined it by arguing that it was decadent. On the other hand, the younger women who opposed the visiting, as I discuss more fully in Chapter 4, sometimes noted that women's "going out" in the past was perfectly fine. Such conflicting ideas about the past (not only between the different generations but also within the different perspectives about visiting) affected people's understandings and concerns about proper behavior in the present.

In particular, they revealed significant transformations in people's ideas about proper religiosity. Underlying the shifts in people's perspectives about sociality were changes in people's understandings, not only about the proper relationship of the individual to the social world, but also about religion itself. Clifford Geertz (1968) once described religious experience in Morocco and Indonesia as transforming from "religiousness" to "religious-mindedness," from embodying religion to making statements about belief. As such, religion and religious experience were becoming distinct domains of life, objectified and functionalized.[3] As I was trying to grapple with the layers of meanings, practices, and tensions around social life, and the ways people understood it to have changed, it became increasingly evident that Bahlawi notions of what it meant to be "good" were shifting such that religion there too was coming to be understood as a distinct realm of life that required definition. For some, everyday visiting could no longer be included within religion's sphere.

On Being Social and Neighborly

The vast majority of married, widowed, or divorced women in Bahla belonged to a *gīrān* and would visit their neighbors every day. They would gather (often rotating between the houses of the group and often accompanied by their

Figure 3.1 Woman walking in Bahla. Photo courtesy of the author.

youngest children), greet each other with a handshake, drink coffee from each other's thermoses, eat the dates that each woman would have brought, and sample the fruit or snack (chickpeas or other beans, sweet angel-hair pasta, fried bread, or tiny pancakes with honey) that each woman might also have brought. And finally, before departing, the women would also often perfume themselves with incense or essential oils and discuss whether they might meet to visit someone else later in the afternoon.

The visits themselves were highly ritualized and, with some variation, quite similar throughout town. They were also, as described by Christine Eickelman (1984), quite similar to visits in Hamra, a town thirty kilometers from Bahla. As the women would sit down, one might say "let's start" (*bidiyan*) and place one of the containers of dates on a tray, take off its cover, and send it over to the person to the right of the coffee server.[4] As Anne Meneley (1996) beautifully described for the Yemeni context, the order of service could reveal and help reproduce social hierarchies. In Bahla, the person serving the coffee was usually the host, but sometimes someone else would take responsibility, either as a way of helping or because it was expected of someone of lower status.[5] In the neighborly group, everyone sat in a circle around the food and coffee. In the larger gatherings, the server would stand in the middle of the circle and move from one drinker to the next. The woman pouring the coffee would hold the thermos in her left hand and a stack of several small coffee cups in her right. She would pour about a quarter of an inch of coffee into the top cup and hold the small stack out for the other woman to take a cup.

The woman drinking the coffee would take the cup from the top of the stack and hold it with her thumb and index finger at the rim. As one person would drink, the server would serve the next person, following the same routine. The cup that was placed on top of the stack would be used for the next person in the circle. When a woman would finish her cup, if she wanted more she simply held it up. If she did not want another cup, she would shake the cup a few times and then hold it out to place it back on the stack. It was possible to refuse to drink another cup, especially when the crowd was large and there were many thermoses to go through. However, this was rarely done and considered rude. So, if someone could not drink "another drop," she simply refused to drink the coffee she brought. Because women tried to have different thermoses by choosing distinct colors and shapes, they knew when their own coffee was being served and could, without offense, refuse to drink.

Indeed, unlike almost all other goods, the women that I knew were particularly keen to distinguish their coffee from other people's, both by using a distinct method of roasting and brewing as well as by looking for a distinctive thermos. As I heard multiple times, and as Omani scholars discussing neighborly relations also noted, neighbors were expected to share things that were distinctive. In order to get around this expectation, many people would consciously try to have similar things, thus diminishing the need to share. Coffee, however, was different, and women worked to distinguish theirs from other women's.

Who was served first depended on who was in the group. In a neighborly coffee group, the person to the right of the pourer was usually the first person to drink and eat. Sometimes within a family, when both men and women were sharing a coffee break together, the men would drink first. Among women alone, however, no one was usually expected to eat or drink first. While this egalitarian arrangement could shift with the arrival of a visitor of stature, in the daily neighborly visits and group visits, there was no serving order determined by status. This had not always been the case, however. In the past, I was told, former servant (*akhdām*) and "Arab" women were sometimes offered coffee and dates separately.[6]

As the coffee and dates would begin to circulate, one of the women might comment on the weather and a few others would agree: "It is so cold these days" or, more often, "It is so hot now."[7] The conversation about the weather would often move to a discussion about someone's health, generally associated with the weather. Maybe one of the women's children or relatives was sick that day or the night before and had been taken to the hospital. Going to the hospital was not reserved for serious illnesses; men, women, and children frequently would go for minor ailments. "How many shots (*bra*)?" would be a common follow-up question serving as a measure for the severity of the illness. Then, the women might speak of their own illnesses, aches, and pains: the older women would complain about their legs (aching legs being the ailment most commonly associated with aging women). There might be a pause in the conversation where the women would insist that the others eat the dates, fruit, or snacks being passed around with the next round of coffee. A woman would get up and change the water in the bowl used to rinse their hands.

As the conversation would start and stop, often returning to questions of health, the women would also continue to drink coffee, eat dates, and then to snack on fruit. The topic of conversation might change to the price of kitchen utensils, cloth, or ready-made children's clothes: "So-and-so is selling trays for five rials, can you believe it?" Or, "Do you know for how much so-and-so is selling plastic containers now?" From there, the conversation might return, once again, to health, "So-and-so is sick, poor thing, we should go visit. When should we go?" And, then, the women would discuss when they might visit the sick person, often the same afternoon. "Ok, what will you take?" And the women would discuss what they might take.

The conversation might turn to an event in the present: "Did you hear that someone in Hamra was in a car accident?" From this, someone might remember another accident in the past: "Do you remember when it flooded and those people were swept away near Hamra?" The conversation might turn to someone's dress or to a comment someone made about appropriate behavior and then, often, to complaints about what "the youth" (al-shibāb) do or don't do, have or don't have. The conversation might then change again to someone's travel plans, or to someone who recently arrived in Bahla, or to a new building in the town. It might turn to someone's husband being away or returning—maybe even a bit of giggling about his return and that the woman will be "busy" for a while.

Some neighborly groups were notoriously loud, while others were notoriously quiet. Being too much one way or another brought with it its own set of criticisms. Too loud and the group might be considered vulgar, too quiet and the group might be considered cold and inhospitable.[8] Speaking was as integral to the neighborly group as coffee and dates. Depending on the occasion—a daily meeting of the intimate neighborly group, a larger neighborly gathering, a visit with family, or another specific event—as well as who was in the group, conversation topics shifted. Nevertheless, whatever the subject matter, just as it was considered rude not to eat or be hospitable, it was rude not to speak.

And, when all the women had drunk coffee from each thermos, eaten dates, snacks, and fruit, and rinsed their hands in the bowls of water continually being brought in and passed around, then it was time for incense (bukhūr) and perfumes. The incense was usually a premade mixture of frankincense, sandalwood, rosewood, and sugar. It was bought from the back of a truck (from Salalah, the capital of the Southern Dhofar region) that was parked in front of the hospital. It would be sprinkled on top of heated coals in a clay incense burner and passed around the group. The incense burner would be held under dresses, under armpits, and under the cloth of headscarves, allowing the smoke from the burning incense to float through the cloth. At the same time, a small tray, basket, or bowl with different types of perfume essences and sprays would also rotate, and women would pick out one, two, or three and perfume their clothes and necks. During the perfuming, one of the women might say "*khali,*" "Ok, let's go, enough," and stand up, shake the other women's hands, slip on her sandals, and return home.

Of course, not all women in Bahla belonged to neighborly groups. There were many who would spend their mornings cutting alfalfa for one Omani rial ($2.60 in US dollars) per day, baking bread in a women's cooperative, or working as janitors, nurses' aides, babysitters, or teachers at one of the state schools. Other women were deemed "crazy" or "possessed" (*magnūna*), and were excused from the obligations of hospitality. For the most part, however, respectable women, including female-gendered intersexuals, belonged to neighborly groups and performed the daily rituals of sharing coffee and dates, reproducing both their "woman-ness" and the ethic of reciprocity and hospitality that was said to produce social solidarity.

The obligation to be social and to uphold social bonds—to belong to a neighborly group, to visit other people, to be visited, to host and provide hospitality, and to take food to others—was made particularly evident in comments people made about those who did not participate in this social world. Not only were those on the "fringes" of society or those who were deemed crazy or possessed sometimes excused from participating, but people's lack of participation could also serve as proof of their positions on the margins of society. Majid, one of my landlord's elder sons, once said that sorcerers (*sāḥir*) could make people crazy, and as proof of this craziness stated that there were some people in Bahla "who won't leave their homes, they're crazy." Another time, Majid spoke specifically about a friend of his who he and others declared was crazy, and again, as proof that this friend was possessed, Majid said: "He used to visit his neighbors, but not anymore. He stays at home and only visits his family. He never goes with his neighbors. He has read too many books." The books, here, were meant to suggest that in reading about and trying to participate in the use of occult knowledge, Majid's friend was no longer able to control the knowledge that he had acquired. Instead, the knowledge controlled him, making him "crazy" and "asocial." Similar comments were made of women who did not participate in neighborly groups. Indeed, the obligations of visiting that Majid placed on his friend applied to women in even more acute ways, especially since women were expected to visit with their neighbors every morning and then sometimes in the afternoons as well.

It was understood that those who did not visit their neighbors were somehow marginal, either because they were "crazy" or because they had entered an economic world where they worked for wages. Similarly, women's greetings also assumed a social world structured around neighbors. As women passed each other on the street, they often greeted each other by saying: "How are you, how are your children, how are your neighbors?" The assumption that people knew how their neighbors were (even if the function of this greeting was not literally to extract this information) suggests a specific and perhaps even intimate personal relationship beyond the limits of home and household and introduces the social world of a neighbor group as part of who women were, with whom they belonged, and for whom they might speak.

Ethnographers of women's worlds in the Middle East have long examined the economic, political, and social importance of neighborly relations and networks for reproducing social hierarchies and for sustaining economic or political lifelines, giving people access to needed resources. In 1974, for example, an entire issue of *Anthropology Quarterly* was devoted to tracing women's networks in the Middle East (Vinogradov 1974). Focusing primarily on elite women and their political connections, many of these articles examined the ways women maintain and reinforce hierarchies in their gatherings. Suad Joseph (1983), a decade later, illustrated the direct intervention in women's networks in Beirut by political leaders trying to undermine any potential threat to their authority. Anne Meneley (1996) examined women's lives, local hierarchies, and the ideals of reciprocity in visiting practices in a small town in Yemen; Diane Singerman (1995) focused on political networks in a working-class neighborhood of Cairo; and Homa Hoodfar (1997) described the importance of women's social networks for household economies in another working-class neighborhood of Cairo. Jenny White (2002) examined religious activism through social networks in Turkey. In work on Central Asia (see, for example, Cynthia Werner 1998 on Kazakstan, Deniz Kandiyoti 1998 on Uzbekistan), scholars have also examined the hierarchies involved in the ways women provide economic lifelines to each other. And, of the few ethnographies on Oman, both Christine Eickelman (1984) and Unni Wikan (1982) analyzed visiting as an important aspect of everyday life. Focusing on neighborly relations in particular, scholars working in Israel have described how "neighboring" allows women in urban settings to establish personal bonds within the alienating environments of large apartment complexes and cities (Ginsberg and Churchman 1985) and how daily and prolonged contact between neighbors does not necessarily foster intimate relations (Birenbaum-Carmeli 1999). From a different perspective, Hildred Geertz (1979) argued that when examining women's networks in Morocco, the concept of "family" included friends and patrons. I draw from such work, but I am particularly interested in the ways that practices of and notions about sociality are historically contingent.

Neighbors and neighborly relations, of course, have not only been of interest to ethnographers of the Middle East. Attention to the figure of the neighbor has also been one of the hallmarks of scholarship on urban environments, as well as a focus of scholars of Islamic law.[9] While this chapter does not concern itself primarily with neighbors' legal relationships, it recognizes that the neighbor has also stood as a marked legal and moral figure.

Bessim Selim Hakim (1986) has outlined some of the basic guidelines of neighborhood-building in Maliki law,[10] noting that cases involving disputes between neighbors comprise a large part of the corpus on property rights and relations. This attention to the relations between neighbors also emerges in cases involving water rights (in Maliki and other schools of Islamic law as well) and will be discussed briefly in Chapter 5. While the administration of neighborhoods has taken on new significance in the bureaucratic shifts of the post-coup Omani state, neighborhoods and neighborly relations have long been the subject of debate and public discourse. Hakim has outlined seventeen "principles and values" that judges in medieval Tunis, for example, used to settle cases of property disputes. These principles although distant in time and space from contemporary Oman, have Qur'anic references or prophetic pedigrees (or both) that Bahlawis also mentioned to me. Such principles included building rights, laws of preemption, thoroughfares, water shares, *fina* (interior courtyard and space adjacent to exterior wall), cleanliness, as well as trust, respect, noise, drainage, and peace.[11]

Neighbors figure prominently in these cases not only as purveyors of complaints, but also as those with "rights" (*ḥuqūq*) who should be protected from the offenses about which they are complaining.[12] The complaints are often voiced not by the "community at large," an "offended member of the public," or a "citizen," but by a "neighbor," giving this figure a particularly salient role in the management of social life.[13] Although in contemporary Oman the figure of the neighbor as a legal subject has tended to give way to the figure of the citizen, who lives within the administrative unit of the neighborhood, the neighbor continues to play a salient role in popular legal and moral discourse. Indeed, people would often invoke the *ḥaqq al-jār*, or "right of the neighbor," in discussing relations between households. Shaykh Abu Zayd, the governor of Bahla from 1916–1945, when studying with the famous twentieth-century theologian Abdullah bin Humayd al-Salimi (otherwise known as Nur al-Din al-Salimi), asked his teacher a series of questions about building in empty lots, building roads, and different interpretations of what and who a "neighbor" was. Some of these questions have been published in Oman in a book, *Kitāb Ḥall al-Mushkilāt* (al-Riyami n.d.). Although not as popular or as widely distributed as Nur al-Din's classic works, this book is important for understanding Abu Zayd's administrative and scholarly concerns as they pertained to Bahla.[14]

Beyond their roles as plaintiffs about property access and nuisance, neighbors are also recognized in (religious) texts as people with mutual responsibilities in terms of hospitality, sharing, and kindness. One famous and oft-quoted hadith,[15] which reappears in multiple contexts, reports: "The Prophet said that Gabriel had so enjoined me to behave well with my neighbors until I became convinced that he was going to include them among those who have a fixed share in inheritance."

In his most popular work, the *Jawhar al-Niẓām*, Nur al-Din al-Salimi also dedicated a chapter (1989 [n.d.]: vol. 4, 319–320) to the neighbor. The neighbor in this case, as well as in Nur al-Din's other texts, is a male neighbor. My landlord would sometimes repeat to me these lines as well as the famous hadith about neighbors:

> Visiting neighbors is like [visiting] relatives; it is obligatory (*lāzimat*) for people
> It has been said that the neighborhood includes forty houses; and that is how our Shaykhs told it
> And, among the Bedouin, if you see their fire, they are your neighbors
> The right (*ḥaqq*) of the neighbor is not only to prevent you from harming them, or to [encourage you] to be generous to them
> But, to tolerate their harm against you and to defend them from whomever is harming them
> It is said that he who asks help from his neighbor, in permissible things, must be helped
> If you bought luxurious foods, put them away because it is a duty (*wājib*) to give them [some] if you display them
> And, this is [also the case] if you cooked a dish, [either] hand some over or hide it as a secret
> And, a person should not hold back from relatives and neighbors

useful things in his house, without the right reasons, unless for someone
more deserving

And, it is said that God will visit and grant mercy to he who visits his
relatives

And thus, God will protect he who protects his neighbors

And, it has been said that a bad neighbor is one who reveals secrets and
exposes you and shows malice to you

Riding the waves [i.e., traveling on a ship] is better than a bad neighbor who
makes you miserable

And, he who brings harm to his neighbor, God-Almighty will have the
neighbor inherit his house

Thus search for good neighbors before [buying] the house so you will be
spared living among malicious people

Nur al-Din wrote about the responsibilities of neighbors to each other in his
children's primer *Talqīn al-Ṣibīyan* (n.d.: 66–67):

The connection of neighbors to each other is a permanent right (*ḥaqqun
thābitun*), and neighbors near and far should be welcomed. Neighbors include
both kin and non-kin (*al-jār al-junub*). The Prophet (PBUH) said that Gabriel
so insisted that I treat my neighbors with kindness that I thought he [God]
would assign them a share of my inheritance. The neighborhood is that which
is practiced in custom, whether it is in a village or a desert or a settlement [i.e.,
town/city], or on a journey. And the obligation of the neighbor to his neighbor is to promote what he has and to prevent his neighbor from suffering. The
neighbor is a partner. It is his duty to join him in his times of joy by joining in
his happiness, and in his times of grief (by sharing) his mourning. It is a person's
duty to share with his neighbor things that the neighbor does not have, especially when the neighbor learns of the difference. God knows best.

Responsibilities for providing for neighbors, for protecting them, and for
looking to be at peace with them suggest, to be sure, that there were often tensions among neighbors. Tensions over property, status, and acts of black magic,
for example, were part of neighborly relations while I was in Bahla. Indeed, a
short poem that my landlady mentioned several times when speaking about tensions with one of her neighbors indicates the prevalence of such difficulties:

In the eye of the jealous, there is intensity
In the eye of the neighbor, there is fire

The hazards of neighborly relations, although evident on numerous occasions during my time in Bahla, were particularly striking in one incident. Nearly eight months into my stay, one of our female neighbors, who belonged to a different neighborly group, became extremely ill. Zaynab and I went to visit her, and I was alarmed at her condition. Many people in the neighborhood accused my landlord, who was rumored to have access to occult powers inherited through his father, of trying to "eat her," another way of saying of trying to kill her. The neighbor's health, after nearly two weeks of bed rest and multiple visits to the hospital, did not improve. Tensions continued to escalate, and one evening as the family and I were sitting together after dinner, we suddenly smelled a distinctly sweet and unusual odor. One of the sons said that it must be a burnt offering protecting the neighbors from his father. He and I went outside and found a small concoction burning next to the wall of the house. He snuffed it out with his feet and covered it with dirt. Everyone in the house was disturbed and angry. My landlady attempted to calm the situation by hosting a large neighborly gathering. Hardly anyone came, and Zaynab was deeply embarrassed and upset. Eventually, the woman recovered, although many in the neighborhood continued to blame my landlord for causing her illness.

To be a "neighbor" in Bahla meant to be a figure with moral and legal obligations. But for women, it also meant to belong to a neighbor-group. This structured sociality, however, was fraught, as I have suggested, with tensions about class and race, jealousy and property, as well as with "the risks of representation," as Webb Keane (1997) has illustrated. Indeed, the ill woman and her family described above were of a servant caste and tensions between them and my landlord's family were certainly entangled in the histories of these hierarchies, as I discuss in Chapters 5 and 6. But, sociality in Bahla was also fraught with tensions connected to broader shifts in understandings of the past, of appropriate religiosity and individual focus on God, and of the very practices within the moments of visiting and exchanging.

Of the Past (bū qabl)

Many of the women I came to know in Bahla would speak about the past, often beginning with statements about how their lives used to be much harder and then equally often nostalgically inserting comments about how, although life was difficult, women would also cooperate in their chores. While I would often try to draw out the shifts in the social and economic life in Bahla over the course of the last fifty years or so, I was also continually frustrated with responses that insisted on collapsing time into "before" and "after," "before Qaboos," "before oil," and after.

Once when I asked Ruwaya, one of my landlord's elder daughters, about how women would get together in the past, she told a story of collaborative work, organization, and little coffee. Some of her account was culled from what she remembered as a child before the export of oil and before the 1970 coup, but most of it was from only twenty years earlier, when she had already been married for some time and had begun working in the fields and meeting with other neighborly women. Except when she detailed the history of types of coffee pots, Ruwaya constructed this generic past as a way of marking distinctions with the present. In describing the past, Ruwaya was implicitly contrasting a memory of collaborative work and little coffee in general to what she knew I had observed in the daily social life of most women in Bahla, structured around the highly organized obligations of hospitality and visiting.

She began her account by describing how women neighbors would meet early in the mornings and go to the fields, cutting the alfalfa or wheat, grazing the animals, and chopping wood. "We used to *work* together," she emphasized. The collaboration and sense of community in work had given way, she implied, to a time of less collaborative work, a time when women would simply visit each other, eat, and talk. Ruwaya described how, if someone had given birth, the women would stop by her house on the way home from the fields: "Not everyone could provide coffee, especially the poor and the servants." At that time, Ruwaya explained, merchants would bring coffee from "Yiman," not like now when coffee comes from Costa Rica. "With the coffee," Ruwaya continued, "we would have dried dates or fresh dates, sometimes chickpeas, red sugar, and coffee. There was no fruit." Coffee, in Ruwaya's description, was not only limited to special events like childbirth, it came first while the other foods (dates, chickpeas, sugar) would accompany it. Ruwaya's statement that there was "no fruit" at that time does not mean that there was absolutely no fruit—mangoes, papayas, and bananas grow in Bahla and pomegranates, grapes, and melons grow elsewhere in the region—but that the amount did not compare to the quantity available in Bahla in the late 1990s.

Ruwaya then described how women would meet again in the afternoons during another break from work and, once again, in the evenings. In the evenings, however, they would not drink coffee, she said, but would discuss their plans for the next day. These gatherings were like meetings, Ruwaya emphasized, where the women would discuss their work: the pasture, grinding wheat, cutting wood. The "meetings" suggested an air of work, professionalism, and seriousness.

Returning to the activities of the morning, Ruwaya explained how every day it would be the turn of one or two women to take all the animals. The women would rotate this responsibility and would, if necessary, switch days if something arose that prevented them from going to the fields. Because the women who took the animals would not be able to join the others in the morning break, they would take water, yogurt, and dates with them.

The other task performed by women in the mornings, which they would discuss in the evenings, was wheat grinding. They would not discuss who would be responsible—this was not as much a communal job as taking the animals out—but simply review how much each had ground or planned to grind. "Women tended to grind the wheat every couple of days. There was a special room in the old neighborhood, you've seen it," Ruwaya said, "where women would go to grind wheat."

The grinding machine was called *al-raḥā*', "the mill stone." She detailed that there were two flat circular stones. The bottom one would remain still while the one on top moved. The top stone had a hole in the middle where the women would pour the unground wheat. They would attach a stick to the edge of the upper stone and turn it, grinding the wheat between the stones and allowing it to pour out of the sides. It would take the women about an hour to grind two kilos of wheat.

Women were also responsible, Ruwaya added, for collecting drinking and cooking water (*tarwaya*) from the wells, sometimes three or four times a day depending on how much they needed. In addition to taking the animals out to pasture, grinding wheat, and bringing water home, women were also responsible for collecting wood for cooking. Two or three women would go together to collect wood from the fields. In one day they might go back and forth three or four times from the fields to get enough wood to last them four or five days.

Ruwaya then returned to discussing the visits and how women would visit for a birth or mourning. Although these visits did not usually include coffee, when they did they would also include dates and sugar. For a wedding, they would have *ḥalwa* (a pasty dessert), coffee, dates, and sugar. "But," Ruwaya noted, "it is not like now, there was no banquet, no lunch." Again, the place of coffee in the gatherings arose: coffee, she explained, used to be kept in small pottery jugs, *dilāt*, where it would stay warm for about half an hour and could be reheated when cold. Then there were metal ones, like the "traditional" ones that were shown on television among the Bedouin, but these were not as good, Ruwaya pointed out, since they could not keep the coffee warm. This was before thermoses.

Ruwaya then briefly described what men would do in the past. Her description of men's "chores" and "coffee time" was limited. The men would meet every day at 7:00 in the morning, in a fixed place. They had coffee every morning, offered by one of the group's members; "every morning," she repeated. Ruwaya emphasized that the women did not have coffee, while the men did, though she did not explain why. The men, she continued, had many important matters to discuss: irrigation, agricultural seasons, needed repairs, the cleaning of the canals, the pollination of the palms, or the date of the palm auction. The men's meetings were like the "consultation council" (*majlis al-shūrā*), Ruwaya explained, emphasizing again their even more official, formal, and important character.[16]

I had not prompted Ruwaya specifically about coffee, yet coffee figured prominently in her description of the social or collaborative work of neighbors in the past: "not everyone had coffee," "we would take coffee," "we would not have coffee in the afternoons," "there was not always coffee for births or mournings," "there was coffee for weddings," "men had coffee every morning." The presence or absence of coffee punctuated her account of what women did in the past and how that compared with the present. In her construction of the past Ruwaya linked collaborative work—time spent in the fields, collecting wood, or carrying water—with the relative scarcity of coffee. As such, they can be contrasted with the neighborly gatherings in the late 1990s. For Ruwaya, coffee was part of how she defined the past and the present.

The Seduction and Dangers of Coffee

The omnipresence of coffee in contemporary Oman—one cup after another in everyday encounters and gatherings in Bahla—belies its history.[17] In the late 1990s, men would buy forty-kilogram burlap sacks of beans imported mostly from Costa Rica or Brazil.[18] The cost of coffee in the late 1990s fluctuated between forty and one hundred Omani rials per sack. Despite the sometimes high cost, it was rare to find a family unable to serve coffee when a guest arrived. After the men brought the coffee from the market, the women of the household would sort and roast the good beans. "If one bad bean gets into the coffee, the whole thing becomes bitter," Zaynab's mother warned me one day. "You have to be very careful." In many families, a woman roasted the coffee beans once a week and set them aside to be ground for each thermosful she made.

Although coffee was often described as an integral part of Arabian life, of hospitality, and of honor when I was in Bahla, its widespread and broad-based consumption was a phenomenon of the post-1970 period. What was not new about coffee was its association with excess. In classical Arabian poetry, the poetry of Bedouin of central Arabia, coffee is referred to as *kīf,* "that substance that sets the mood right" and the substance critical for the smooth performance of hospitality (Sowayan 1985). This substance, however, is also a fraught "classic," and one that has long carried with it a sense of luxury.

If broad-based consumption is a recent phenomenon, the coffee trade in Muscat goes back centuries.[19] European travelers to Muscat in the eighteenth century testify to large amounts of coffee either in the port or in the hands of Omani merchants.[20] Carsten Niebuhr, who visited Muscat in 1765, wrote that Omanis were "the best mariners in all of Arabia," responsible for a large portion of the coffee trade (fifty tranki ships annually)[21] from Jedda to Basra (Niebuhr 1792: II, 123). In 1775, with the Persian occupation of Basra, John G. Lorimer wrote, the coffee fleet stopped, but was immediately resumed with the end of the occupation (Lorimer 1915: II, 652). In the same year, a traveler to Muscat, Abraham Parsons, noted that Muscat sent twenty thousand bales of coffee to Basra (Ward 1987: 8).[22]

How much of this abundant coffee was reexported from Muscat to Nizwa and Bahla in the eighteenth and first half of the nineteenth century is unknown. Captain Cole, a British naval officer from the ship Palinurus who traveled to Nizwa in 1845, described how in crossing the Jebel Akhdar there was no coffee until he reached Nizwa, where he had coffee with the governor (*wāli*) (Ward 1987: 165–166). It seems that only the most powerful had coffee even when there was plenty coming through the Muscat port. Thirty years later, however, Samuel Miles described how in his visit to Nakhl in 1876, he witnessed shaykhs and leading Arabs discuss local politics in their "council hall," where "the *inevitable* coffee-pot is in full requisition, and the sheikhs' slaves may be seen close by busily engaged in roasting, pounding and cooking the berry for the company" (Ward 1987: 347; my emphasis). On the one hand, Miles's reference to the "inevitable coffee-pot" suggests that coffee beans may have been more readily available in the interior regions than might be supposed. On the other hand, this coffee seems to have been brewed mainly for elites: the shaykhs, leading Arabs, and visiting diplomats.

In addition to imported coffee, several nineteenth-century travelers to Oman mention locally grown coffee.[23] James Wellsted, who traveled to the Jebel Akhdar in 1835, mentions seeing coffee bushes (Ward 1987: 218), and Miles stated that on his trip in 1876 from Nakhl to Nizwa (also over the Jebel Akhdar) "a few coffee plants may be seen here, and it is the only place in Oman where it still lingers, the flourishing plantations that formerly existed having now all disappeared" (Ward 1987: 351). Captain Hamerton, another early nineteenth-century traveler to Bureimi, writes that "Coffee, too, was formerly cultivated on the hill Hafeet, but from the indolence of the inhabitants, or other causes, its growth has been abandoned" (Ward 1987: 438).

Throughout the twentieth century, the availability and price of coffee fluctuated. Indeed, the price of coffee increased 410% during World War II (IOR, R/15/6/339), even while the number of bags of coffee imported (mostly from Africa) into Muscat more than doubled from 4,972 in 1942–1943 to 12,616 in 1943–1944 (Muscat Trade Report 1946a, 1946b). In 1939, the Muscat government established a price control committee that implemented measures to prevent profiteering (IOR, L/PS/12/2972). The committee attempted to fix prices and limit the amount of foodstuffs people could buy in Muscat as well as the amount of foodstuffs exported to the interior. Explained by British consuls and the Sultan as part of an effort to ration goods during World War II (which were, for the most part, coming from India to Oman), the restrictions on supplies to the interior continued late into the next decade.

In January 1943 shaykhs from al-Dakhiliya and al-Sharqiya gathered to discuss and formulate a complaint about these measures, especially about the "export" of rice from Muscat to Oman (IOR, L/PS/12/2972). According to the British annual administration report for 1943, even as the Muscat government was profiting from the war (the elevated prices of imports led to an increase in customs duties), "the poorer classes were very near to famine conditions" (IOR, R/15/6/339). This era is now remembered in Bahla as the period of control, *mudat al-quntrūl*.[24] In 1945 the Muscat government formalized what it called the Control Department,[25] which further regularized the restrictions on goods sold to individuals on the coast, established a system of rations, and restricted exports to the interior.[26] And, again, in 1945 when the British consul traveled to the town of Sumayil, local shaykhs met with him and raised the issue of the control system, asking whether it was necessary, given the end of the war and whether the idea was a British one (IOR, R/15/6/242). Custom duties as well as the experience of the period of control meant increased restrictions on the movement of coffee to the interior. At the same time, however, the complaints about control and about the duties also revealed that coffee, although one of the most important imports into Oman in this period (after rice and textiles), was not a necessity and was not the focus of complaints.

Once the Control Department was eliminated in the late 1940s, coffee again became more readily available in Oman. Despite the fluctuations and the uncertainty of the amounts entering the markets in the interior of Oman throughout the twentieth century, it is safe to say that until the early 1970s, coffee was a luxury item affordable only to more wealthy and powerful townspeople.[27] I was often told that for those who could not afford coffee, in moments of required hospitality such as when there was a death in the family, neighbors, patrons, or the wealthy would often provide the poor with coffee and sugar.[28] Thus the requirement, or at least the pressure to provide coffee in moments of hospitality, although not as urgent as it became in the late twentieth century, was clearly important. An elderly woman explained to me that in the mid-1950s she would pay about five baisas (110 baisas = one qursh fransī)[29] for a handful of beans, using and reusing a few beans for each pot (the coffee from reused beans was called *raga'a*, literally "returned"). Generally, another wealthier woman explained to me, coffee cost between five and ten baisas for a quarter kilogram and a family could last an entire week on one qursh worth of coffee. Otherwise, people would mix chickpeas (*dingiū*) or ground date pits (*nawa*) into the coffee to make it sufficient.

While coffee was one of the most important trading goods at the end of the eighteenth and beginning of the nineteenth centuries, Muslim scholars also debated its legality.[30] John C. Wilkinson has noted that coffee was forbidden for Ibadis until the scholar A. Nabhan Jaid b. Khamis al-Kharusi (c. 1735–1822) wrote a *fatwa* [legal opinion] in its favor (Wilkinson 1983: 192 n. 3). The legality of coffee, clearly still in question, was reaffirmed by his son, Nassir bin Abu Nabhan al-Kharusi.[31]

Nur al-Din al-Salimi, in the early twentieth century, explains the debate about coffee in two sections of his *Jawhar al-Niẓām*: the last fifteen lines of the chapter on drink in volume 2 and, in volume 4, in the chapter on customs of eating and drinking. In his chapter on drink, he writes:

> And [as for] the coffee bean, the differences among the ulama is reported
> That it is forbidden is mentioned in the canon of our excellent scholars
> And they have a reason for it and this reason has light

And, this is because foolish people made [drinking] it a custom and depend
    on it

And they used it in places of entertainment, replacing their wine in this way

Its cup circles like the cup of wine, and it is named after wine when it is men-
    tioned [in memory] (*dhikr*)

It is called "wine" and "coffee" and "cup" in a pleasing way for the drinker

Because for them it is like drinking that which intoxicates, the prohibition of
    this is not denied

[But] it is only this forbidden mimicking, which is not allowed, not the desire
    [for coffee] itself

Oh God, how farsighted that vision is in preventing the substance of the cor-
    ruption if it occurs

And after time passed and disappeared, so did the intended target of our
    ancestor-scholars

Some people, who do not know the origins, deny any saying that is permis-
    sible (*al-ḥall*)[32]

And, so the imitating [of wine] has disappeared, and the reasons for allowing
    coffee have [correctly] proliferated

There might be something that is forbidden by the definition of it but the
    forbidden is annulled when the description no longer applies

There are counterparts to rulings, it is impossible to count them all

According to Nur al-Din, the problem with coffee is neither coffee itself nor the
desire to drink it, but rather the practices associated with it: drinking coffee in
a way similar to wine, in a way that "mimics" (*yiqallid*) wine drinking. When
people drink coffee just as they drink wine, then coffee drinking should be prohibited. Nur al-Din does not discuss the drinker's "intention" (*niyya*)—that is,
whether it is legal or illegal based on people's intentions to drink coffee like they
drink wine, but rather whether they do drink it like they drink wine. The legality of coffee has to do with the social practices involved in its drinking.

In another poem about coffee's legality, Nur al-Din al-Salimi's teacher and
the one-time judge in Hamra, Majid bin Khamis al-Abri (AH 1252–1340
[1836/7–1921/2 CE]), wrote:

Oh wineserver (*sāqī*) of the bean,[33] be generous, serve cup (*kās*) after cup, and
    it is a pure liquid (*ḥall*) that has nothing wrong with it

How strange that people would forbid it, and they prohibit it (*hajarhā*) with-
    out any reason

They forbade it without bringing any evidence from the book,[34] the Sunna, or
   analogy

And it is a bean that is roasted without sin,[35] the water is pure without doubt

Is there any intoxication (*sakar*) or pollution in it, so that it is made forbidden, like a pollutant?[36]

And, it is from a cell (*khalīya*) and is considered tremendously useful for all
   kinds of drowsiness

Coffee [in the meaning] of wine, God forbids it, but not coffee [in the mean-
   ing] of beans, and the truth is like the lantern

We are not denying those who say an opinion, because in the opinion [one
   sees] the argument of intelligence

If it [the opinion] is not arbitrary, it is [from] the blessed scholar and leader
   (*walī*) of the people

And peace be upon the Prophet and his family and the highly-respected
   people, who are like unmoving mountains

While Nur al-Din points to the social context in which coffee is drunk as ob-
jectionable, al-Abri simply notes that there is nothing wrong with coffee and
that its effects are not harmful, but rather useful. Although interested in his
opponents' arguments, al-Abri states that it is a valuable medicine for staying
awake and that there is no analogy with wine. If it were wine, it would be illegal, but it is from a bean that is not illegal.

For others, however, there is something seductive and dangerous about coffee itself, a seduction that appears in an anonymous poem commonly known in
Bahla today. Although the allure of the social aspect of coffee drinking is noted,
here there is also something specific to coffee that gives it its seductive quality:

How many jewels in coffee; jewels of red, yellow, and green

A brunette exhales fragrance from her medicinal cups like aloe, musk or
   amber

He did not know when drinking it, whether he was drinking a mouthful of
   an intoxicant, sugar, or Kawthar[37]

It is more delicious for the obsessed lover, sipping it than kissing a graceful
   gazelle with a seductive voice, pitch-black irises and with the white of the
   eyes pure

It distracts the foreigner from [remembering] his nations until he returns late
   not having realized [this]

It heals the sick, so tell who is passionate about cures, seek no more and use
    coffee instead
If their tombs are sprinkled with it, it makes the dead alive; you will see the
    day of resurrection
If a cup circulates, its scent guides both the arrogant rich and the stingy poor
And, if a humble man is drinking it, you will see him in a proud and haughty
    state
[he] wipes the sides of his beard as if he were awarded the throne of
    Alexander
It distracts people from their work until it restrains; their earnings become
    difficult
They are infatuated by it until they forget, from love for it, to earn a living in
    time of hardship
So, you will see them walking in crowds to it like the pilgrims walking to
    Mina and al-Masha'ar[38]
They are racing to places to drink; morning and afternoon in all eras
Welcome al-Nubi boy,[39] carrying coffee to us and with it he buys and sells the
    people
Give me, pour me some, I am madly in love with it, fill up the cups, do not
    weary and give more
Give me, pour me a cup and another cup and another cup and another cup,
    raise and repeat
Give me, pour me with a coffee-pot and keep these small cups away, which
    never grow up
Give me, pour me some, I will never get bored even if seven seas of coffee
    drowned me today
It is what makes me alive and living in the world and I cannot be without it
    for an hour

In another version of this poem, the insatiable desire for coffee has the narra-
tor demand from the coffee server to continue pouring, even if that means that
the drinker is "led astray":

Get up, and pour us husk coffee, it surpasses all the kings and Caesar
    together
Get up, and pour us, there is no hope [for me], even if seven seas of coffee
    were to lead me astray
Get up, and pour us cup and another cup and another cup for me and repeat it

Another short poem by Abdulrahman al-Riyami (d. AH 1374 [1954–1955 CE]) refers to the smell of coffee, saying that it attracts, that it flirts, that it smells like musk, and that those who smell it will not get lost, just as the Magi did not get lost when they were following the light from the north star:

> It appears to us like the blood of the gazelle and its fragrance is like sharp musk
> Whoever seeks the shadow of the wineshops (ḥānātahā), I swear he will not lose the road
> If the [star] had not shown for the Magi, they would not have worshipped the flame of the fire

These poems,[40] repeated in Bahla from time to time, testify to the problems of the practice of coffee drinking as well as to the power of coffee as an intoxicant and as a medical cure. The sexual associations of coffee are not particularly surprising given not only its connection with wine in terms of its intoxicating effects, but also the necessarily social character of coffee drinking.

When coffee requires sociality (either because of its luxuriousness or because it needs managing), both coffee and sociality are subsequently also imbued with meanings of seduction, intoxication, and forgetting God. When sociality requires coffee (because of etiquettes of hospitality), both become associated with leisure, the waste of time, decadence, decline, and overabundance. In either case, coffee not only becomes a synonym for social gathering, but also ensures that sociality becomes both a means to control desire and a producer of risk, potentially corrupting those who partake in it. One could even argue that coffee is not simply a metaphor or even a metonym for leisure and luxury, but a synechdoche for sociality.

Hayden White's (1973) discussion of the differences between metaphor, metonym, and synecdoche can clarify some of the relationships explored in this chapter.[41] As E. Valentine Daniel, drawing from White, summarized, "In synecdoche . . . it is not merely a case where the part stands for the whole in which the whole is reduced to one of its parts [as in metonym], but the part selected to represent the whole suffuses the entire being of the whole that it represents" (Daniel 1984: 107). While in metonymic relationships, the whole is reduced to a literal although, at times, qualitative part, in synecdoche the part that stands for the whole infuses that whole with sets of meanings. In the case I have examined, coffee is a synecdoche for sociality; sociality is not only sometimes reduced to coffee (as the phrase "Have you coffee-ed?" suggests), but coffee also suffuses sociality with some of the symbolism associated with its drinking and its effects.

As the anonymous poem suggests (and as al-Abri mentioned), Bahlawis also used coffee as a cure. Zaynab once explained how drops of brewed coffee were good for earaches, while coffee grounds were good for cuts. Another time, in talking about her father's occult powers, Zaynab described how a young man once laughed at a magician (*sāḥir*) and when the man went home he collapsed. His mother and father sat around him crying and giving him coffee, hoping that the coffee would help, but this time it was not enough. One of the parents went to Zaynab's father to explain what happened, and he went to visit and saw them sitting around the young man. Zaynab's father then went home and took a nap; the next day another family member returned to Zaynab's father and described how he was cured. In this account, the ability of coffee to cure was not sufficient on its own, and the young man needed the help of a scholar whose ability to cure (even while or through resting) was remarkable. And, as with other cures, coffee's healing power is the obverse of its power to harm. Coffee can cause one to lose one's head, to forget to work, to think one is someone one is not, or to induce one to worship as though he or she were performing the rituals that show love of God. On the other hand, it can raise people from the dead, cure an earache, or give energy.

The question of the legality or appropriateness of coffee and coffee drinking had not been forgotten in Bahla. Indeed, while I was conducting fieldwork, some people refused to drink coffee because of its association with forgetting God and intoxication. They also complained of coffee's centrality in social life, and the way that both had become so much a part of daily life in the post-coup oil-economy era, to the point of excess. Coffee had come to stand for the material abundance, over-consumption, and ease of modern Omani life. It is therefore somewhat ironic that coffee and coffee drinking have also become one of the primary symbols of Arabian hospitality.[42]

Dates, Words, and the Attempt to Balance

In the daily neighborly groups, women would often tell me that they had to maintain a balance, a *ta'ādul*, between hot and cold, between bitter and sweet, in their eating and drinking.[43] Such balance, women would explain to me, was made possible with dates. Whereas coffee was an ambiguous item, dates were considered fundamentally good. The bitterness and "coldness" of coffee was balanced by the fundamental sweetness and "hotness" of dates. While coffee, in many ways, signified the excesses of daily consumption in the oil state and a "waste of time," dates signified the basic wholesomeness of the earth. Unlike coffee, which should be shared, dates could be consumed alone. Of course, as Webb Keane (1997) illustrated with regard to ritualized exchange in Indonesia, such attempts at balance also create the space for slippage and the possibility of imbalance. And indeed, the risks of imbalance were evident in the rituals of these daily gatherings, especially with regard to the words that the exchanges required.

While Bahlawis that I knew understood that the sweetness and hotness of dates balanced the bitterness and coldness of the coffee, the contrast was not only one of taste; it was also one of history. While coffee pointed to a world of luxury and potentially of excess, dates were a necessity of life. Dates were also enmeshed in the politics of taxation and even seen as evidence of divine ire in the form of drought and the diseases particular to date palms. The history of coffee as an imported luxury item was contrasted with the history of dates as a staple food, a local product, and an export item (a distinction that Bahlawis made when speaking of most products, but especially those that they ate).[44] While one was associated with conspicuous consumption, the other was entangled in the history of production.

Indeed, dates were still considered one of Oman's most important exports, even if since the early 1970s revenues from dates had not come close to the revenues derived from oil.[45] According to the Omani Ministry of Information, Omanis produced between 150,000 and 175,000 tons of dates in 1998–1999. Compared to the annual income from the approximately 700,000 bpd (barrels per day) of oil at that time, dates represented only a tiny fraction of the gross national product.[46] But, until the discovery of oil, dates were the largest export item from al-Dakhiliya. This dependence on date exports sometimes created local difficulties in the nineteenth and twentieth centuries, especially as Omanis relied more on international markets. At other times, the Muscat government changed the taxing system for dates from the interior. These political and economic fluctuations, in addition to the problems of drought and disease, made the production of dates a precarious enterprise. Nevertheless, dates were considered in many ways "sacred."[47]

Tracing the history of the date trade in Muscat and in the interior of Oman is beyond the scope of this chapter. Nevertheless, a few words about the date trade will highlight the centrality of dates to the economy of the interior. European travelers from the early sixteenth through the twentieth centuries invariably mention dates in the markets of Muscat and Matrah, and British records from the nineteenth century indicate that most dates were exported to India.[48] Although the main market for Omani dates has been India, they were also exported to Zanzibar. At the beginning of the nineteenth century, to the US as well.[49] By 1865, the American W. J. Towell Company had established a branch in Muscat and was the largest supplier of dates to the US.[50] Because there was not enough supply to sustain the American market in the second half of the nineteenth century, there was an attempt to plant Omani *farḍ* dates in Arizona (Lorimer 1915: I, 2295).

Although early travellers often mentioned the destination of Omani dates, they rarely noted the origin, whether they came from the interior regions of al-Sharqiya and al-Dakhiliya or from coastal Batina. In the mid-nineteenth century, however, Captain Cole, visiting Sur, wrote that caravans of five to six hundred camels laden with dates were leaving from al-Mintirib daily, with the dates then being shipped from Sur to India (Ward 1987: 158). British residency administrative and trade reports from the early and mid-twentieth century note that most of the dates exported to India came from the coastal Batina area.

Although Omani shipping in general declined after the 1860s, dates were still the major Omani export through the mid-twentieth century (Landen 1967: 147). The political upheavals during Sultan Faysal bin Turki's reign (1888–1913) did not help the export trade, since caravan routes from the interior to the coast were periodically closed and subject to attack, and the destruction of groves of date palms was a common practice in attacks on villages and towns. Date traders also suffered from periodic droughts and from the fluctuations in the value of the Maria Theresa dollar.[51] Nevertheless, at the end of the nineteenth century, under the reign of the Sultan Faysal bin Turki, dates were the most valuable export and source of exchange, earning over $MT 750,000 annually.

By the early twentieth century, date growers in the interior had become dependent on the ability to trade with the coast. The dependence on date exportation for the economy of the interior is evident in the struggles over the system of taxation and trade controls.[52] With the declaration of an Imamate in 1913, a series of battles ensued between Imamate supporters and the Sultanate, which had the backing of the British. The Imamate confiscated lands belonging to members of the Sultan's family, and the Sultanate demanded their return.[53] In May 1920, the Sultan's government, with the support of a reformed administration, declared a sharp increase in taxes on goods from the interior in order to punish the Imamate supporters. The tax on a case of dates rose from 5% to 25%; on a case of pomegranates, from 5% to 50%.[54]

According to British documents and to Wilkinson, it was the imposition of this punitive export tax on dates that led the Imamate administration to agree to the 1920 Treaty of Sib, by which an ambiguous dual state was established (Wilkinson 1987: 70).[55] In the treaty, the Sultanate and the Imamate eventually agreed that the Muscat government would charge no more than a 5% duty on dates from Oman (what is now al-Sharqiya and al-Dakhiliya) that would be exported from any Muscat port. However, the Muscat government at Sur continued to charge a fee of $MT 1.50 per camel-load, which, according to Omanis, equaled a 12% duty on the value of the dates. In 1924, the Imamate government filed a complaint about Sur, and by the summer of 1936, merchants from Oman, exasperated that nothing was being done, boycotted the port of Sur and began to talk about establishing another port with the shaykh of the Beni bu Ali tribe (IOR, L/PS/12/2972, Muscat Diaries: News and Intelligence Summaries, August 1–15, 1936). The reorganizing of Muscat's finances in 1932 once again affected date producers.[56]

That people in the interior relied on dates both for sustenance and for trade is evident too. In July 1945, for example, it was rumored in Muscat "that the export of dates from Oman will be forbidden and that the Imam has recently appealed to the people to store the crop in order to avoid famine and starvation" (IOR, L/PS/12/2972, Muscat Diaries: News and Intelligence Summaries, July 15, 1945). In addition to the control of exports, international bans and price fluctuations also affected production and life in the interior. Clearly, this export, like the import of coffee, was tied to political relations and international markets.[57] Unlike coffee, however, dates have come to be seen as belonging to the Omani landscape; they are local. In the late 1990s they were recognized as a source of life: they sustained people in Bahla when there was nothing else to eat.

The nutritional dependence on dates and their value to the local moral and administrative order is evident in accounts of drought and the organization of cultivation. Dawood's biography of the early twentieth-century governor of the town, Shaykh Abu Zayd, explains how he, in addition to rebuilding the walls of the town, also worked to replant date palms. Abu Zayd's main projects, according to this and another local history as well as to many Bahlawis, were to rebuild the wall, fix the water canals and wells, and plant more date palms when the drought ended. Thus, as the taxing of date exports from the region was becoming a struggle for traders from the interior and frustration over the wartime system of *qunṭrūl* was mounting in the 1940s, Abu Zayd was working to make sure there were enough dates for people to eat.

In these histories and in conversations I had with Bahlawis about Abu Zayd, his actions in taking care of the date palms were particularly heralded, especially by older generations. Dates, many would tell me, should not be wasted. The sight of dead date palms would often conjure up discussions about the disinterest of the youth in caring for important things. Abu Zayd created, according to these local histories, a workforce for taking care of the dates on the *bayt al-māl* lands, and he punished people for wasting dates. Abu Zayd's attitude towards dates, like his attitude towards many things, tended to be viewed as the correct way to be. Abu Zayd's humility and modesty, his piety and forceful determination to administer God's laws, often appeared in people's accounts of what one should do. Thus, in descriptions of his work on the land, his care for date palms can be read as emblematic of correct behavior: recognizing the blessings in fruit such as dates, prohibiting the wasting of dates, and supporting date farming in order to bolster the community, both in terms of income and nutrition.

When Abu Zayd became governor of Bahla in 1916, the town was afflicted by a serious drought. According to Dawood, "in the first days [of Abu Zayd's governorship], the river of Bahla dried and the wells dried and Bahla closed up from fear and hunger and lack of fruit [dates] and that is what the people earned from their deeds from the wisdom and justice of God" (al-Mufarji 1995: 7). The punishment from God was due to Bahla's support for or, at least, acquiescence to, the ruler Nassir bin Humayd, as well as to the town's opposition to the Imamate of Salim bin Rashid al-Kharusi. Divine intervention, seen in the drought and the lack of dates, appears again in the miraculous survival of the date palms in the *bayt al-māl* lands. Although many of the date palms of al-Sifāla (lower Bahla) died during this drought, the palms on the *bayt al-māl* lands, those lands belonging to the religious state, did not suffer.

Dawood also recounts that "if the shaykh was walking in the street and he saw a fallen date he [would] take it with his noble hand and [would] wipe away the dirt from it and put it in his turban and [would] say: 'it is not distinguished to be indifferent to blessings [of God] and the people do not understand where there is blessing and perhaps it is in the fallen date and it is not permissible to trample it with steps and a neglect of blessings causes poverty and God forbids it'" (al-Mufarji 1995: 10). Dawood also recounts how Abu Zayd once saw that the wind was blowing a large pile of dates off of the roof of a tanner's house. One of Abu Zayd's guards called the tanner, Zaher bin 'Isa al-Hamaymi, to the fort. When Zaher arrived, Abu Zayd said that summer and the cultivation of that particular date, the *farḍ*, had ended two months before and that the Prophet had said that it was prohibited to waste water. What, Abu Zayd asked, was preventing him from properly storing his dates? Zaher responded that as a tanner, he only ate a few dates every day for work and that he was nowhere near eating them all. Abu Zayd then threatened to imprison Zaher, unless he "protect the blessings" (al-Mufarji 1995: 10). Zaher did so.

When the rains finally came, Abu Zayd undertook to replant date palms. First, he hired a workforce to uproot the dead trunks and chop them up for firewood. Abu Zayd hired Salih bin Salim al-Malaqab, who was a specialist in cutting down the trunks of dead palms and planting young date palms. He planted many palms in a short time, especially *khalāṣ* dates, the best kind.

Abu Zayd had noted that there were few *khalāṣ* palms planted in town and asked why the townspeople were not planting good dates. The townspeople responded that *khalāṣ* palms attract more bees than others and that therefore it was necessary to harvest the dates using fire. Abu Zayd reasoned that if the number of *khalāṣ* dates increased, then the bees would be filled and God would protect the people from the bees' evil. God, of course, created bees for a reason, even though this reason was hidden from humans and even though humans were given the capacity to interpret. So, the people of Bahla began planting more *khalāṣ* palms, and the people were able to eat due to God's increased blessing and the blessing God had given to the shaykh. Practical measures were also taken to protect the *khalāṣ* palms from bees: Abu Zayd hired another man, al-Abd bin Suayd Mawali al-Kunud (a servant of the Kindi tribe), ordering him to cover all the date palms. When the numbers of bees increased, Abu Zayd ordered the bees destroyed. Abu Zayd also instituted money for a religious endowment for the collection of rodents and bees.[58]

Not only were date palms important for providing the town with food, but the revenues from the annual date palm auctions also worked to support the mosques and the central administration. Abu Zayd, according to Dawood, used auction revenue to redistribute food to the poor. Dawood attributes the reorganization of the religious endowment properties to Abu Zayd. Abu Zayd selected agents for each mosque and had every date palm of the mosques counted. The agents would be responsible for organizing the monies and properties of the mosques and would receive a percentage of the mosque's revenues. For the auctioning of the date palms, Abu Zayd would have the auctioneers begin with the *bayt al-māl* palms and then move on to the palms of the individual mosques. Because palms could be donated to a mosque on privately owned land, however, it was not enough to know which plot of land belonged to whom or to which mosque; the agents needed to determine who or what mosque owned each date palm. In addition to the agents for the mosques, Abu Zayd also hired a scribe, someone from his own hometown of Izki, who would write down the transactions. For the poor who could not afford to pay for user rights[59] to date palms, Abu Zayd would write a note to the auctioneer giving the individual an amount that he or she could spend for date palms for that year.

The annual date auctioning, which, according to Dawood, was originally instituted and organized by Abu Zayd, continued in Bahla in the late 1990s. But by then, it seemed to serve almost as much as a rite of summer as it did as a source of income for the mosques or a source of dates for the community.[60] Indeed, during my fieldwork the yearly date auctions were attended by hardly more than twenty men, compared to the forty to one hundred men that Fredrik Barth noted in 1974 (Barth 1978: 59). This is a significant decrease,

Figure 3.2 Auctioning a date palm. Photo courtesy of the author.

especially given the increase in the town's population. People would, instead, buy most of their annual supply of dates from the government farms in Wadi Quriyat, which provided the popular *khalāṣ* dates, the variety that Abu Zayd had planted in town. When the government built its own state-subsidized date farm in Wadi Quriyat, near Bahla, it provided Bahlawis with more affordable *khalāṣ* dates, but it also limited the interest in cultivating dates in town.

The annual date harvest not only introduced the summer, but also marked time more broadly in Bahla. In discussions with older Bahlawis, I would ask when they went somewhere or when something happened, and they would often say, "I'm not sure exactly, but it was when the dates were being harvested." Sometimes, they marked time even more specifically according to which kind of dates were being harvested. In Bahla there were nine major types of dates, which ripened at different times.[61] "When did you arrive from Zanzibar?", for example, would be answered with, "During the monsoon, when the *khiṣāb* dates were being harvested." Or, when I asked my landlord when he returned from his trip to Dubai thirty years earlier, he answered: "I arrived when the first dates were being harvested." Sometimes, though, someone would answer a question about when with "when the dates were being pollinated." Unlike the Ḥijrī Islamic calendar, which is lunar, the agricultural calendar, remembered according to the date harvest, can indicate the cycle of the seasons.

The cultivation of dates, like the reliance on their exportation, was not of course a perfect process for everyone. Fredrik Barth, who visited Bahla in 1974, illustrated how factors of production—land, labor, and water—reproduce inequality in Bahla. While Barth described the structure and circulation of the factors of production in Bahla, he also highlighted the moral import of dates. According to Barth, Bahlawis did not buy or sell dates from Bahla in Bahla: "Indeed, no Bahla person can honourably offer God's bounty (the crop of dates) for sale within Bahla, nor can he without loss of face refuse a request for dates in bulk from a neighbour or townsman" (Barth 1978: 58). Although I found no ethic about selling dates in Bahla to Bahlawis, Barth's analysis of date production, circulation, and consumption in Bahla reveals the centrality of dates to a moral universe.

The moral universe of dates was one in which a lack of dates signified either the disrespect of the youth towards the difficulties of life or the ire of God in punishment for wrongdoings. The tragedies of droughts that often afflict Bahla were visible in the late 1990s in the remnants of dead palm trees, left as reminders of impending death and the instability of life—a life that necessarily relies on the elements and, ultimately, on the limits of natural resources. Given the importance of dates in Bahla, it is not surprising that some families with the means to do so planted date palms at the birth of each child.[62] Each of my landlord's ten children, for example, had a date palm planted for them when they were born. Date palms were thus part of a symbolic world of fertility, sweetness, and life.

Two poems about dates, and about *khalās* dates in particular, suggest some of the associations of dates with sweetness, life, and honor. This short, two-line poem was sometimes repeated to me when *khalās* dates were being served:

I do not like the *khanayzī* date, even though it is red, and I like the *khalās* date
Although it is big and full of honey, later on, it will be a fire in people's hearts

A longer poem, also about *khalās* dates, reveals the differences between dates and coffee. Whereas coffee, in the poems quoted earlier in this chapter, seems dangerous and can cause one to forget his responsibilities, *khalās* dates are irreproachable.

The Delicious Khalās Dates
Honor the *khalās* and praise it honorably and judge it as the winner because
    it is the best
Oh, you, who are a very precious treasure and who became a soaring palm
    tree carrying the garland
They accused you wrongly if they compared something to you, and they
    abandoned you if they made something like you
They came to me with what they promoted, and they spoke about it nicely,
    but did not show any evidence
And what they said vaguely about it and pretended, they departed from the
    reasonable and substantiated
Courage resigns in us and we refuse to be humiliated or submissive
Where is the *khalās* compared to this [other] palm tree date, even though in
    its color and length it is the same species
The color of pure gold describes its color and the oleander flower is similar
But there is nothing like your taste even if they exaggerate similar palm trees
They said there were two swords, one is solid and the other sharp
Oh, this sword and sharp tongue, the slaughtered stallions broke away from
    their fleet
If they tried to be proud they would be taken there and slaughtered

> Oh you have mastery over all the dates, increase your beauty and wear the
> garland
> You are superior in taste and in smoothness, your color is precious and you
> taste like honey

Unlike coffee, dates are sweet, soft, honorable, and virtuous. It was important
for Bahlawis to care for and respect the date palms, even though by the late
1990s it was clear that many palms were being neglected. Dates were understood to balance coffee, not only because they were considered sweet and hot
against coffee's bitterness and coldness, but because they were local, nutri-
tious, and "good." And, because they were not dangerous or ambiguous in the
ways that coffee was, dates also did not require sociality.

The everyday requirement of sociality in Bahla, of visiting with and caring
for neighbors, of exchanging and "balancing" coffee and dates, was fraught with
tensions and imbued with historically shaped meanings. Sociality was both a
requirement and condemned as a waste of time, useless (*ghayr nafa'a*), and full
of "gossip." Sociality in Bahla was increasingly considered an activity that drew
attention away from the correct running of households (a complaint that I often
heard from female professionals) and, more importantly, from the individual's
direct focus on God. Sociality was also complicated by the fact that the activities accompanying visiting—consuming and exchanging coffee and dates—
carried with them histories of war, trade, blockades, and famine, as well as good
governance and piety. The activities and objects of exchange reminded women
of the surprising "good fortune" of the present.

Adding further to the tensions surrounding sociality was the status of
words. While dates, as I have argued, provided a balance of goodness and
sweetness to coffee, words—which were also required social interactions—did
not function as neatly. Just as women were expected to provide coffee and dates,
they were also expected to greet each other, to ask about each other's children,
and to inquire into each other's health. Women were expected, in subtle ways,
not to share certain words—not necessarily words that might seem offensive or
risqué—but rather words that might compromise their families or friendships.
At the same time, suspicion about words could be mitigated if the focus of talk
was on what came to be recognized as "religion," as I discuss more fully in the
following chapter. The third part of the triad of sociality, after coffee and dates,
then, is words. As one young man explained to me, coffee, dates, and words are
"together . . . they are one unit."

The "consumption" of words, therefore, can be understood to be similar to that of coffee and dates. All three can be ingested; they leave traces and yet they also seem to disappear; they can be remembered and yet they no longer "exist."[63] And, indeed in some forms of healing, people literally ingested words: a common cure was to drink Qur'anic words written with saffron on water. At the same time, the dangers and power of eating are apparent in the Bahlawi use of the verb *to eat* to mean "to kill." At stake here, then, is not only the materiality of words (Irvine 1989; Keane 1997), but also a specific kind of materiality. Words, like food and drink, stand apart from the body, but they can also enter it, affect it, and affect its relations with other bodies.[64]

The study of language as an economic resource (Bourdieu 1977), as a source of authority that gives objects their full exchange-value, or as an object which is exchanged for cash or other goods (Irvine 1989), has provided varied and substantial examples of the materiality of words and the relationships between language and political economy.[65] Keane illustrated the relationships among people, things, and words in formal ceremonial exchanges, and in particular that "people's relationships to words and things are shaped by the demands, dynamics, and risks of interaction with others" (1997: 225). Keane's focus on ceremonial exchange and ritual speech could be extended to people's everyday relationships with words and objects. While the force and weight of exchange is certainly more acute in formal ceremonial exchange, the coffee, dates, and words that formed the fundamental components of women's mundane neighborly exchanges in Bahla also illustrate the interconnections of things and words. People's relationships to things and words are shaped by their relationships with each other; these relationships and exchanges are also fraught with hazards.

The importance of speech for the smooth performance of hospitality, together with coffee and dates, was regularly noted in Bahla. People often explained to me that the most common way of indicating displeasure with someone's actions was to serve the basic coffee and dates, but to sit in silence, exchanging only a few words of greetings. The moral obligation of appropriate sociality—to perform as host or guest and to be socially hospitable—did not negate the possibility that that obligation was not performed or was limited somehow as a meditated way of insulting a visitor, showing disrespect, or voicing displeasure, or as a less meditated act of performing the markers of status distinctions.

In other words, the requirement of generosity does not in itself preclude deliberation about action. James Hagen (1999) has argued that literature on the gift has abandoned Marcel Mauss's (2000 [1924]) original concern about

whether (and, I would add, how) to give for an approach that considers it almost impossible to behave differently. The question of deliberation also raises
the issue of the degree to which individuals decide to engage in reciprocity,
through the sharing of edible things or words. In Bahla too, although generosity and hospitality required particular acts, there were many ways that this hospitality could be enacted, and this was often indicated through the profusion or
limitation of words. Judgments about the relationships between talk and hospitality or talk, gender, and gossip are not, to be sure, particular to Oman. There,
however, this metalanguage reveals unease about time and leisure.

One proverb that I often heard in Bahla, "there is more news among neighbors than there is from London," also points to the ambiguity of the place of
words in women's daily neighborly groups. On the one hand, words were necessary for the appropriate performance of hospitality, and this proverb suggests
that neighbors were regarded as the purveyors of a great amount of information. On the other hand, too much talk among women was frowned upon.
Information gained at neighborly groups was sometimes dismissed as "only
women's talk" that did not "mean anything," even though much town news
came from women's visiting networks.

My landlord revealed a similar attitude to words (rather than deeds) when
he responded to a poetry reading being broadcast on television one day by saying: "The poets, they are rich with speaking, not with doing." In fact, as will be
noted again in the following chapter, much of the criticism of the neighborly
groups was precisely framed around "useless talk" among women, which required repentance (*tawba*). Not wasting words was similar to not wasting dates,
as in the example of Abu Zayd's picking up the fallen dates and putting them in
his turban. In Bahla, then, just as coffee and dates provided for the smooth performance of the social (and, often, economic) exchange, words also facilitated
these moments of interaction. And, as with coffee and dates, words not only facilitated the production of the correct context, but were also in these moments
themselves objects of transaction—objects to be ingested, objects that might
disrupt the very balance of dates and coffee.

Conclusion

Every day in Bahla, women would visit with their neighbors and exchange coffee, dates, and words. They would drink coffee from each other's thermoses and
eat dates that they had each brought. They shared news that they had heard
at home the previous evening. They discussed their personal and children's

ailments, and they remembered people, events, and places that had recently or long since passed. Women would also go, either on their own or together, to visit other groups of women or family members to offer their condolences, share their congratulations, or simply to express their greetings. The daily repetition of these gatherings affirmed community belonging as well as social hierarchies. But, these visits were also tied to historical trajectories and people's notions about the past. They were inflected by the histories of the production and consumption of the objects (the coffee, dates, and words) themselves.

The daily repetition had the effect of making the visits appear customary. And, in some ways, of course, they were, as Nur al-Din al-Salimi and Abu Zayd's works outlining the obligations and responsibilities of neighbors illustrate. Clearly, a similar form of sociality had existed at least since the early twentieth century. Likewise, national representations of Arab hospitality, which extended images and examples of positive traditional generosity to women's neighborly visits, also helped produce the notion that these visits were traditional. Many Bahlawis themselves viewed such sociality as essential to proper conduct and personhood; not participating in social life implied that the person was not behaving as a person ought to behave. Not participating in such activities sometimes resulted in comments by others, both men and women, about a woman's selfishness, greed, and even madness—all signs of inappropriate asociality, "religious" or otherwise.

At the same time, the debate about whether or how these practices were rooted in the past (and how they helped shape proper womanhood) was precisely where the tensions around them lay. Some argued that these practices were not possible in the past because the objects and conditions of exchange were less available then. As a result, these visits came to be seen as decadent and as emblems of the leisure and waste that the new oil wealth made possible. This was made especially the case as coffee shifted from luxury to common commodity (or as life shifted from one that emphasized production to one that emphasized consumption). Others argued that while visiting may have been practiced in the past, it was less an example of good personhood than of previous religious ignorance. Sociality was thus associated both with modern waste and with some older women's lack of religious education and knowledge. Indeed, it is precisely such concerns about proper piety and religious knowledge, as they were coming to be understood in Bahla, that the following chapter explores.

4 Circles of Knowledge
Religious Learning, Pious Pasts, and Alternative Sociality

AISHA, A STUDENT AT A TEACHER'S TRAINING COLLEGE, first mentioned the summer classes a week before they began. I had gone to visit her sister and her sister's husband one day for lunch, and Aisha, who was visiting them that day as well, said that she and her friends were starting summer classes for high-school girls. They had not done this before in Bahla but decided that it would be a good time to study and teach Qur'an, hadith, and Ibadi history. She and another woman, Mawza, would run the class for their neighborhood, and two pairs of other college women would hold classes in two other neighborhood meeting-rooms. I asked if she would mind if I attended and recorded her classes and she said she would ask her friend but thought it would be fine.

In the previous chapter, I analyzed everyday visiting in Bahla and noted that to be a good person meant being social. Indeed, not being social could be a symptom of "possession." I described that despite such expectations, sociality was not ahistorical, but tied to shifting economic conditions as well as to changing ideas about religiosity. Not only were the primary aspects of visiting (time, coffee, and dates) newly available, but younger people saw sociality as an impediment to proper religiosity. In this chapter, I explore the ways that several groups of young women harkened to an idealized Ibadi scholarly tradition to structure new forms of sociality—organized around religious study—in opposition to the visiting practices of their mothers, grandmothers, and sisters, and in so doing helped shape new notions of religiosity. Although the number of young women and girls who, during my fieldwork, actively participated in these study groups was small (about seventy-five students altogether) the standard created by these gatherings and the local discourse around them affected people far beyond the small groups directly involved. Rather than socializing with and belonging to neighborly groups, Aisha, Mawza, their fellow teachers, and their students were constructing a moral universe in which one would belong primarily and explicitly—and at times in divisive ways—to a religious community of students, scholars, and what they understood to be a pious public.

This chapter focuses on two intersecting processes in the activities of the study groups. First, this chapter illustrates how young teachers in Bahla defined, invoked, and drew from different forms of education, thereby producing a new religiosity. By invoking local practices and well-known histories of study circles among Ibadis as well as by critiquing the new state schools, the teachers and students were expressing their deference to and admiration for "traditional" religious authority and knowledge. Arguing that the new state schools purposely worked to produce secular citizens, the young women insisted that religious knowledge must be pursued independently—and in the forms of "traditional" education—lest they forget or not learn what it means to be good Muslims and good Muslim women.

The desire to pursue traditional education, however, was complicated by the fact that these women simultaneously admired and saw as unauthoritative older generations of Bahlawis. Similarly, although critical of state-school education, the structure of the study group and the pedagogic methods of the group drew heavily from the religious studies classes at the new state schools, and from the new education system in general. Indeed, the teachers derived and established their authority from pedagogic methods borrowed from the state schools: lectures, direct question-and-answer techniques, and high-involvement repetition strategies being three of these methods. Their experience of attending the state schools, therefore, conferred on the young teachers authority to hold such study groups and to demand respect for their religious knowledge in the first place.

Perhaps most significantly, these women believed that they *needed* religious classes to learn about Islam and Ibadism, suggesting a distinctive and shifting understanding of the process of cultivation of good personhood. While there is a long history in Ibadism and Islam in general that emphasizes the cultivation of good personhood and proper community through study, this emphasis on the necessity of formal classes is distinctively recent, and not simply the continuation of age-old Ibadi traditions.

Indeed, the various schools and branches of Islam have historically emphasized different paths to proper piety, depending on particular notions of the origins of human goodness and the role of human reason in achieving piety. Many

Bahlawis maintain that individuals are discreet, autonomous beings, born good (*fiṭra*) and quite responsible for their actions and beliefs. Contemporary (as well as classic) Ibadi doctrine, while emphasizing that God is the creator of all human acts, is thus not absolutely predestinarian. Many Ibadis emphasize the individual capacity to reason (*'aql*) as paramount to the human achievement of goodness and proper Islam. The emphasis on individual reason means that while learning from others and texts and performing the acts of religious obligations (*'ibādāt*) are critical for becoming and being a proper Muslim, individual and God-given capacity to choose and to reason, it is argued, confers on the individual the ability to distinguish good from bad. It also enables the individual to deduce from the Qur'an and hadith correct interpretations of such obligations when there are textual discrepancies.[1] This approach, it should be noted, is distinct from other theological and legal interpretations that suggest that humans learn deductive reasoning and must rely on literal readings of God's words and hadith, rather than on a possibly flawed human and individual ability to reason, in order to fulfill God's aims and expectations.[2] The difference between what are called rationalism and traditionalism is a classic distinction in Islamic theology and the subject of countless texts of Islamic scholarship. This distinction was evident in Bahla as many people insisted that humans, both men and women, are reasoning beings. Suffice it to say that to the extent that individuals are understood to require literal readings of the Qur'an in particular, they are considered inherently less capable of relying on their individual (and according to the rationalists, God-given) abilities to reason.[3]

At the same time, what constitutes a pious person in the Bahlawi and Ibadi context is hardly a fully autonomous individual who becomes *fully* pious simply out of his or her own conscious volition (or even reason). According to many Bahlawis, humans also inherit—through blood—qualities from their parents, they are potentially controlled and inhabited by spirits, and, most important here perhaps, their piety is not *fully* self-produced, willed, or reasoned. Learned and textually based theology or ritual is necessary for the fulfillment of becoming a good person.[4] However, whether this learned piety can evolve from everyday interactions or must emanate from classes and individual study marked the difference between younger and older generations.

The second process this chapter examines is the ways women and girls in these Bahla study groups were struggling with how to speak of themselves, as good humans as well as gendered and sexual beings. Although the women felt entitled to demand space outside their homes for their classes and were, in fact, encouraged to study by national and "religious" discourse that valued knowledge, much of the talk within the study groups revolved around limiting their own and other women's movements. An examination of these tensions among the sense of entitlement, the duty to become knowledgeable, and the desire to limit movement and control bodily and moral comportment revealed that the path to proper womanhood for younger generations who advocated more visibly devout conduct was hardly without its internal conflicts.

The young women's activities and their expectations for their own and other women's behavior also revealed the nonliberal nature of their actions. The authority vested in these young women from their education and their deference to the continuation of a religious tradition did not translate into what liberal feminists might recognize or expect as liberatory discourse or practice. As Saba Mahmood (2005) has argued, "agency" in liberal and radical feminist analysis and politics has often been incorrectly conflated with "resistance."

These women did not encourage "public piety" in the form of large gatherings in public spaces (Deeb 2006) or in the form of attending classes in mosques (Mahmood 2005). In fact, these women actively discouraged such publicness, even while they demanded a "publicly" acceptable space to study. Rather, the publicness of these women's piety centered on their interest in being "visibly" pious through a set of limited symbols: primarily, through their clothing. Although clothing could always be said to be symbolic of certain forms of piety (or any social, economic, or political subjectivity), older women in Bahla did not view their clothing choices as obviously projecting signs of piety in the same ways that younger women did. In other words, while older women wore what "women" wore (colors as opposed to white, something covering their hair as opposed to bareheaded), younger women wore what they *consciously* understood as conveying a woman's piety. In comparison to this form of pious visibility in town, the younger women who organized these study groups were much less comfortable with the movement, activities, and conversations of their mothers' and grandmothers' visiting, as well as being conflicted about their own missions of studying outside of their homes.

These missions, however, were continually fraught. On the one hand, these young women were clearly creating an alternative sociality, a sociality that was structured around religious knowledge and what they understood to be traditional learning. On the other hand, this alternative sociality also encouraged solitary or household-bound life, a life in which going out even to study might be suspicious. This encouragement of nonsocial activity appeared primarily in comments and hesitations about "going out" and movement as well as through comments about "useless talk." This is not to say that the students were explicitly guided to study on their own before coming to class; they were not. However, they were encouraged to pursue individual study in general and in private at home, just as supposedly used to happen in the times of the more appropriate past.

Ultimately, by bringing different styles of or approaches to religious knowledge and religious education together, the young women were attempting to create for themselves a space where they could practice their emerging religiosity, in dialogue with their male colleagues and as opposed to their mothers and grandmothers.

Modern Mass Education

It is no surprise that education had become the focus of debates about the socialization of proper religiosity, proper womanhood, and about the changes in Oman since 1970. Official Omani publications and foreign commentators have continued to herald the dramatic increase in "modern" (non-Qur'anic) schools since the 1970 coup d'état as one of the most important developments since the coup.[5] Histories and newspaper articles about Oman rarely leave out proud statistics about or references to the increase in schools since 1970.[6] On a local level too, men and women often mentioned the construction of schools as one of the primary changes in Oman since the coup. While many young people acknowledged the importance of this change, they also questioned the implications of this kind of schooling. They were proud of their training and abilities. At the same time, however, they were also confronted with tensions surrounding their status in the social hierarchy as well as how to maintain the values of what they saw as traditional knowledge and practice. Learning, although critical to becoming a good Muslim, had not naturally evolved into classes, even though the young women of the study group understood their activity as an extension of traditional Ibadi practices.

Anthropological research on education in the Middle East has tended to focus on the specifics of traditional teaching and learning in Qur'anic schools and more advanced seminaries (D. Eickelman 1978, 1985; Fischer 1980; Houtsonen 1994; Wagner 1982; Wagner and Lotfi 1980) or, inspired by Foucault (1977), on "methods of ordering" in schools in British and Ottoman colonial contexts (Mitchell 1988; Messick 1993). For the most part, scholars have focused on one system or the other. A few, however, have also noted how in particular contexts, these schooling systems have changed and, sometimes, how they influence or inflect each other. Brinkley Messick, for example, notes the internal transformations of traditional schooling in Yemen (Messick 1993: 102). Jennifer Spratt and Daniel Wagner (1986) discussed the transformations of the Qur'anic schools in Morocco with the introduction of modern educa-tion at the beginning of this century and with the formation of the national education system after 1968. Gregory Starrett (1998), in particular, explored the ways that the modern state schooling system in Egypt has appropriated and transformed religious learning.

Focusing on policies and philosophies of Islamist movements, Anne Sofie Roald (1994) outlined the different ways Islamist intellectuals in Jordan and Malaysia have discussed education. While these intellectuals have insisted that Islamic learning and teaching is comprised of both everyday experiences and particular schooling practices, their policies center on formal schooling, where most demand the "integration" of different schooling styles such that all fields of a "modern" school would be "approached from an Islamic point of view" (Roald 1994: 59, 94–95). Although Aisha and her colleagues also considered it essential that modern schools conform to "Islamic points of view," they were, unlike the groups and people that Roald described, much less opposed to what they saw as traditional schooling. While the educa-tional philosophies of the movements that Roald examines argue for modern schooling, which would teach and be based on religious principles, in Bahla, the young women were much more inclined to praise what they considered to be traditional education.

In fact, the young women I knew in Bahla expressed respect for the older generation, at least older men, when it came to religious knowledge. Unlike in countries where independence movements of the 1950s and 1960s were tied to nationalist languages and ideologies, in this part of Oman, the older gen-eration was generally seen as religiously righteous, supportive of a theocratic state and remembered to have fought the British-supported Sultan in the Jebel Akhdar war in the 1950s. This admiration, however, was complicated by and intertwined with gender dynamics. While many older men were respected for their devoutness, many older women were more often castigated for their "ig-norance." Nevertheless and despite this respect for older men, younger men and women, with their access to mass state schooling, had not only gained access to the cultural capital that distinguished them from the older generation, but were also asking different kinds of questions about themselves and their religiosities.

Education not only provides a source of authority and cultural capital, it helps, as Messick (1993), Mitchell (1988) and many others have illustrated, produce notions of personhood. Dale Eickelman (1992), in particular, reflected on the implications of the introduction of modern mass education for religion in the Middle East and suggested that this change is related to the emergence of new forms of religiosity and shifts in communal identity: a shift from experiencing religion in local symbols to identifying with particular, shared statements about belief and practice. Drawing from Eickelman, other anthropologists have analyzed how the new institutions of schooling transferred religious socialization from private to public worlds resulting in the formation of public religious discourse, public pronouncements of individual and collective religiosity (Fahy 1998; Starrett 1998).

On the one hand, such processes were clearly at play in Bahla. On the other hand, I found another simultaneous shift, at tension with such emphases on public discourse and public religiosity. While public religious discourse and appropriate religiousness were becoming the legitimate forms of life in public, what qualified as religion was shifting such that other forms of what might be considered public life—of sociality, for example—were becoming excluded from the domain of the religious. At the same time, while religious learning came to seem the most legitimate form for women of participating in appropriate public life, private and reflective study was also being encouraged, especially for women.

Speaking to the construction of gendered subjectivities in religious education, Azam Torab (1996) and Mahmood (2005) focused on the question of the relationship between agency, feminism, and religious knowledge, illustrating specifically that agency and resistance to patriarchy are not coterminous.[7] My concern here is specifically how young women's understandings and expressions of what it meant to be Muslim women were related to their mass education, from how they responded to the state schools and their ways of seeing their responsibilities for upholding the integrity of a good home to the necessity of studying and the ways they spoke of their bodies and sexualities. Their responsibilities, their bodies, and their sexualities all became objects of scrutiny in the state schools and in the study group, a place where they critiqued the new schools. At the same time, in the discussion around and in the study group, it became evident that these young women were struggling with a tension between the desire to be respected as politically active public intellectual figures and their responsibilities as "good women," bound to spatial and bodily restrictions. The tensions that these young women faced were in part related to a growing sense that they needed to participate *in* religion, confirming the idea that religion is a distinct category in life and one that requires participation, and to an equally growing sense that they needed to determine what constitutes gendered participation and what constitutes religion.

Following in the Footsteps, Sort Of

It was no coincidence that Aisha organized a class. When I was in Bahla, she was training to be a teacher at the Teacher Training College in Rustaq, a town on the Eastern side of the Jebel Akhdar mountains, and was home for the summer holidays. I met Aisha through her older sister Zuwayna, who was married to Hilal, an English teacher in Bahla as well as the co-owner of a store that sold agricultural equipment and material like seeds and fertilizer. Aisha and Zuwayna's father, Gamal, was the shaykh of their neighborhood and an Islamic studies teacher in one of the Bahla boys' schools. He was the only teacher in Bahla who had been a teacher before the introduction of mass schooling in the 1970s and continued to work in the new system. He had also been a teacher at the now-closed state-run alternative religious elementary school in Bahla.[8] Teaching ran in Aisha's family: from her father to her older sister's husband and to herself. While Aisha was following in the steps of her father, she was also challenged with the prospect of negotiating a role for herself in the changing and gendered world of authoritative religious knowledge.

Although many people in Bahla saw teaching as a good job, several young men I spoke to complained about how it was no longer a desirable profession for them: there was neither enough money nor prestige in teaching. Like Hilal, many others had a second profession, usually in some kind of business endeavor. Male teachers at the new state schools did not have the same respect that Qur'anic teachers and scholars once had. Young women, however, generally saw teaching as one of the most desirable professions, since they could gain money independently in a job where they did not have to worry about mixing with men. While scholarship and the pursuit of knowledge in general had not lost prestige in Bahla for men or for women, for men, teaching in the state school was simply another job that paid less than one might gain in business. For women, on the other hand, teaching provided a source of income in a respectable profession. Their schooling could be put to good use. The main drawback for many young women was that they might not work in their hometowns. If they came from a town with enough teachers, it was most likely that they were sent to another town.

Aisha was well on her way to entering the job market, though it was unclear where she would be teaching. The family tradition of scholarship and teaching was being taken up less by the other men in the family, and more by the young women. Taking up this role meant, for Aisha, demanding the same respect that had been accorded to her father and her brother-in-law; it meant being entitled to the same respect and to the same access to places to study: meeting rooms, schools, libraries, and bookstores.

The State Schools

Despite Aisha's criticisms of the state schools, she was a product of them, using the same pedagogic methods in her lectures as what was practiced in the state schools. The first modern state school for girls in Bahla, the Aisha Riyamia school, opened in upper Bahla in the early 1980s. At first, girls were divided by approximate age into several classes and taught the basics of writing, reading, and arithmetic. There had been some opposition to the opening of the schools, I was told, but soon, everyone was sending their girls. Some of the girls had already attended Qur'anic schools and had writing and reading skills, but most did not.

When I was in Bahla, there were four girls' schools in town, all outside the walls, either in Ma'amūra or in Jumāḥ.[9] The twelve-year school system in the late 1990s was divided into three divisions: six years for primary ('ibtidā'ī), three for elementary (i'dādī), and three for secondary (thanawī). At the time of my fieldwork, the Ministry of Education was reforming the school system and, in particular, parts of the curriculum.[10] Most of the new textbooks for English, science, and mathematics were complete and the schools had begun to introduce some of them. It was unclear when (or whether) there would be reforms in history, social studies, and Islamic studies. Although the reforms seemed to be extensive and the structure of three levels was changing, the style of teaching and the division of the subjects were expected to remain the same for some time.[11]

At the time of my fieldwork, students from grades one to three kept the same teachers throughout the day and the teachers would divide the day into subjects (mathematics, history, religion, science) according to a national academic schedule. After the third grade, teachers would teach particular subjects, moving from one classroom to the next. The organization of the classroom was similar to many classrooms in the United States and Europe: rows of individual desks with each student at an assigned seat. Teachers had plans of the classrooms and used them to check attendance and to call on the students. Several teachers explained that since they had many students, they were not able to remember all the students' names. The teachers used the students' first names, sometimes adding the father's or tribal name to make clear which student was being called. For the most part, the students call their teachers *mu'allim* or *mu'allima* and their first names.

In the last two years of secondary (or high) school, the students were divided into those who wished to study humanities and those who wished to specialize in the sciences, the better students going to the science division, or at least, that was the assumption of the teachers and school principals. Students also assumed that the better students went to the sciences, although many did say that it was harder to do well in the humanities. While some of the textbooks were different for the two sections, the Islamic studies textbooks were the same.

Islamic studies was mandatory for all students from first primary through third secondary, or in other words, from first to twelfth grades. The twelfth-grade religious studies textbook was divided into two parts: one for the first semester and one for the second. The first semester textbook was itself divided into sections on the Qur'an, hadith, doctrine ('aqidah), jurisprudence (fiqh), prophetic biography (sira), and economic system; the second semester into those plus the social system. The few references to Ibadi history in the textbooks was indicative of concerns about Sunni-Ibadi relations in Oman. While some Sunnis complained that the textbooks assumed that Oman was necessarily Ibadi, many Ibadis said that the textbooks were very vague and only emphasized a "generic" Islam. For the women's study groups in Bahla to focus one section of their studies on Ibadi history indicated their awareness and desire for specific attention to their distinctive religious ideologies, practices, and histories—features, according to them, that were insufficiently attended to in the religious studies classes.

As for the method of instruction, I observed (from my numerous visits to the various state schools) that emphasis was on lecturing and, from the first grade, students' (both boys and girls) abilities to engage in direct question-and-answer: students were expected to answer teachers' questions as directly and quickly as possible. Teachers asked questions and students raised their hands, hoping to be called on to answer. When the teacher called on a student, the student would stand up and attempt to "shoot back" the correct response. In the more advanced classes, the students remained seated, although they too were expected to respond directly and quickly. Students were discouraged from pausing and were sometimes verbally reprimanded if they paused or filled in pauses in their answers with "umm's."

In the classes I observed, sometimes students who were called on were unable to answer the question or recite the memorized phrase: it was as though these students were pretending that they knew the answers by raising their hands, but were expecting that they would not be called on to respond. This way the teacher might assume that they knew the answer. As the classes averaged between thirty and thirty-five students, some students could count on slipping through unnoticed. If a student did not know the answer, the teacher would ask if someone else wanted to try and again, the students raised their hands. This would continue until someone answered correctly.

The emphasis on direct question-and-answer demands what linguists call a perfect "adjacency pair" (Levinson 1983; Schegloff and Sacks 1973), whereby a particular question requires and expects a particular response. In this case, it was important that the response was both composed of a certain sequence of words and, further, that it not have any interludes or "holds." While in everyday interactions strict adjacency is, as Stephen Levinson points out, too strong a requirement for the coherence of a conversation, in this school context the concept of the adjacency pair is quite appropriate (1983: 303). Since there was a limited number of acceptable responses, some of which were dismissed because they were prefaced with a delay, such as with an "uhhh," the students were being trained to answer as succinctly and directly as possible.

In addition to direct question-and-answers, schoolteachers in Oman (in the state schools as well as in the summer classes) employed another method, encouraging students to engage in a topic; a method similar to Deborah Tannen's "high involvement repetition strategies" (Tannen 1989). Teachers would begin an utterance, then slow down and raise their voices slightly before the end of the utterance. Slowing down and raising their voices would key the students into finishing the phrase. Some or all of the students would shout out the last words of the sentence in unison. This method was particularly effective after the students had heard the phrase or topic already. The students would have heard the phrase already either because they had read the chapter with the teacher in class before or because they had completed their homework. Homework usually consisted of copying out verses from the Qur'an or hadith reproduced in their textbooks and then answering a series of questions at the end of the section. Sometimes the teachers simply made a statement and then immediately repeated it, slowing down near the end so that the students could finish it. The students were expected to complete the sentence they just heard. These two methods of engaging the students in the class material—direct question-and-answer adjacency pairs and high involvement repetition strategies—were distinct from the modalities of teaching in the Qur'anic schools and more advanced study-circles in Bahla.

In many ways, Aisha's study group was unlike the classrooms of the school year. The students were less formal with the teachers, there were no grades, they all sat together in a semicircle on the floor, and they only focused on religious education. At the same time, however, there were clear similarities both in terms of the style of instruction and the content of the lessons. The classes were divided into Qur'an, hadith, and Ibadi history as distinct categories of religious knowledge. Although the style of the classes both invoked the traditional approach of the study group and, in some ways, replicated the assumptions of the state schools, Aisha and her colleagues did make a claim as to where their allegiances stood and what their goals were for organizing these classes. It was clear that their goals were to rescue religious education and to make the students recognize that they could or should study Islam outside the confines of the new schools, and yet also outside their homes.

A Question of Place

Aisha held her classes in her neighborhood *sabla* or meeting room. Her neighborhood, like most in Bahla, was walled with close, mud houses, narrow alleys, and neighborhood gates (although by the late 1990s these gates were always open). This *sabla* was a cement room next to the new town library, in the courtyard just outside the entrance of one of the neighborhood gates. The courtyard stood at the edge of the neighborhood: it was not quite part of the old neighborhood and yet it was clearly attached. The courtyard, housing the new library and the meeting room, hinted at a separation between a space of more official gatherings and the daily gatherings of men and women in their neighborly groups: the new library and the meeting room were two neighborhood institutions distinct from other daily activities.

The new library and *sabla* were also separate from the mosque. Some of the mosques in Bahla used to have small libraries and schools either in or next to them. Until the early 1980s, most of Bahla's Qur'anic schools were set in rooms attached to mosques or held within mosques.[12] At the beginning of the 1980s, the Ministry of Islamic Affairs and Religious Endowments began building Qur'anic schools in separate buildings on religious endowment property, corresponding to an approach to education as an activity distinct from prayer and parallel to "secular" schools outside of the town walls.[13]

Sablas were usually reserved for men's gatherings such as mournings and speeches. The government also used these rooms for distributing monthly payments to widows, the disabled, and the poor. Aisha told me that she did not want to hold the gatherings in someone's house and, she said, as long as no one died, the girls could use the neighborhood meeting room. She had tried to get permission to hold the classes at one of the schools, but this request had been denied. A male official from the Ministry of Islamic Affairs and several other town citizens held summer classes for elementary and high school boys in one of the schools, but for some reason the men organizing those classes had been granted permission. When I asked why she could not get permission and the men could, she responded with a shrug of her shoulders. Aisha's presumption of holding classes in the schools, although in line with a general emphasis on the pursuit of knowledge in Oman, seemed to have raised an institutional question of who would be willing to take "responsibility," supposedly, for the "safety" and, more likely, the content of the girls' and women's discussions. Having young women leave the town walls regularly for two hours made too many people nervous. It was probably better, I suggested to Aisha, trying to lessen the blow, since it would be harder for the girls to reach the schools. At least this way, the girls could walk to the class.

Aisha's determination to hold the classes in a formal setting, ideally in the school building and by necessity in the *sablas*, and her refusal to host them in someone's house is an indication of her self-conscious intention to break with the social roles and places usually reserved for unmarried, local young women and girls. Aisha and her colleagues also assumed that if they held their classes in their homes, people, including the girls themselves, would not take their intellectual goals seriously, not to mention that they might be interrupted by young siblings, parents, grandparents, or neighbors. The conceptualization of a separate space for their intellectual endeavors suggested an idea of institutional education as necessary to learning. As part of a complex next to the library, the meeting room seemed a good place to hold the classes.

A struggle for space was not limited to the case of the class. Before the summer classes, the library next to the *sabla* opened for the town. Besides private collections and the school libraries, it was the only library in town. It was more convenient than the school libraries, however, because it was set within the walls and open to everyone. The library was a tiny room covered in bookshelves and filled with the usual list of Ministry of National Heritage published Omani history books, collections of hadith, law manuals, biographies of the Prophet and his companions, dictionaries, literature and poetry, children's books, school textbooks, and some magazines, as well as cassettes and video tapes of sermons. There were also folders with legal opinions (*fatawa*) of Shaykh Ahmed al-Khalili, the leading religious scholar (nationally sanctioned through his position as Grand Mufti), and research projects by local students on Bahlawi scholars and Omani history. In the middle of the room was a plastic table and chairs where the visitors to the library could write and read as they did at school. The library was open for women three hours a week on Friday mornings, which, Aisha said, was not enough time for all the women and girls who wanted to use it. Sometimes the tiny library got so full on Friday mornings that everyone had to stand, holding books up in front of them. Aisha explained that she had written a letter to the organizers of the library asking that they provide a second time for women, but this request was also denied. This time, it seemed that her demand that more time be set aside for women to use the library was less a question of who would take responsibility for the girls, and more a problem that Aisha was transgressing boundaries expected of young women.[14]

The Meetings

Aisha held her classes three times a week: Saturdays for Qur'an, Mondays for hadith, and Wednesdays for Ibadi history, from 8:00 to 10:00 or 10:30 in the morning. Each Saturday, Monday, and Wednesday for two months, the group of approximately twenty-five girls met in front of the metal *sabla* door. Each morning, we shook hands and waited for Aisha's younger sister to arrive with the key. I knew two of the girls from lower Bahla, where I lived, and recognized most of the others from the library: Aisha told me they were from her neighborhood.

About fifteen of the girls wore black *abayas* over their dresses and black scarves covering their hair.[15] The other ten girls wore colorfully patterned dresses and scarves. Five of the fifteen in black *abayas* also wore black socks, but no one's face was covered. Aisha and her sister both wore the black *abayas*, headscarves, and socks. The different styles of covering not only marked modesty, but the way in which the *sabla* was perceived, its place in town, and the girls' activities there. Some of the girls wore *abayas* any time they left their houses, others when they went to school or beyond the boundaries of their neighborhoods, and yet others wore *abayas* when going to particular places, such as the meeting room, for a talk or class. How the women related to the spaces they were passing and going to partially dictated their dress codes.

Abayas come in many different styles, from the more fashionable to the more simple. All the young women and girls who wore *abayas* to the class wore the plain style, without sequins or sharp angles. To school, young women also wore overcoats in either black or muted tones, signaling a kind of professionalization that older women did not exhibit through their style of dress. None of the girls wore these overcoats to the summer class, indicating that this was not *really* school. The socks were particularly important for identifying the degree of covering that a woman might consider religiously recommended. Only young women wore socks, however, indicating their different approach and interpretations of Islam as well as their unwillingness to engage in agricultural work. Although some of the girls wore colorfully patterned dresses and headscarves, none wore the shorter knee-length dresses and colorful pants that are seen as the traditional dress of interior Oman. These were clothes that their grandmothers might wear.

The changes in approach to dress and dress codes could be read as part of a shift in religious discourse more generally, as I mentioned earlier: whereas older women, as women, necessarily wore headscarves, younger women instead wore particular emblems to index their religiosity.[16] As religion took on a particular place in everyday life, headscarves became indexical of religiosity. In addition to the differences in approach to religion, there was also a mix of former-servant and free families, as well as girls from different economic backgrounds.

When Aisha's sister would arrive with the key, she would open the metal door and we would enter, following Aisha and her colleague, Mawza, to the one corner of the room where there were plastic mats. The *sabla* was a large room with wall-to-wall carpet, divided in half by a low wall against which people could sit and still be within the same room together.[17] There were two air conditioners and several ceiling fans. Sometimes Aisha would bring a tape recorder for us to listen to a Qur'anic recitation or a lecture from a famous scholar. Once in the room, she would put down the tape recorder, close the windows, and turn on the fans and air conditioners. The girls would sit in a semicircle with their backs to the long wall of the rectangular room and the low dividing wall. Aisha and Mawza would sit at one end of the semicircle, along the wall at the end of the room, and I would usually sit at the other side, farthest away from the two teachers. Occasionally, I would move to sit closer to Aisha and Mawza, since my own tape recorder would not always pick up their voices above the hum and whirr of the air conditioners and fans. Even though the teachers did not assign a seating arrangement, the girls tended to sit in the same place every class, usually next to the girls with whom they had arrived.

At the library the Friday before the classes began, I saw Aisha ask some of the girls whether they were going to attend the class. Her questioning had an air of pressure and it is possible that some of the girls sensed the moral burden of attending the class. In addition to expanding their religious knowledge, Aisha said, through summer study, the girls could improve their grades at school. In either case, because of an ethic of furthering their religious knowledge for its own sake or because they wanted to improve their grades at school, the girls would not be wasting their summer vacation if they attended. While Aisha put some pressure on the girls, I doubt that parents pressured their daughters to attend. I knew that the girls from lower Bahla were responsible for watching their younger siblings and I suspect this was the case with most of the other students. Parents tended to discourage their daughters from being away from home in the mornings when they did not have to be at school, especially since that was the time their mothers visited neighbors. The combination of self-motivation and peer pressure was evident in the girls' behavior in and attitude towards the class. Although by the end of the two hours, the girls would fidget and chat, they were, for the most part, very attentive and serious.

Instead of devoting the entire two hours to one of the three topics (Qur'an, hadith, or Ibadi history) as they had planned, Aisha and Mawza usually spent the first hour on one of these and the second hour listening to taped lectures, watching videos, playing quiz games, or simply giving lectures. Sometimes, however, they would discuss two of the main themes in one class and then spend the next class on a video or lecture. There was not much general discussion, although occasionally Aisha and Mawza would open the class to asking questions about a particular issue from one of their discussions, lectures, or videos.

On the one hand, these were most certainly "classes" where students learned from teachers who controlled the stream of discussion, who lectured, and who would sit at one end of the semicircle, against the wall at the end of the room. The students were not expected to study on their own, arriving with questions, or to come together to read and raise questions. These summer classes were very similar to the state-run classes during the school year. Like in the religious-studies classes in the schools, the topics of discussion were divided among these three particular themes; and the style of teaching—the lectures, established questions and answers, and memorized responses to well-known debates—marked the teachers and students as participating in the pedagogic style of the new schools.

On the other hand, Aisha, her colleagues, and the students were also aware that they were in some ways pursuing a "traditional" education. The similarity between their basic practice of sitting in a semicircle, as opposed to the straight lines of the classrooms, and the oft-invoked national representations of traditional scholarship was not lost on the girls. The fact that they were discussing religious issues, no matter the style of teaching or the particular issues raised in class, also connected these summer study-groups to a particular past, when education necessarily meant religious education. As these young women and girls negotiated their relationships with different styles of schooling, they were also participating in the formation of a new religiosity in relation to their mothers and grandmothers, as well as a new understanding of what it meant to be women in a world where they, as well as men, had the authority to interpret religious doctrine and demand respect for their interpretations and initiatives. In these classes, the young women were also struggling with learning how to be women, how to talk about their bodies and about their relationships with men, and how to fulfill their responsibilities as devout, serious, and intellectually aware women.

Circles of Knowledge: The North African Legacy

In Bahla, the girls were not only expected to be good Muslims, but also good Ibadis. The importance of the study circle (*halqat al-ʿilm*) in Ibadi history and its continuation, in spirit, in the summer classes was one way the girls were connected to their shared identity. The girls were not only supposed to be trained in "real Arabic," the language in which God revealed himself in the Qur'an, but were also supposed to learn about the differences between their interpretations of Islam and other schools. For the most part, Ibadis I knew stressed how similar they were to other Muslims. Discussions of differences did emerge, however; especially when Ibadis felt they were being accused of being heretics, which was, at the time, a salient issue.[18] Trying to outline differences between Ibadis and non-Ibadis was not always easy for these women. Nevertheless, these young women felt it was important to recognize and try to define what made their approach to Islam distinct.

In a lecture on July 13, 1997, for example, Mawza explained how people misunderstood Ibadism and accused Ibadis of accepting anyone who believed in God to be a Muslim. This accusation, however, derives from a misinterpretation of classic Ibadi doctrine that emphasizes that the first step toward proper piety is belief in or knowledge of God—a quality that is inherent in humans, as they are born good (*fiṭra*), but from which people are easily swayed.

Mawza then complained that critics accuse Ibadis of being particularly violent and attacking defenseless people. Mawza's complaints clearly reveal both a contradiction in the claimed criticisms (too lenient or too violent) and the vague quality of her defense of Ibadism. Her lecture then jumped from defining Ibadism by what it is not, to a brief mention of the close connections between Omani and North African communities, leaving an impression that Mawza was not exactly sure of the significance of their particular brand of Islam, besides the fact that it is distinct from other schools and that Omanis share something with some people in North Africa. She continued her lecture mentioning that although Ibadis are moderate, which she defined as "loving people," they always have problems with other groups when they go to Mecca and Medina. Finally, touching on the early study groups in Basra as part of the establishment of Ibadism, Mawza noted the importance of study circles and knowledge in Ibadism.

In order to understand Aisha's initiative better and to place it in the context of changing forms of religiosity in Oman, it is necessary to consider briefly the history of circles of knowledge and its relation to the study groups in Bahla. The practice of gathering small groups of students in study circles was a popular and continually invoked practice of "traditional" Ibadi scholarly life while I was in Oman. Ibrahim, the son of my landlord, also held one such study circle. Unlike Aisha and Mawza's summer class, I was unable to attend Ibrahim's group because it was restricted to men. Ibrahim's father, my landlord, explained some of what they did, however. He said that they were about six men who would meet in the evenings and read a predetermined text, taking turns in the circle to read. They would meet in Ibrahim's old house, which he had converted into apartments several years before. He then converted one of the apartments into a Qur'anic school for young boys, which he then also used for his own study group.[19] When I asked who the leader of the group was, my landlord responded curtly that there was no "leader," only someone who would comment (*yifassir*). As the members would take turns reading, he explained, someone might raise a question and the group would discuss the point or defer to the commentator. My landlord's emphasis on the egalitarian character of the group, on the fact that there was no leader or head of the group, signaled a difference with the women's classes that I attended. Ibrahim and the other participants consciously modeled their meetings on the Ibadi tradition, in its emphasis on egalitarian rule and in the name they used to describe the group, *ḥalqat al-'ilm*.

The gathering of a *ḥalqat al-'ilm* is a well-known practice particularly among Ibadis of North Africa and is part of the often-invoked story of the spread of Ibadism.[20] Besides Oman, North Africa (and in particular the Mzab region of Algeria) is the primary site of Ibadism. According to Amr K. Ennami (1972: 61–64) and C. Grossman (1976), these circles derived from the original secret study gatherings, or *majālis*, of Ibadis in Basra (Iraq), at least from the end of the Umayyad rule at the beginning of the eighth century CE.[21] It seems that they became more established during that century under the leadership of the second Ibadi Imam, Abu Ubaydah Muslim bin Abi Karimah.[22] Basra was the center of the Ibadi movement at the time, and young men would study with Abu Ubaydah or other scholars to become missionaries sent throughout the Middle East spreading the message of Ibadi learning and faith to North Africa, Yemen, Hadramawt, Khurasan, and Oman.[23] These Ibadi missionaries would, in turn, establish schools or study groups for interested Muslims or soon-to-be Muslims. While these gatherings were first established to ensure the safety of the community and the continued transmission of Ibadi knowledge, they later became a place of refuge for students, a kind of hostel or college. This story of the gatherings and the spread of Ibadism with an emphasis on serious study is often repeated in Omani accounts of the early development of Ibadism.[24]

The first reference to such groups in North Africa dates to the tenth century CE, and the first set of rules seems to have been established in the beginning of the eleventh century CE by Abu 'Abd Allah Muhammmad bin Bakr (Lewicki 1965: 95; Wilkinson 1985: 236).[25] These earliest rules focus on the daily obligations of the *azzabi*, or "recluses," who were the students and teachers at the hostels. Bin Bakr outlines the particulars of the ascetic lifestyle in the hostel: rules about how and when to eat, how to dress, and when to study or recite the Qur'an; and the precise schedule, methods, content, and punishments of the classes held in the hostel.[26] According to Bin Bakr, the shaykh of the hostel would appoint an *'arīf* to run some of the meetings, organize the food, and teach the classes.[27] In the section on the teachers of the Qur'an, Bin Bakr writes that each student should have a small blackboard and that the teacher should hear each student's recitation from the previous memorized passage, starting with the student on his right around to the student on his left. Then the *'arīf* should dictate the next verse to the students, correct their mistakes, and then have them memorize the verse. Bin Bakr explains the number of mistakes the students at different experience levels are permitted before they are punished. Throughout the section, Bin Bakr repeats that the teachers must recognize what the students are capable of doing: the teacher should not punish a student who is slower than the others if he is less capable of learning. At the same time, if a student is capable and is simply lazy, the teacher must punish the student.

In the section on the Qur'anic students, Bin Bakr writes that the students should study their verses by propping their small blackboards against pillars of the mosque. The students, Bin Bakr repeats several times, must not lean anything against themselves. The only thing these students should do, besides the obligatory devotional practices, is study the Qur'an. Students of the (religious) sciences, that is the more advanced students, should, in addition to studying with their blackboards, also gather with other students to discuss their readings. The students should make a habit of coming together at a particular time and then meeting with their teacher. They should spend the morning reciting and asking questions to the shaykh. Bin Bakr suggests several ways this can be done and says they are all acceptable: the students can take turns like in the Qur'anic school, or they can choose one of the students to ask the questions for all of them, or the person who is in the most hurry can ask. The shaykh should also be aware that if there is a question that someone else in the group is more capable of answering, the other person should answer it. There is no expectation that the students would study individually and then come, individually, to the shaykh. In the more advanced study circles, then, students were expected to study and discuss together and then come to the shaykh with particular questions. Lecturing was restricted to the Friday prayer sermon, or *khutba*.

While Bin Bakr as well as al-Darjini and al-Barradi centuries later use the phrase *halqat al-ʿilm* to refer specifically to study circles and hostels, the twelfth-century scholar Abu ʿAmmar ʿAbd al-Kafi states that the *halqas* were also responsible for "maintaining order in the town" (Lewicki 1965: 96; Rubinacci 1961: 46–47).[28] While it is not clear to what extent al-Kafi's rules reflected political and religious life in Wardjalan where he lived, according to Rubinacci (1961: 46–47) and Tadeusz Lewicki (1965: 97), the communities of the Mzab did adopt al-Kafi's rules as the basis of their approach to religiously appropriate governance.[29] According to Lewicki, this political role is also evident in several other documents. In these documents, the phrase *halqat al-ʿilm* implies several things: a political council with judiciary powers and moral authority, a gathering of the most advanced scholars in a study group, and a place where students would learn from teachers. With the application of al-Kafi's rules, the *azzaba* councils came to be seen as the replacement of the Imam during the time of *kitmān*, or age of secrecy, an age that North African Ibadis had entered after the tenth century CE (Ennami 1972: 235).[30]

References to *azzaba* political councils also appear in ethnographic accounts of the Mzab in the early twentieth century. In his 1922 ethnography *La Civilisation Urbaine au Mzab*, Marcel Mercier notes that at that time the religious class had its own hierarchy, with the top clerics forming the *azzaba el halga*, which administered justice in the communities of the Mzab (58, 133). In his 1927 monograph on religious endowments in the Mzab, Mercier describes how the *H'alga des Tolbas* was made up of about twelve *azzabi* who were responsible for the religious life of the community. To emphasize the importance of this group, Mercier notes that the director (*wakīl*) of the mosque would not make any serious decisions without consulting the *ḥalqa* and, further, that the shaykh of the *ḥalqa* acted as the judge (*qāḍī*) instead of the person who had been assigned as judge by the French colonial government (121–122).[31] In addition to the political councils, Lewicki also notes that, in the early 1960s, there were *azzabas* of women that did not hold any political role in the communities. Overall, however, it is clear that at the beginning of this century in North Africa, the term *ḥalqat al-'ilm* implied administrative council as much as study group.

Although Omani Ibadis, like Ibadis of North Africa, did not always have Imams, it seems that Omanis did not form *ḥalqat al-'ilm* political councils as became the practice of the *azzaba* in North Africa. Wilkinson notes that while in North Africa "the institution that eventually emerged to replace the Imam was the circle of the learned, the halqa[,] in Oman the position was much more fluid. There was always ulema present with a degree of open authority and the most important of these might have a pre-eminent influence" (1987: 162). Perhaps one of the reasons that this institution was not established is that in Oman the Imamate was considered to be either in the state of manifestation or defense rather than in a state of *kitmān*.[32] Indeed, there was some discussion while I was in Oman about whether Oman was currently in a period of *kitmān* since the last Imam, Ghalib bin Ali, who was living in exile in Dammam, Saudi Arabia, was said to have abdicated his position before his departure from Oman.[33] However, even if the Imam abdicated, this would not necessarily mean that Oman was in a state of *kitmān*.

Despite the difference in institutional histories, many Omanis in the twentieth century were aware of North African practices of having *azzaba* councils, and Ibrahim certainly admired the political and moral control that such councils exercised on town life. At the beginning of the century, when the famous North African Ibadi scholars Muhammad Atfayesh (d. 1914) and Sulaiman al-Baruni (d. 1940) traveled to Oman, they solidified contact between the two communities as well as shared literature, thus bringing more attention to work such as Abd al-Aziz bin Ibrahim al-Thamini's (d. 1808) influential book *Kitāb al-Nīl* in Oman.[34] In his 1903 *Le Droit Abadhite chez les Musulmans de Zanzibar et de l'Afrique Orientale*, the lawyer Alfred Imbert notes how in his time *Kitāb al-Nīl* was the most important book on Ibadi law used in Algeria, how Muhammad Atfayesh had written a commentary on it, and how the French courts in Algeria were using these two books (al-Thamini's original and Atfayesh's commentary) to decide cases involving Ibadis.[35] While the *Kitāb al-Nīl* was well known in North Africa, the awareness and interest in North African Ibadism and its literature were also evident in Bahla. Not only did Sulayman al-Baruni visit Bahla,[36] the *Kitāb al-Nīl* was popular too: my neighbor Gaukha once mentioned how in the "old days" people read the book a lot. And, this was the very book that Ibrahim's *ḥalqat al-'ilm* was reading during the time of my fieldwork.

Although Ibrahim and his father called their reading group a *ḥalqat al-'ilm*, there were, of course, certainly differences between their group and the rules described by various scholars mentioned in this chapter. Nevertheless, Ibrahim's *ḥalqa* resonated with the earlier gatherings. On the one hand, Aisha's study group diverges even further from the specifics of the *ḥalqat al-'ilm* described here. On the other hand, she, her colleagues, and the students were also aware of the connections between their quest for knowledge, their potential moral authority, and the rich and long history of the study circles in Basra and North Africa. Whatever similarities there might have been between Aisha's group and North African *ḥalqas* derive from the level of instruction: Aisha's class was neither a beginning Qur'anic class where the students only focus on recitation (although they did do that sometimes), nor were they a gathering of equals who learn from each other as with the more advanced groups. Instead, here, the teachers instructed the students through lectures and questions and answers. At the same time, however, that the study groups in North Africa also had a moral influence on the communities, resonated with Aisha's project of establishing the summer classes. For Aisha, as well as for Ibrahim, it was less important to determine the exact ways that the practices corresponded to the *ḥalqa* system in North Africa than it was to recognize their relation to the long and well-theorized history of learning and political councils in Ibadi scholarly life. Aisha recognized that her classes were not only continuing a tradition of local Qur'anic schools and more advanced methods of learning in Oman, but also—and perhaps more poignantly—they resonated with and were drawing their authority from a political and scholarly Ibadi tradition dating to the eighth century CE and practiced in towns as far away as central Algeria. This emphasis on continuing this tradition was, in many ways, tied to the emergence of the new state schools.

Responding to "Modern Education"

While the women were drawing from different styles of education as well as from national representations of Ibadism as scholarly and studious, it was also clear that the teachers, at least, firmly believed that there were problems with the new state schools. On July 14, 1997, Aisha gave a twenty-minute lecture on the history and dangers of the schools introduced in Egypt after the British occupation. Her main argument was that the introduction of this "new" (*jadīd*) education was a colonial plan to diminish the role of religion and religious education in the Middle East. Aisha began the lecture after the students had listened to a tape of another lecture by a Saudi man on the dangers of Western calls for "liberating" women in the Middle East. The connection between the new schools and the demands for women's liberation was clear, yet Aisha pointed them out again in her own lecture. The demands for liberation, Aisha noted, would cause the demise and weakening of the Middle East. This point, however, was not the only one of the lecture. Aisha began her lecture by explaining how Egypt was the first Arab country that submitted to the British and where the British installed "education" (*ta'alīm*).

> In Egypt, at the beginning, the education was like ours: the system was of "*makātib*," that is Qur'anic schools (*madāris al-Qur'an*). With this system, the students would study everything. Then, there was also the glorious university of al-Azhar where those who graduated would become imams, teachers, or judges. If a family had a graduate from this university or mosque, his house would be well considered. The British government in Egypt had a minister who was responsible for education and who introduced government schools (*madāris ḥukūmīya*). At first they didn't have schools like ours now. The name of the minister was Dunlop, and he wanted to change education so that education was not only religious education. He was not open to Islamic education. He made education like ours is now. He first opened primary, then elementary, and then secondary and like that. The important thing is that those who graduated from Dunlop's school received higher salaries than those who graduated

from the al-Azhar university. Those who had graduated from al-Azhar would receive as a salary three qursh, and three qursh was enough, it was good. But, then if they went to the other schools, they would get more. This encouraged people to send their sons [or children] (*awlād*) to these schools. Why did Dunlop do this? At first, the teachings were fine, normal, and so people would send their children, but when people began sending their children, they made Islamic studies elective. This came at the expense of religion, Islam. And even now, in Egypt, there is no Islamic teaching, and those female teachers who teach Islam are not specialists in Islam or even specialists in Arabic. At first they would teach classical Arabic (*fuṣḥa*), and they would teach it in schools, and then they started to use colloquial Arabic (*lughat ammīya*), they Egyptian-ized Arabic (*tamṣīr lughat ʿarabīya*). Instead of writing true Arabic (*ʿarabīya ṣaḥīh*), they would use the Egyptian dialect (*lahga Miṣrīya*). This was all orga-nized by colonization (*istimār*). People did not know at the time, they did not know what was planned for them. Small things changed and it was like a water pipe that gets clogged first by little stones. It is the same as this: it starts like this. It begins with only one time that there isn't Islamic education. It happens slowly. Like women in Egypt. They used to be good. They would not leave their homes. They would only go out if they were decent. Now it is not like that. There was an Egyptian princess, her name was princess Nadi, who had private contact with the British, and once there was a meeting with men. And she went with the men and she took off her veil.

Egyptian women are no longer decent. Even if it says on their birth certifi-cates that they are Muslim, they are not. This is because of education. Education is an important way of Westernizing society. If I ask any one of you a historical or religious or cultural (*thaqāfī*) question, you would not be able to answer. This is because of education. Novels are used for this [making ignorant]: you learn to read and write, and you read and write stories. The amount of pages used for novels and those used for religious books is fifty or sixty to one—for every one page of religious literature there are fifty for stories. What is one or two pages? Another method of lessening the importance of religion is putting the classes at the end of the day, when the students are tired. And, yet another way is to have subjects for girls that are not important: for example, fashion and makeup. Also, they talk about problems (*mashākil*)—are these religious problems? [girls respond "no" in unison] No, these are problems of character, like problems of love. In these, there are poems, stories of love. Fine, even in the television programs, there is love. And when there are historical series or cultural series, there are always women in them. We want them to bring Islamic programs and movies, but they rarely do. And, when they do, you see women, almost naked, even if a television series is about the companions of the Prophet. These women cover themselves with makeup and certain clothes. Is this how women used to dress? Ruining one woman is much more dangerous than using a thousand canons; and, without us knowing. They know how powerful wives and women are in the families.

You know, when there is a girl at home. And her brother is at home too. The girl and boy are at home. And the boy asks something from her father, his father will never do it. But, with the girl, the father will agree. Why is this? Because God has given women certain ways of getting things. She will cry and men will immediately do anything. [girls laugh] Women are beloved by every-one. This is not just mere words, but it is fact. Women or girls cry and men can't do anything, they can't control their feelings. Her emotions are very powerful.

Ok, so women had their places, from the beginning of Islam, when she would learn, she would learn at home. She does not go to the *souq* [market] un-less it is necessary. There were places for gathering for girls, normal. But, then they began going out, girls have changed. Girls, now go out, they go to the *souq*. What do they do in the *souq*? They put on makeup and perfume and contact men. What do you expect? The main place she should not go is the *souq*. A woman has a father, brother, husband. Can't they go get what she needs from the *souq*? Why should she go herself? To be with men. There are no places as hated to God as the *souq*. The *souqs* are the most hated places for God. Because many of the problems are found in the *souq*. The last thing are merchants: merchants promise, really this is cheap, but they trick her easily. I went to the *souq*, I wanted to see what was going on there. I did not go to see someone. For example going to the hospital when you go to see a particular person, but just to go. And what is there? There are Indians. They are not Muslims. They do not have respect. And, I returned home. Then there are the people who see the fash-ion magazines for sewing (*mudilāt*): Are these styles Islamic? Are there veiled women? I'm sorry. Who sells these magazines? Girls, when they are young, they get used to it and like it and then they get older and she wears them.

Women are keys to destroying the Muslim world and the keys for pro-tecting it. She can protect the Muslim world by her awareness. She should study and learn. For each Muslim man and Muslim woman this is neces-sary. The Prophet said, one should continue learning from the cradle to the grave. But, Islamic knowledge is true. That means Islamic books are the light of the religion. This does not mean stories for little children, or other stories. Cartoons are dangerous, they teach three-year-old children about sex. They teach them about love and wrong things. And television series too. We lack the basic necessary knowledge about life, such as prayer, fasting and pilgrimage, particularly women. One does not know how sweet life is until one knows the difference between what is permitted and what is forbidden.

Aisha's lecture revolved around distrust of Euro-American (and, by extension, Egyptian) education systems and respect for "traditional" religious knowledge. As it was her new education that gave her the authority to hold such classes and give such lectures, however, she was also caught between nostalgia for traditional knowledge and changing social hierarchies, between the tensions arising from a desire to maintain the values and knowledge of the older generation (and from a classic Ibadi tradition) and the authority emerging from her own, new status as "educated." Such tensions were also evident in her hesitant attempts at instructing her students about where and how one should learn, where and how girls and women become good.

Aisha began her lecture with a discussion of how the British introduced a new education system in Egypt. Although she focused on Egypt, she barely hid her worries about the education system in Oman. Attention to the role of colonial government in the transformation of the education system in Egypt reflected recognition of the influence of European—and Egyptian—powers in Oman. Colonial governments in the Middle East, Aisha pointed out, work to make religious knowledge less important in society, both by making religious education tangential to education and by insisting on tying the question of development to women's rights. She switched back and forth between Egypt and Oman suggesting, although never explicitly stating, parallels. Moving from the past in Egypt—both before and after the introduction of the new schools—to the present in Oman, which she used as a point of reference for explaining the types of schools she was describing, suggested the connections between the two places. While discussing Egypt, she marked a linear trajectory from Qur'anic to "new" schools; in reference to Oman, she at first seemed to imply that the two styles coexisted. As the lecture continued, however, it became clear that Aisha was arguing that while there might have been Qur'anic schools in Oman, religious knowledge and practice in Oman were in danger of decreasing, just as happened in Egypt. The schools that were in Oman were, in fact, too similar to the new schools in Egypt.

Aisha spoke about how, with the colonial government in Egypt, graduates from new schools received higher salaries than al-Azhar graduates, how religious studies became an elective, and how Egyptian Arabic was the language of the schools. It soon became evident, however, that she was not restricting her discussion to Egypt: were only students in Egypt encouraged to write and read novels or taught irrelevant subjects? Aisha made the point about the decline of historical, religious, and cultural knowledge in Oman directly. She said that if she asked any of the girls present in the room a historical, religious, or cultural question, none of them would be able to answer and that this was because of their education. In other words, although some of the issues that she raised about the Egyptian education system might not have applied to Oman, there were still problems with what the students in Oman were learning in these new schools.

In her description of Egypt's colonial history, Aisha was suggesting that Oman may also be influenced, not only by Britain, but by Egypt as well. Many of the teachers and doctors in Bahla and throughout Oman in the mid-1990s were Egyptian. And, animosity between Omanis and Egyptians when I was in Bahla was hardly hidden or subtle. Egyptians were considered arrogant and stingy; many women openly stated that they would much rather go to an Indian doctor than an Egyptian, be taught by a Sri Lankan than an Egyptian, or be neighbors of a Bengali worker than an Egyptian. In her lecture, however, Aisha recognized that many of the shopkeepers in the Bahla market were Indian, which led her to assume that they too had different and un-Islamic morals. Her simultaneous criticism of Egyptian education, and by extension, Egyptians cannot be separated from local experiences. Irrespective of a shared religion and a shared language, and, at times, a shared politics, Aisha's condemnation of Egyptian education spoke directly to the presence of Egyptians in Oman's schooling system, and Egyptians in Bahla.

From this critique, one was led to conclude that the girls must, on their own, join study groups such as this one to further their own intellectual paths. They must recognize the benefits of the "old" system and complement their education with these older values and knowledge. From these study groups, the young women and girls were confronting questions of local and international culture and politics. Religious education and knowledge must continue in order for Islamic values to be perpetuated. A tension arose, however, when Aisha also insisted that women and girls should not "go out." Thus, on the one hand, these young women accepted the need for and encouraged group religious study. On the other hand, the pursuit of group study ran against their desired restrictions on going out. Indeed, she made a point of saying that "in the past," when Omanis were properly religious, women would study "at home."

Aisha's distrust of the new school system and the literature, religious or otherwise, that students read, was reflected also in the books that she had the students bring to class as well as the books that she relied on to teach. When Aisha mentioned the book she was going to use for the hadith class and I asked if the book was something that she learned from school, Aisha answered with an emphatic "no"—the book was from her father's library. The book, the knowledge she was going to be passing on to the young students, was not going to be mediated through the state schools. It was something outside, something that belonged to the traditional world of her father's generation, the generation of religious knowledge unmediated by state interference. Aisha was continuing the respect for religious knowledge and education that she saw pervasive in the local practices of her father's youth. The respect and authority that her father was accorded would now be accorded to her. Even though her father had become a teacher in the closed state religious schools and in the regular state schools, he represented, for her and for the rest of the community, the religious knowledge and education of a previous generation.

Aisha's relationship to the new schools was also, of course, ambiguous: despite her strong criticisms, she was studying at the Teacher Training College and, furthermore, the students in her summer class were all students at the new schools during the September to June academic year. Aisha's insistence on using the school to teach this class and her maintenance of the pedagogic methods of the new schools complicated the picture of Aisha's critique of the new state schools as well. Aisha was neither denouncing the state school system outright nor criticizing the students in the class for attending the state schools. Instead, she was warning the girls about the possible future of religion in Oman as well as implying how the girls could maintain their religious integrity through their further religious education. Becoming good Muslim women demanded that they be aware of the dangers of the educational system, of their responsibilities as inherently powerful women, and of the need to continue to study.

For their part, the students, it should be noted, did not all approach religion and religious education in the same way. Some of the students were more "advanced" in their abilities to recite the Qur'an than others; some more readily answered the questions that the teachers raised. In addition to their "abilities," the students also had differing attitudes towards religion and education, some of which was indexed by their clothing. While many agreed with the way that Aisha outlined the responsibilities of women, some also considered her style too restrictive. As the girls were responsive and considerate, this attitude was not necessarily apparent in the class.[37] Regardless of the students' personal behaviors or attitudes, however, this particular lecture was one that they would have heard in one form or another before, in lectures in town, on cassette tapes, and even, perhaps, in school. The issues and questions that Aisha raised in her lecture were common enough to be commonsensical.

Becoming a Good Woman

In the lecture about education in Egypt, Aisha not only spoke about religious knowledge and modern state schools, she also discussed what it means to be good women, their strengths and their responsibilities.[38] She criticized notions of "liberation" by arguing that this demand was intricately tied to development politics, which weakened the cohesion and values of Middle Eastern society. The problems that the girls were supposed to be having, according to development politics, were not really problems at all, she pointed out. These "problems," which one presumes were those associated with "women's rights," were only distractions. Religious issues were the only serious problems. Making problems out of nothing, making the "problem" of women's liberation central to discussions about development and progress, not only shifted attention away from the important issues of religious obligations and practices, but also undermined the strength of Omani culture.

At the same time, Aisha pointed to how these "problems" became important precisely because Western policies were based on the knowledge that women and girls in Islamic countries were the foundation of the society as well as essentially powerful. Respect for women, Aisha implied, is central to Islam. God gave women an inherent power to control men through their emotions. This strength, Aisha told the students, is well known and one that the Western powers have attempted to use to their advantage. They have tried to make Muslim women weak by making them un-Islamic, just like in Egypt. Beware, she said to the girls, that the same does not happen here in Oman. The way to prevent this happening, the way to protect the Islamic world is for women to study, to learn about Islam and Islamic behavior. Learned and schooled knowledge is critical.

In constructing a space for their gendered authority, for demanding respect, and expounding on their religiosity, Aisha and Mawza also referred to women as sexual beings. Acknowledging that women have sex and that men can be sexually interested in them was also part of the discussions in these groups. In this discourse, avoiding places where men spend time was one of the ways of preventing illicit interaction: Muslim women become corrupt, or rather, one of the ways that their corruption is visible is that they "go out." On the one hand, it seems that going out was not a problem in itself, but rather, the problem was where one goes: *souqs* and, by extension, shopping centers, were considered the most vile places. Going to the *souq* is not like going to the hospital; going to the *souq* must have no other purpose than to see men. Why else would a woman go to the *souq*? Everything she needs, she can ask her male relatives to get for her. In contrast to the *souq*, there are no problems about going to the hospital to visit sick friends and relatives. The acceptable places for women to go are limited by the fact that mixing with unknown men is necessarily shameful and prohibited. Maintaining women's seriousness of purpose through visiting sick relatives is acceptable and encouraged.

On the other hand, Aisha's discussion about "going out" suggested a significant tension in her project, and that a great gap existed between a desire for public legitimacy and her sense of piety. Aisha briefly noted that "in the past," in the time when women were respectable, women would "study at home." Aisha's voice lowered as she said this, mumbling the phrase to the point of almost being unintelligible. Throughout the rest of the lecture, Aisha had spoken loudly, with certainty and authority. Her sudden shift in volume and tone suggested that, at that moment, she recognized that her quest for public approval and authority conflicted with her vision of the women's acceptability and religiosity. In fact, Aisha quickly recovered and stated, more assertively, "there were places for gathering for girls, normal." The desire for public approval, from both men and women, boys and girls, which meant—for the teachers—organizing the classes in the schools or in the neighborhood meeting rooms, conflicted with this discourse on movement and limits.

The debates and concerns of these young women were directed not only towards colonialism, Egypt, and general religious strength, but also specifically towards their understandings of local social practices. From their positions as "educated," and using the language of devoutness, these young women opposed some of the social and religious practices of their mothers and grandmothers, and in particular their "going out." Although not usually stated directly, this opposition nevertheless appeared in comments about movement, talk, use, and waste. As I described in the previous chapter, every day in Bahla, women would walk to visit each other, either individually to join neighbors or together to visit other women. While the streets of the town were not predominantly male, they were, in some ways, an ambiguous space where the dynamics of male / female relationships were constantly being played out. Not only was it important to avoid the spaces of ambiguity such as the street, but avoiding "idleness" and "uselessness" was critical too.

Indeed, in organizing the group, Aisha had been particularly concerned about what women did when they convened, or how they might be perceived. Part of Aisha's determination to have the classes outside the house was tied to her concern that her classes would not be taken seriously. Despite her approval of women who used to study at home, Aisha, instead, acted on the idea that gatherings at home could not be serious.[39] Thus, on the one hand, the home was safe in terms of providing security against the ambiguities of gender relations. On the other hand, however, it did not provide the proper context for Aisha's desire to be respected as a local intellectual. This lack of seriousness of purpose was not a small matter for Aisha and her colleagues. Their determination to establish their religious seriousness, their devotion, and their goals of intellectual enhancement was also reflected in a comment Aisha made the same day as her Egypt lecture. At one point, she said that useless (*ghayr nafa'a*) talk is a sin that requires repentance (*tawba*).

With this brief comment, Aisha touched on many of the tensions in Bahla: her tainted Euro-American / Egyptian education gave Aisha the authority to make such comments and to act upon them, to start a study group that hoped to define what was right and what was wrong, and to help define who the women were and who they were not. According to Aisha and her colleagues, older women walked through streets and visited with each other, engaging in useless talk. This activity was not only disapproved of by religion, it required repentance. The notion of usefulness in religion has a deep history in some Islamic traditions. Indeed, 'Abd al-Jabbar, who was one of the key theological scholars of the Mu'tazilite school, not only influenced Ibadism, but wrote specifically about uselessness and evil.[40] And, for many of the young women, because the older women were not involving themselves in a recognized, distinctly religious activity, they were wasting their time and engaging in useless talk. The possibility that older women discussed religious matters (although not in the same ways as the younger women did), or were caring for the sick or even monitoring each other's activities, did not seem to mitigate any of the criticisms. For Aisha, such practices required repentance.

Aisha's opposition to the socializing practices of the older generation was related to her form of religiosity. Religion, for Aisha and her colleagues, was not simply a part of being a human or a good human. Rather, religion, and Ibadism in particular, required classes: specific definitions and lectures, study, and concentration. Religion was based on defining, categorizing, and lecturing. It was also something that needed constant individual self-monitoring. Theirs was a religiosity that stood apart from that of the older generations, who were less concerned with defining absolutes or even, who they were. Aisha tended to begin from defining rules, rather than the goals of religious precepts that should be related to specific circumstances and contexts. Religion for Aisha was a subject to be studied, separate from the mundane world in which she lived. In this context, older women's visiting practices were not seen as providing any useful service since they did not further the goals of learning—in a certain way—about the subject of religion. On the contrary, for young women such as Aisha, visiting was precisely the kind of activity that distracted from serious religious reflection.

Conclusion

Through the formation and discussions of this summer class, some of the difficulties and tensions facing young women in Bahla became apparent. On the one hand, these young women respected the ways that, in the past, religious knowledge was part of what it meant to be a Bahlawi and Ibadi. Many of the women felt that the dramatic changes in Omani society since 1970 had resulted in the loss of former religious values and awareness. The tradition of religious scholarship and the transmission of religious knowledge were, according to this idealized vision of the past, an integral part of Bahlawi life, in contrast with everyday life in the renaissance. On the other hand, the young women's authority to interpret and discuss theology and doctrine as well as their views on what was appropriate behavior (including sociality) led to conflicts with older men and women whose perspectives and practices differed from theirs.

As these young women believed that they must participate in the formation of a public, religious good, they also considered that their participation should be through their education—an education that required individual attention, was circumscribed by a "classroom," and was focused on defining what was and was not Islam, what was and was not Ibadism, and how to be a good Muslim woman. While drawing from this general sense that religious scholarship must be maintained, these young women were also shifting what education meant: education and knowledge should be a distinct form of activity; it must be "useful," it must take place in sites designated for learning, and it must involve the defining and articulating of absolute precepts. Just as education was required for being gainfully employed, it was required for being appropriately religious.

But, these young women were not only helping to reformulate what education and knowledge were, they were also reformulating religion and what it meant to be a good person: moving away from the idea that the responsibilities and obligations of sociality were good, to the idea that if the focus of everyday life was not on God, then the activity was not appropriately religious and did not qualify under the category or definitions of proper religiosity.

The establishment of modern, mass state education, one of the most heralded features of Oman's renaissance, thus produced in its wake tensions about Oman's past scholarly knowledge, about education, and about what qualified as religion. These issues mattered so intensely for these young women not simply because they were disappointed with contemporary religious life, though they were that too. Rather, such issues mattered because these women understood that their era, the renaissance, would not necessarily last forever; though, of course, what the future might hold only God knew. Their mission, therefore, was to improve the quality of religious life as they saw it now, but what might become of Oman no one could predict; indeed, it might even be redemptive.

5 Senses of Water

Nostalgia, Private Ownership, and Bodily Privacy

ABDULRAHMAN, ONE OF MY LANDLORD'S ELDER SONS, came over for dinner one night early in my stay in Bahla and asked if I had seen the *zaygra*, a well whose water is pulled up by animals. As I had not, the following afternoon, Abdulrahman and his wife and two of their children came to pick me up to see the well. My landlady, who had also never seen this particular *zaygra*, decided to come too. We piled into Abdulrahman's pickup truck and drove to the other side of town. When we arrived at the well, there was no one there. Abdulrahman walked towards the well, we all followed, and as we got closer, he turned around and proudly proclaimed that this was the *zaygra*. After circling the well several times, we all piled back into the truck and headed home: a short trip to show the anthropologist and the women something "traditional."

A few weeks later, I was in the capital, Muscat, and went to visit an American historian, who also asked if I had seen the *zaygra* and whether I would be willing to take pictures of it for someone who was building a model of one for a museum in Muscat. I agreed to help and when I returned to Bahla a couple days later, I walked back to the well, which still stood quiet and unused. This time, though, two young children, who saw me walking around the well, ran out and explained that their father, Hamad, was the owner of the well. Soon, the owner came and I introduced myself, explaining that I wanted to take some pictures and measurements. He said that I was welcome to look around but that I should really come back that afternoon when he would have it working. When I arrived in the afternoon, a group of older men was sitting near the path that a bull and donkey were using to pull up the water from the well. One man was walking the bull and Hamad, the owner, was walking the donkey.

As I walked towards the men, Hamad looked up and on seeing me, tied the donkey to a rope that ran along the path. He came over and welcomed me to the *zaygra*. Without me needing to ask, Hamad began to explain the different parts of the well: every little part, he insisted, has a name. He listed the parts so quickly that I felt I wasn't supposed to learn them, only recognize his expertise. I jotted everything down as quickly as I could, thinking that the exhibit organizers in Muscat might find the names useful. He also began to explain the reason he had rebuilt the well a few years earlier: first, he said, the youth, *shibāb*, do not know anything about the past and second, he missed the sound of the turning wheel. Listen . . . all you can hear is the sound of the mechanical pumps. We stopped talking and in fact, all around I could hear the quick fire of mechanical pumps. I was tired of that, he added. He said that now, he comes here in the afternoons and works, irrigating his fields the old way, and the other men come and sit, enjoying the outdoors together. After our conversation, Hamad returned to work and I continued to take pictures, draw, and measure. I soon noticed that on the steps on the side of the well, there were about four or five small tape recorders.

I finished as the sun was setting, and Hamad kindly offered me a ride home, saying that he would pray later. Although it would normally be inappropriate for a woman to get into a car with an "unknown" man, because I was a foreigner and because Hamad's neighborhood was quite far from my own, it was more acceptable for me to accept the ride home. The call to prayer came and all the other men started to leave for the mosque. We walked quickly to Hamad's car, got in, and as he started the engine, he pushed the cassette in: it was the sound of the *zaygra*. The screeching sound of the turning wheel played on, and I realized that all those other tape players were making similar recordings.

I could not stop thinking about Hamad's rebuilt *zaygra* and the tapes he and the other men were making and might listen to in their cars, or about the model, soon to be built, from my snapshots, untrained drawings, and inaccurate measurements. The juxtaposition of the two projects suggested that Hamad, in particular, was struggling with how to remember his past, how to present his past to future generations, and, ultimately, his recognition of the limits of official memory. Hamad's struggle over how to remember and how to represent his past emerged, however, not from encounters with violence, pain, and the limits or workings of "cultural anesthesia" (Feldman 1994), as many scholars examining the politics of memory have illustrated, but from a mundane experience of nostalgia, a nostalgia that was spilling over and moving beyond the stills of national visual representations of heritage. This nostalgia was being legitimated by national representations of Oman's former water practices. And yet, for Hamad, such representations could not completely capture what he sensed he was missing.

This chapter examines discourses and perceptions, sensory regimes, and memories struggled over and entangled in shifting technologies and practices of water distribution in Bahla. In particular, the chapter examines how the changing water distribution system produced in its wake tensions about the past, women's religious modesty, and neighborly obligations and ownership. As the material forms of new water pipes became the norm, the social experiences and senses of sociality associated with sitting around the well, with bathing, and with neighborly obligations to share water also transformed.

In the previous two chapters, I focused on notions and practices directly related to sociality, either in the form of older women's visiting practices or in the form of the study groups that spoke against such practices and also provided an alternative sociality. In this chapter and the subsequent one, I examine how ideas about neighborliness, sociality, and community are entangled in changes in basic infrastructure and memories of life in East Africa. This chapter analyzes the introduction of piped water and how Oman's past as well as proper sociality and community were being reimagined in its wake.

In Oman, water distribution practices fall squarely between naturalized assumptions that development, in the form of piped water, mechanical pumps, and sprinklers, is necessary for the fulfillment of successful statehood and notions that older forms of water distribution are emblems of Oman's past values and knowledge. At the same time, however, previous and new forms of distribution are also entangled in shifting forms of and struggles over the meanings and policies of authoritative knowledge, religious ethics, sociality, and the economy of an oil-state. Embedded in a variety of globalized discourses and policies, including development, heritage, Islam, and labor, are memories and sounds, the appropriateness of sight and bodies, and the meanings of ownership and belonging that become the sites of everyday tensions.

The Development of Water in Oman

It is hardly necessary to highlight the importance of water and water distribution in Oman. Besides the Southern Dhofar region, which receives the tail end of the later summer monsoon rains from the Indian Ocean, the country is extremely arid. Annual rainfall in northern Oman ranges from twenty millimeters per year in the desert regions to three hundred millimeters per year in the mountains. Instead of rainfall, people in Bahla rely on wells and a network of underground canals, or *aflāj* (singular *falaj*), which probably date from before the advent of Islam in the seventh century CE.[1] Not all wells and canals work all the time, and Omani histories tend to describe the establishment or destruction, prosperity or demise of a town in terms of the state of its canals. The water system becomes, in many ways, emblematic and an index of the status of the community. References in contemporary Omani histories to these canals mention how the governor of Bahla at the beginning of the twentieth century restored three of the town's five canals, suggesting that they had been badly damaged or were not working at all during the reign of the previous governor. In the late 1990s, three of the five were still in use. Until the late 1960s, local wells and canals provided water for drinking, bathing, and irrigation for the town, distributed according to customary and religious law and a complex system of water-share ownership, rents, auctions, and rotations.

As described throughout this book, with the exportation of commercial crude oil beginning in 1967 and especially with the 1970 coup d'état, the Omani government precipitated extensive development projects, including building schools, hospitals, roads, and a new water distribution network. There is no doubt that a lot changed in Oman in the first years after the coup. For example, the dramatic transformation in infrastructure is evident in the amount of building supplies and equipment imported to Oman in those years. From 1970 to 1972, the import of cement increased from 125,000 Omani rials (1 OR = $US 2.60) to 576,000; the import of other building materials from 286,000 to 1,450,000; and the import of machinery and parts from 232,000 to 1,799,000.[2]

Water policies and distribution were of primary concern to the young post-coup state. The new state began its initiatives by sponsoring surveys and research projects with the Food and Agriculture Organization of the United Nations; Renardet-Sauti-ICE, an Italian engineering company; and the Centre for Middle Eastern and Islamic Studies at the University of Durham, and by establishing government ministries to manage water distribution, initially for the capital area and then for the rest of the country. The early research projects and ministries were concerned with documenting and establishing inventories of the wells, canals, and water levels throughout Oman.[3] The development of water policies also meant laying down pipes in the capital and opening and subsidizing a new market for selling pipes, pumping equipment, and pumps throughout the country. By 1973, most of the houses in the capital area were connected to a piped water network.

A 1973 *Middle East Economic Digest* report on Oman announced that the forthcoming five-year plan (to begin in 1975) would be a great opportunity for suppliers of irrigation equipment: "Development schemes likely to be included in the forthcoming five-year plan are large-scale irrigation projects (of interest to suppliers of pumps, pumping equipment, pipes and irrigation equipment)" (*MEED* 1973: 25). Not surprisingly, all the advertisements accompanying this early 1970s English language magazine article on Oman were for banks, suppliers of building equipment, or Omani trading companies that are agents and distributors for these suppliers. Through the support of the research projects as well as the subsidizing of equipment and the encouraging of new irrigation practices (not to mention the change in the economy itself), diesel and electrical pumps, sprinkler systems, and hoses quickly entered the Omani market and soon became part of the landscape of small towns and villages.

Certainty and determinism about development and about the necessity of improving water distribution and irrigation was evident in the literature and statements of the new state: Oman's progress depended, in part, on the "modernization" of irrigation practices (which assumed that surface irrigation systems, such as the *aflāj*, incur high water losses) and would be measured by the numbers of people who had water piped directly into their houses.[4] The Omani state was not alone in looking to water distribution as an indicator of successful development. The United Nations, for example, has long calculated the percentage of people within a given settlement that have water piped into their homes as one of the determining factors for categorizing communities into "rural" or "urban" (see United Nations 1998). Similarly, the International Monetary Fund (IMF) is increasingly including water privatization as a condition for loan agreements.[5]

Recognizing the importance of access to water for determining progress and yet also recognizing that Oman's statistics would not be as favorable if calculated according to piped water into homes, Oman's own 1993 census enumerated, instead, the percentage of people who had easy access to clean water (Sultanate of Oman 1993). In the 1990s, the Ministry of Water Resources appointed a consortium, led by ABN Amro, the Dutch banking group, and including the UK-based law firm Denton Hall as well as the UK-based technical consultants Mott MacDonald Ltd., to assist in the privatization of water and provide the technical support for new water distribution systems. Mott

MacDonald Ltd., in particular, began working to design and construct supervision for new wells, pumping stations, tanker points, towers, reservoirs, and 215 kilometers of new pipes to serve twenty-one towns and villages in Oman. These "necessary" moves towards the development of water distribution systems were encouraged by international development organizations and administered by a consortium of multinational corporations. However, these changes confronted other forms of water distribution in Oman, forms with complex histories and practices, not to mention the Omani state's own recognition of the ancient water system as an emblem of historic knowledge and practice.

The constant emphasis on progress, achievement, and development has not meant that the past is ignored. On the contrary, in Oman, as in many parts of the world, progress is almost inevitably accompanied by the language of tradition: although the previous era is vilified, the spirit of age-old values and memories of ancient glories are heralded as both necessary to and constituent of contemporary Omani society. The past, as a spirit and a value, is said to continue in the new era. The spirit of the past, expressed in terms of hard work, religious piety, seriousness of purpose, purity, and ascetic grandeur, is relegated to the realm of "culture." Although at times contradictions and tensions emerge in official articulations of this relationship between development and tradition, for the most part, an unsteady and continually shifting equilibrium has been maintained: the spirit of the past, rather than the mechanics of its hardships, continues in the age of prosperity. And, it is this seemingly successful balance of the discourses of development and tradition that stands at the heart of Oman's distinctiveness in the Arabian Peninsula. According to the state, unlike the other countries of the Persian Gulf, Oman has retained its culture of religious purity and village humility; and unlike the other Gulf states, Oman has not squandered its (limited) oil revenues. Water systems and the *zaygra* and *falaj* in particular stand as common emblems of the great and difficult past.

Hamad's *Zaygra*

While Hamad's and the museum's interest in the well were not surprising, given national attention to past values, Hamad's personal quest to relive the past, through bodily reenactments and sounds on a cassette, revealed that a simple fascination with the past cannot fulfill local struggles to come to terms with personal memories and the late twentieth-century changes in Oman. While the museum presented a static remnant, in miniature, of tradition whose spirit should continue in the time of "progress," Hamad was confronted with more

Figure 5.1 Hamad's *zaygra*. Photo courtesy of the author.

than this apparently simple relationship between tradition and progress. As Jonathan Boyarin (1994) notes, memories are neither strictly individual nor collective, and it is precisely this in-betweenness of memory that allows for its complexity. Both Hamad and the museum were attempting to capture his reenactment: he, working with his re-creation and continuing to listen to its sounds; and the museum, preparing a static miniature and presenting it to the capital area Omani residents and foreign visitors. Modernity's duality of nostalgia and fascination with technology were evident in Hamad's longing for Bahla's not-too-distant past: he both rebuilt the old well and listened to its sounds on his car radio. Like Hamad, the museum, also playing with nostalgia and technology, hoped to teach the sophistication of "ancient" indigenous practices while at the same time illustrating the everyday hardships of the previous pre-coup era.

The sight of a miniature in a museum would hardly have been enough for Hamad, however. He needed to recapture the past. However, even the rebuilding, the bodily reenactment was not enough. He had to continue to listen, surrounding and enveloping himself in his car, through his car stereo, with sounds of the screeching wheel as well as with the sociality of his friends. The landscapes of memory are not only visual, Hamad's recording reminded me, but enveloped in sounds and sociality. These encompassing background sounds,

Hamad hoped, could be recaptured through individual listening on his car stereo. The inadequacy of the museum to capture the loss, the failure of the national discourse of tradition to be a consolation, is evident in Hamad's need to rebuild and listen to the sounds of the well. On the one hand, the model in the museum and the tape of the sounds of the well were similar: both rarified forms in enclosed spaces. On the other hand, however, moving through the town in the car highlighted Hamad's need to be completely surrounded as he moved through space.

Hamad's insistence that the other men would often spend their afternoons there, reliving their past, alerted me to the possibility that their presence at the well was not as customary as he would have liked. Although Hamad claimed that the men had made the well their usual meeting spot in the afternoon, no one had been there on my previous visits. It was most likely that the well was not a usual meeting spot, where the men came to enjoy nature, "the outdoors," but rather that the men occasionally came to watch and that my visit had simply marked an occasion to put the well on show and for the men to bring their tape recorders. The men's choice of this particular day for recording the well suggested as well that recapturing the sounds was a recent interest and that they did not often have the opportunity to record. Perhaps, unlike Hamad, these men would keep the tapes as mementos, souvenirs, and future documents for their children.

Even Hamad himself did not always use the animals to water his fields. At the end of the animal path that I mentioned, there was a mechanical pump and well not in use at the time of my first visits. On another visit several months later, Hamad had both the mechanical pumping well and the *zaygra* working. When I asked him about it, he said that he did use the other well, but that it ran out of water after fifteen minutes. It is very possible that the mechanical pump well did run out of water more quickly than the *zaygra* but at that visit, the mechanical well was being used and ran the entire time I was there, which was about an hour. Nevertheless, the limit of Bahla's local water supply was not lost on Hamad.

Hamad's claims—that he often used the *zaygra*, that the mechanical pumping well ran out of water after fifteen minutes, that the men had made this their usual afternoon gathering spot—revealed more than simple inconsistencies in his story. They revealed his desires, desires that the technology of water distribution had, along with all the Omani discourses about progress and tradition, stirred, and that no model in a museum could even possibly begin to fulfill. The technology of diesel and electric pumps, of pipes and of sprinklers, had almost erased the sounds of his youth. In turn, the youth, who were the supposed audience of Hamad's project, were neither visiting the well nor listening to the tape.

The Water Cooler

While the *zaygra* was, in its fragmented way, becoming part of a national project on heritage and local customs, other water-related "customs" about communal responsibilities were being challenged. One day in the early spring of 1997 as I walked to my house, I saw that a group of men was digging up part of the street and laying a new pipe. I soon learned that the government was going to begin piping drinking water to this part of Bahla.

In the twentieth century, from the restoration of the canals until the introduction of piped water in the mid-1970s, canals provided the water for washing, bathing, and irrigation while wells provided water for drinking. This division of water labor was not absolute, however, and wells have also been used for the irrigation of lands not connected to the main canal system.[6] Among these various categories of water use, the only type of water that, until the early 1970s, one would have had to purchase was for irrigation; even then it was argued that it was not water itself that was owned or purchased, but water-time. While one could own or purchase water-time for irrigation, water for washing, bathing, and drinking in particular, were, by moral and religious recommendation, free and open to the community.

As I was occasionally reminded in Bahla, *sharī'a*, the term generally translated as "Islamic law" or the "right way," also technically means access to a source of pure water. The Prophet Muhammad is known to have said that people hold three things in common: water, pasture, and fire. In another account, Muhammad is recorded to have said: "The man who holds back water from another will have God's mercy held back from him" (see Varisco 1983, 369–370). This is not to say that no one can own water; the general rule is that water belongs to the person who first exploits it, to whomever undertakes the enterprise of digging or carrying it. However, one can only use what one needs and cannot make a profit from selling the rest. Therefore, if someone builds a new canal, that person—in effect—can own only the water from that well or that canal that is needed for drinking, bathing, washing, and irrigating the fields (two ankles deep, according to the Prophet); the rest must be given away or sold at the cost of upkeep of the canal or well. Speculating is illegal, and portering water is acceptable only if one does not profit from it. These, however, are some of the basic formal prescriptions, and most people and towns have tended to follow the spirit of the Prophet's sayings rather than attempt to apply them systematically, especially since in many towns water is not owned by an original founder but in corporation, organized around the figure of the ʿarīf.[7]

In Bahla, time rather than quantity regulated the system of the purchase of water from the canals for irrigation.[8] One man, an auctioneer and water canal organizer known as the ʿarīf or "specialist," controlled the water distribution system. He was responsible for knowing who or which mosque owned how much water-time as well as when and where they should be receiving water. Individuals and mosques owned certain amounts of water-time within a cycle of about two weeks. The twenty-four hour schedule of the day began with sunrise and was divided into thirty-minute units called āthār. Other units of water-time division in Bahla were: Baʿada (twelve hours or twenty-four āthār), Rabiya (three hours or six āthār), Qama (seven and a half minutes or one quarter āthār), Daqīqa (one minute). A twenty-four hour day, therefore, had forty-eight āthār. Individuals could own units of time as small as a quarter of one minute, and there was no limit to the amount of time an individual could own, although water-time, like all property, would have to be divided upon death. In Bahla, records of exactly how much time each person or mosque owned were kept, updated, and guarded in a leather-bound book at the house of another town elder.

To maintain the fairness of when a mosque or individual would receive water, each cycle would include two rotations of its own, alternating between day and night. In other words, if someone owned time, thirty minutes say, during the day in the first rotation of the cycle, his or her thirty minutes of water-time would be allocated to the night during the second rotation. Whatever was left over from the ownership of water-time, which was usually about one third of the total time available, the ʿarīf told me, was auctioned off for that cycle. The proceeds of the auction, or mawqid, would go toward the maintenance of the canal. The ʿarīf received about three US dollars for each auction as well as a small salary from the Ministry of Religious Endowments. He was not supposed to make a profit from this work of water trade. Indeed, I was told that the son of another ʿarīf had made his father stop auctioning water because he believed his father was profiteering. Therefore, even though one had to buy water-time to irrigate fields, no one was supposed to make a profit directly from water.

Unlike Karl Wittfogel's "hydraulic society," here water—as the main means of production—was not controlled by a centralized power (1957). Certainly, while the rich were more easily able to buy permanent water-time or rent water-time for a particular cycle, ownership of that time would quickly divide through inheritance. Furthermore, rent prices were generally difficult to fix by the 'arīf because of the auction and the prohibition against making a profit. Rather, the main beneficiaries of water-time in Bahla were the mosques, the religious endowments of which could not be divided and which could rent out surplus water-time. Like the Balinese Subaks that John S. Lansing, Clifford Geertz, and Robert C. Hunt and Eva Hunt have described, however, even with the mosques, the degree of centralization was ambiguous (Lansing 1987; Geertz 1972; Hunt and Hunt 1976).[9] The emphasis of water law, as an ideal, was clearly placed on providing water, especially drinking water, for the community.[10]

In the early 1970s, when pipes and pumps entered the Omani market in a pronounced way, the town's water distribution system dramatically changed. Although irrigation water from the canals continued to be divided and distributed more or less according to a system of auctions, rotations, renting, and time ownership, other methods of water organization also became possible—other ways of "owning" water became possible. From the mid-1970s, when pipes were brought to Bahla, much of the water for household washing, drinking, and bathing began to come from privately owned wells in town. Each house would decide whose well water they wanted and would pay that well's owner to lay down the pipes and deliver water. From the mid-1970s to the early 1990s, users paid a flat monthly rate, which fluctuated the most during times of drought. In the early 1990s, the well owners decided to install meters so that consumers would pay according to how much they used.

Although it might be expected that paying for water for washing, drinking, and bathing contradicted the emphasis on communal access in law and custom, some people explained that they were paying not for the water but for the pipes and for the service into their homes, just as they would have paid a porter. Further, the canal water, which could not for legal and moral reasons be tapped by pipes, was still available for washing and bathing. Paying for piping into homes did not in itself seem, at least for almost thirty years after the pipes were installed, to cause much consternation. In abiding by the moral recommendation to provide free drinking water, however, many families put a thermos of water and a plastic cup outside their houses for anyone passing by. Although willing to pay for the delivery of water into the house, exclusive ownership of that water, especially drinking water, continued to be a matter of negotiation. While by far the most laws and legal rulings on water were concerned with irrigation and with establishing fairness of access, in Bahla it was, above all, drinking water that was subject to the most adamant moral statements and understandings about providing for the community. It was drinking water, in particular, that should never be held back.

Now the government was bringing piped drinking water, and no one seemed to be willing to pay for yet another supplier—except for the owner of the house where I was living, who believed that this "new" water might be better. My landlord bought a new electric water cooler and placed it near the main entrance to the house. He drilled a hole through the cement wall around the house for a faucet to be available from the road. He then hired someone to build a small cement area underneath the faucet on the ground so that the water dripping from the faucet would not create a pool of mud. Finally, he hung a new plastic cup to the faucet. The new water cooler was ready for the inhabitants of the house and for anyone walking by. Although others in the neighborhood had been providing drinking water from plastic thermoses and clay jugs, there was a difference here: this was the "new" water and it could flow continuously.

My landlord would now be paying three separate water suppliers: the 'arīf for "rented" water-time to irrigate his small gardens and backyard; the local well owner for the delivery of washing and bathing water to the house at a metered rate; and the government for the delivery of drinking water, also at a metered rate. Soon, however, my landlord's "good deed" of providing the new drinking water to the neighborhood turned sour. My landlord's children, in particular, began complaining that it was always a mess in front of their house and that people were not simply drinking a bit of water but taking *a lot* of *their* water to their homes. It became apparent that entangled in these complaints was a problem of class (or caste) tensions. The "people" my landlord's children were complaining about were migrant laborers and young boys from former-servant families.

Although the shift in the mid-1970s to paid private water or, more accurately, paid local distribution from a private well for washing and bathing, seems to have been acceptable in terms of moral and legal ideals (at least from the perspective of the late 1990s), the status of drinking water was more tenuous. By placing thermoses and jugs outside their homes, many families strove to maintain a blurred line of ownership and to provide for the community. In the late 1990s, ambiguities of morality and charity were being played out again, as some boundaries continued to be negotiated and others reinforced: my landlord broke a large hole through the cement wall around his house in order to provide the expected drinking water to the neighborhood, and yet his children resented some of the people who were drinking that water. The uneasy status of migrant laborers in Bahla (integral to and yet separate from what constituted the public community) and tensions between former servant and "free" families were being played out through the dynamics of community obligations and ownership.

The arrival of the government drinking water, piped to the house in the new hoses from tankers brought from Muscat or from new wells dug by the Mott MacDonald Ltd. consulting group, and kept cold in the extreme Bahla heat by a continuously running electric cooler, certainly qualified as an event in the neighborhood, marking a further shift in the organization of water distribution. The water no longer came from local wells, either brought to the house on foot or pumped through pipes; it came from elsewhere. Drinking water had become a commodity derived from unknown origins, "bought," "owned," and "distributed" by the household, its value to be calculated in terms of quantity rather than time. If the privatization recommendations of the ABN Amro consortium were implemented in accordance with new IMF policies, this "government" water was to be privatized by 2009. This is not to argue that the new piped water caused divisions within the community or that there were no tensions before it but, rather, that it made even more possible the children's assumption that they owned certain amounts of the drinking water (after all, they were paying for the quantity that was being used). This possibility, combined with the continuous flow from the water cooler and the tensions revolving around the migrant laborers and between different classes of Bahlawis, helped to reveal and to aggravate discord in the neighborhood. The children were expressing the practical tensions seemingly erased in the Omani state's discursive elaborations about development and tradition.

The tensions surrounding the water cooler, were not, however, only between the children of the house where I was living and migrant laborers or the children of former-servant families. The conflicts emerging here were also between my landlord and his children. The *falaj* in front of the house reminded the father about the importance of dividing water fairly, about forms of water distribution requiring that drinking water be accessible to everyone—that everyone be able to taste the new, cold, and supposedly "better" government water—and finally, that he did not "own" water, only water-time. My landlord was not rejecting new technologies: he embraced the arrival of government water and bought a brand new electric cooler. Nevertheless, by placing the water cooler near the entry and breaking a hole in the wall around the house, my landlord was also setting an example for his children to learn about providing drinking water. The children, however, saw water in terms of the amounts for which they were paying, the meter that would mark how much was being taken. Eventually, my landlord won the conflict with his children, insisting that it was their duty to provide water to the neighborhood.

The Bathing Room

While my landlord and his children were struggling over how to negotiate communal responsibilities about ownership and sharing water, discussions about social appropriateness, bathing, and bodies took place among my neighbor-group. We, the regular group of neighbors, were sitting in front of Rayya's house one afternoon having our usual coffee and dates. Rayya's daughter, Amina, was there that day as well: she was home for the week because of a university holiday. We began to talk of the *magāzī*, the women's wash and prayer room that separated the patio where we were sitting from the main road. This room, like the many other abandoned ones around town, sat over a canal, a *falaj*, with running water. Inside there is an area to pray, with a *miḥrāb* marking the direction of Mecca, and an area to bathe, with a ledge to sit along the canal. "Do you ever use it, Rayya?" I asked. "No, it's too cold for me. Even when it's hot outside, in the summer, it's cold and in the winter, it's freezing. Only the old woman across the street, Fatima, still uses it," Rayya said. "Who used it before?" I asked. While officially "before" marked a generic pre-coup time when there were no schools, hospitals, or roads, when there was no electricity or piped water, it was also a time of living memory for these women sitting on the patio. For Amina, Rayya's daughter home from the university, it was a time learned through constant official reminders, family stories, and my questions.

"We all did," Rayya answered. "All together?" Amina interjected suddenly. "Of course all together; if you needed to bathe and someone else wanted to bathe, we'd bathe together. And, when we prayed, we'd pray together." Amina looked disturbed and added "But, bathing together, that's *ḥarām* (forbidden)." Now Rayya looked disturbed. Her daughter Amina had studied Islam in school, she knew how to read the Qur'an, she knew how to read legal texts: she would probably know if something were *ḥarām*. "But, it's between women," I added, trying to make the older women feel better about their practices. "That's right," Rayya said. "It isn't forbidden if it's between women," she said, tentatively—still not sure of herself and certainly not sure of our religious authority. Now it was Amina's grandmother's turn, frustrated with all the restrictions she saw being imposed by the religious youth: "*Everything* is *ḥarām* now." "Now" the extremely private space of the bathroom in the house, with its piped water and hot and cold taps, was the place to bathe, alone.

Whether Amina had actually read or heard any specific religious statement against women bathing together was not clear, although it certainly is possible that she had heard students discussing this particular issue at university. What was clear was that her religious authority came from her experience of going to the university, which made the older women in the group uncertain of their own practices and interpretations of what was proper. Amina's experiences at the university, however, also would have encouraged particular approaches to ethics and principles about proper behavior and sociality. Such approaches, which I often heard from young people in Bahla and were encouraged by young lecturers speaking in the neighborhood meeting rooms, emphasized the need to apply generalized precepts, irrelevant of specific contexts. In this particular case, it would have meant that because it was generally forbidden for "strangers" (that is non-married adults) to see each other's bodies, the specific contexts in which adult women might see each other's bodies were also expected to be forbidden. It would not have mattered that these women were "neighbors," shared many aspects of their lives, and did not think of each other in sexualized ways. It would not have mattered that the practical considerations of the desire for and requirements of bathing would have meant that it was highly likely that women would have to bathe together. Same-sex sociality was required to abide by some of the same restrictions about bodily propriety as male-female sociality. Another way of understanding Amina's approach is to see it as primarily rule-based, where the main categories for action were either forbidden or required.[11] Amina's reaction expressed yet another ethic, part of the increasingly shared Islamic universe espoused and assumed by many university students; a moral ethic tied to a discourse of individualized and privatized religious modesty.

What was remarkable about Amina's statement, in addition to her recent access to this kind of information and discussion, was that her shock and certainty that these women's activities would be *ḥarām* came only after several months at the university. Amina had grown up in front of the *magāzī* and yet her reaction suggested that this was the first time that she had actually considered what women did inside. It seemed as though, until that moment, Amina, who had lived in the house near the *magāzī* her entire life, had not thought about the fact that women bathed together there and that this bathing would, in any way, conflict with a religious ethic. This sudden realization both defined something as immoral and revealed her intense discomfort at the thought of seeing other women's bodies.

Living communally at the university must have raised questions for Amina about whether it was appropriate to see other women's bodies or how much of another woman's body was appropriate to see. The mere thought of *seeing* the "naked" bodies of those—of women—not part of the nuclear family was almost as abhorrent as seeing a naked man. This was a new control of sight, no longer geared only towards men, but towards all adults. Amina's shock that women would even have thought to bathe in the same room ran counter to what the other women sitting on that patio would have assumed was appropriate and remembered as part of their cultural past. In this moment, Amina and the older women were also struggling with what objects would become sites of authentic Omani tradition. This struggle over whether the *magāzī* was authentic to Omani traditions, however, also implicitly carried with it struggles about what was appropriate to feel and see as well as what could be remembered. The authentication of objects, as C. Nadia Seremetakis reminds us, is also an authentication of the senses associated with those objects: "Crucial to any process of authentication is the moment when certain objects are selected over others as sites of social anchorage. This results in the discarding and marginalization of sensory values, meaning and emotions attached to discredited materialites" (Seremetakis 1994: 136). While for the older women, the *magāzī* carried with it sounds, sights, and a sense of community that they considered an important part of their past, for Amina, it mostly suggested a sight that should have been forbidden.

Rayya had said that the water, in that arid weather and in the shade of the wash room, was cold. Rayya was remembering the feel of that cold *falaj* water, the spray, splash, and dipping that was part of bathing and that she was acknowledging as integral to using the *magāzī*. Rayya was not concerned about what parts of other women's bodies would be forbidden to see, but focused on the feel of that water, of a way of bathing, and of communal life. Like the other women sitting on the terrace that morning, her concern about modesty would have been that they could not be seen by men walking by outside the room.

It was not only Amina who was drawing on religion to authenticate particular practices: Rayya had coupled praying with bathing. Rayya mentioned how the women used to bathe together just as they used to pray together. This was no longer what women did; they no longer shared either of these activities. Praying together, for Rayya and the other women, was just as much a part of her memories of that past as bathing together. In evoking the past of the *magāzī*, Rayya was evoking a past about community, and a mixing of religion and sociality. The coupling of bathing and praying, activities now performed alone, in the singular spaces of individual rooms, was of their communal past.

Amina's certainty and concern about the limits of acceptable distance between the women revealed not only the discrepancies between her assumptions about religiously prescribed modesty and those of the other women sitting on the patio, but also ensured that the lines of privacy would be closed even tighter. Amina's assumed authority to speak against the memories and experiences of the older women, as well as the older women's relenting to her objections, signaled, as well, the degree to which they had all, except the grandmother perhaps, interiorized the state's legitimization and heralding of Amina's "new" knowledge. While the enclosed wash room was clearly conceived as protected and distinct from what was happening on the road, which is what was important for the other women on the patio, and while it held the possibility for the articulation of a gendered heritage, this was not enough for young Amina's university-educated sensibilities.

Conclusion

While I was in Oman, water was a constant image on Omani television: images of clear riverbeds, pools of glistening water, and flowing canal water marked moments between programs. These pure and soothing images were safe reminders of the past as well as markers of the present. They signified "tradition" and the values and sophisticated ancient technologies of village life, seemingly distant from the glitz and oil money of the capital, Muscat. These images also touched on "progress" and the relatively new amenities of piped water, mechanical pumps, electricity, and television, as well as on the wisdom of a state that recognized and supported national treasures and resources. While the discourses of the state, in its smooth official messages, played with an unproblematized relationship between tradition and progress, people in Bahla were confronted in practice with the complexities of changing relationships emerging around and through changing water distribution systems.

The reconstruction and occasional use of the old-style well signaled local nostalgia for a past time, an unfulfillable desire no matter how hard Hamad tried. National attention to Omani heritage supported and justified Hamad's project for rebuilding the well, although perhaps not quite in the ways he would have liked. He neither received funding for his project nor did references to the great engineering and spirit of the past capture all the experiences and memories that he wanted. Hamad spent his own money to build the well and occasionally irrigated his fields using it. His professed goal of teaching the youth who had no memories of a time when farming was an integral part of daily life in Bahla only began to touch on the emotions and desires of his project. More accurately, Hamad was trying to relive the past in some ways, enacting an older ethic of communal and social appreciation for the outdoors and surrounding himself in the sounds that accompanied that ethic.

As Hamad struggled to capture the past through the well, a nationally recognized emblem, struggles over customs of communal responsibility were being negotiated over access to and private ownership of drinking water. The quick installation of the water cooler, however, was also a sign of social status, which required its partial redistribution to the neighborhood. This gesture, however, was doubled by concern that others were taking advantage of the family's generosity. Water ownership, now expressed in terms of quantity rather than time, was possible because drinking water could be owned, calculated by a meter; it had become a commodity. My landlord, an older man who would go to the auctions and who often told me that his sons did not even understand how the *falaj* was organized, went out of his way to provide for the neighborhood. On the one hand, his act was geared towards his neighbors, in terms of establishing his generosity as well as his status. On the other hand, it brought out tensions with his children: for the father, the *falaj* invoked an ethic about ownership that the technologies of piping and meters, electric coolers, and tankers seemed to be overturning.

While private ownership and the obligations to neighbors were being disputed in the events after the installation of the water cooler, private space and individual propriety were being negotiated in the discussion of the bathing room. Amina and her mother also struggled over what artifacts, and the senses associated with them, should be remembered. The argument between the older women and the young university student revealed their struggles in establishing particular artifacts as authentic. The older women were proud of their bathing and prayer room—it stood for a time when people would share more, conjuring up memories of dipping and splashing in cold water, of praying and bathing together. For Amina, instead, the thought of seeing other women's bodies was disturbing. Socializing should not, for Amina, involve seeing other adult women's bodies. Using the *magāzī* was not a practice that raised senses that she could understand or even wanted to understand. Here, in the discussion over the bathing room, the women were also negotiating the lines of privacy. The shifts in the boundaries of private and public, however, should not be seen as simply moving in one direction towards privatization: it is in fact only the "public" position of a university student that allowed Amina to claim a restricted privacy. Amina's authority in proclaiming what was proper or improper conduct and her assumptions about spatial control derived from the public recognition of her schooling and her place in a newly founded university system. Entangled in the general "Islamic" principles that have become common among many students were generational struggles over what could appropriately be seen, revealing shifting assumptions about space, bodies, and gender.

These three stories highlight how the need to negotiate the novelties of "progress" engendered a spectrum of accommodations, conflicts, and debates. From these accounts, one also detects the entanglement of different discourses such as those of the past, gendered modesty, religion, class, and sociality. Changing water distribution practices, made possible by oil revenues and encouraged by discourses on development, have naturalized the introduction of pipes, electric coolers, and diesel and electric pumps as a necessary part of development. These particular machines, however, also came at a time when people were confronting issues of migrant labor, shifting notions and practices of sociality and community, divergent religious ideologies, and the importance of retaining emblems of Oman's great past. Perceptions and assumptions, conflicts and struggles about ownership, about bodies and modesty, authentic artifacts and senses, all emerged as people both embraced and confronted what it meant to live with the technologies of development that seemed so natural, and yet may also be fleeting.

6 Becoming Bahlawi

Race, Genealogy, and the Politics of Arabness

FATIMA, THE THIN BUT STRONG seventy-something-year-old woman who lived across the street from me in Bahla spoke with an accent. She had lived in Bahla for almost sixty years and had never lost it, that trace of her background in Africa. What does it mean in contemporary Oman to have been born in, to have lived in, or to have ancestors from Africa? Of course, it means many things, depending on the context in Oman and on the particular circumstances of life in Africa. It depends on the history of the 1964 revolution in Zanzibar and on the policies of the post-1970 Omani state, a state that relies on but does not acknowledge its "Zanzibari" intelligentsia. It depends on the legacy of slavery in Oman and on memories and practices of injustice, hierarchy, and marriage. And, it depends on seeing an ocean as a boundary and the political organization of nation-states as markers of identity.

In the previous chapters I examined how Bahlawis have understood and experienced the dramatic transformations in their town: from the rebuilding of the town's fort and the construction of asphalt roads to the omnipresence of coffee; from modern mass schools to piped water. Each of these noted changes, as we have seen, is shaped by and helps shape a series of discourses and policies, from development and nostalgia to concerns about appropriate religiosity and sociality. Indeed, this book has emphasized the ways that concern about women's sociality emerged in particular as central to anxieties about Oman's oil economy and modernity. Sociality and what it means to be a good person in Bahla are also, however, embedded in memories and hierarchies of lives and histories beyond Oman. This chapter, therefore, focuses on the ways that Bahlawi practices and notions cohere, not merely to Oman's domestic transformations, but to histories and representations of Oman's connections with East Africa as well.

In Oman, references to East Africa are hardly straightforward. On the one hand, particular aspects of Oman's East African past, especially when signified in limited Swahili-speaking and histories of Oman's great empire, have increasingly become legitimized as "tradition" and celebrated as glorious. References to Oman's connections to East Africa also index the nation's intelligentsia and bureaucratic elite, even though the Omani state has downplayed the background of its bureaucratic elite in favor of emphasizing the nation's Arab genealogy. Omani national representations have increasingly emphasized the nation's Arabness, reorienting its transnational connections away from East Africa and towards other states on the Arabian Peninsula and in the Arab world more broadly. At the same time, references in Oman to East Africa also raise memories of servitude and the continued distinctions between social classes through which these memories are often performed.

In Bahla, unlike in nearby towns such as Hamra (C. Eickelman 1984), hierarchical distinctions between descendants of East African slaves or servants (*akhdām*) and "Arabs" were not often overtly expressed in the daily visiting practices that I witnessed in the late 1990s. Women of both classes often belonged to the same neighborly group; and, within these small neighborly groups, status differences were not often visible in the women's interactions. However, hierarchies clearly existed and were most openly discussed around the topic of marriage. It should be noted that Arabs and servants were not so much racial or ethnic categories (although they are increasingly so) as they were class or caste categories, reproduced through patrilineal genealogy.

Thus, on the one hand "Zanzibariness" and East Africa more broadly reference Oman's bureaucratic elite and remind Omanis of their once-great empire. On the other hand, histories of East Africa are also troubled, linked to tensions around defining Oman as an Arab nation and around the history of servitude.

After an account of Omani history in Zanzibar and a discussion of the relationship between notions of race and patrilineal genealogy, this chapter examines two Bahlawi women's life stories. In these accounts, I emphasize less the ways that everyday visiting practices reproduced or disrupted social hierarchies than how memories of lives in East Africa intersected with people's understandings of work and neighborly obligations, as well as being Arab or Omani in Bahla. In many ways, the two women's stories are similar. Both women lived in Bahla, across the street from each other. They were about the same age. In the late 1990s, they were in their mid-sixties or mid-seventies, and both spent time in East Africa. They experienced many of the same economic conditions in Oman and were products of much of the same history: the poverty and wars of Oman during the first half of the twentieth century, the centuries of travel between Oman and East Africa, the divisions and tensions among different groups and generations of Omanis in East Africa, and the history and practices of the slave trade and slavery. At the same time, however, these women's stories also reveal their differences. The two women were identified through their fathers with different social statuses and through their mothers with different nationalities. One woman's father was from a free "Arab" family and the other was from a servant (*khādim*) family. Yet ultimately, they both constructed their histories, through their fathers, as productive of their "Omaniness." And, both constructed their stories with the recurring themes of loss, of solitude, of productive labor, and of reluctant returns to Oman.

Migrations

By the beginning of the twentieth century, Omanis had been traveling back and forth from East Africa for centuries, mostly as plantation owners, slaves, petty merchants, and traders—of slaves, wood, ivory, and then cloves and coconuts.[1] In the mid-seventeenth century, Omani rulers of the Ya'ariba dynasty, who had expelled the Portuguese from Muscat and "aided" East African ruling families in expelling the Portuguese from Zanzibar, began appointing governors to various principalities on the East African coast.[2] Although Omani merchants had traveled to East Africa before, Ya'ariba expansion marked the time of the first major wave of migrants from Oman to Zanzibar.[3] By the middle of the eighteenth century, internal family disputes as well as an invasion by Nadir Shah's army from Iran paved the way for the fall of the Ya'ariba dynasty at the hands of Ahmad bin Sa'id al-Bu Sa'id, a coffee merchant in Sohar. With support from the mercantile community, Ahmad bin Sa'id defeated the Ya'ariba and was elected the next Ibadi Imam of Oman. Many towns within traditional Imamate territory and along the East African coast, however, did not accept his leadership: Ya'ariba and other local shaykhs continued to rule the territory west of the Jebel Akhdar mountains and, on the East African coast, only the governor of Zanzibar recognized Ahmad bin Sa'id's election as Imam.[4] Therefore, Ahmad bin Sa'id established his "capital" in Rustaq, on the eastern slope of the Jebel Akhdar from where he could control towns along the Batina coast as well as the commercial centers of Muscat and Matrah.

By the beginning of the nineteenth century, al-Bu Saʿidi rule also seemed on the verge of collapse. Not only was al-Bu Saʿidi territory divided into three polities (Muscat, Matrah and Sohar, and Rustaq) after Ahmad bin Saʿid's death in 1783, but a Wahhabi invasion at the end of the eighteenth and beginning of the nineteenth centuries weakened the dynasty further. Despite their unfavorable position within Oman, al-Bu Saʿidi rulers managed to consolidate their power in the Indian Ocean: coffee from Yemen, sugar from Batavia, and slaves and ivory from East Africa all passed through the Omani ports of Muscat and Matrah by the late eighteenth century. And, in the early nineteenth century favorable tariffs and protections for traders attracted Indian Ocean merchants to Muscat.[5]

The shape of Omani trade in the Indian Ocean at the beginning of the nineteenth century was also shifting. Increasingly tied to British, French, and Dutch interests and rivalries, merchants in Indian Ocean ports were not only supplying goods to Asia, Arabia, and Africa, but also to markets in Amsterdam and London. "Neutral" merchants from Arabia were able to take advantage of Franco-English rivalries to establish themselves as critical to the success of European empires. In Zanzibar, trade in ivory and in slaves, who labored on the growing number of plantations on the island and who were sent to the Arabian Peninsula and Iran, dominated the early nineteenth-century economy. The exact numbers of slaves sent from East Africa to the Arabian Peninsula is unknown (Austen 1988). However, estimates are that between 1782 and 1842, approximately 800–1,000 were sent annually; between 1842 and 1872, approximately 2,000–3,000 annually; and, between 1872 and 1902, 50–100 annually (Ricks 1988). Indeed, Zanzibar had become so important for Oman, Omanis, and the fortunes of the ruling family that in 1832 Sayyid Saʿid bin Sultan al-Bu Saʿid moved his entire court, most of his family, and even some furniture to Zanzibar, some 2,200 miles away from Muscat.[6] The Sultan was not simply visiting, but moved to Zanzibar intending to rule his "dominions" on the Arabian Peninsula from Zanzibar.[7] After the first wave of Omani Arabs had gone to Zanzibar under the Yaʿariba, therefore, a second wave followed Sayyid Saʿid bin Sultan. While it was primarily prominent merchant families and petty traders from Muscat, Matrah, and the coast who took advantage of conditions that the al-Bu Saʿidi rulers had made favorable for trade, descendants of the Yaʿariba and their supporters continued their connections with East Africa. Lists of tribal names in East Africa reveal that it was not only merchants from the coast or from Sharqiya, the region popularly associated in Oman today with Zanzibar, that traveled.[8]

It was also during Sayyid Saʻid's time that clove plantations and slave labor on which the clove plantations relied began to play a major part in Zanzibar's economy. Although Sayyid Saʻid signed an antislavery treaty in 1845 with the British (the British consul had arrived in Zanzibar in 1841) to prohibit the export of slaves to Arabia, slavery continued to be legal on Zanzibar itself.[9] Encouraged by the clove market, Omani Arabs who followed Sayyid Saʻid bin Sultan to Zanzibar began buying and confiscating land as well as marrying into some Hadimu (one of the largest "native" and Swahili-speaking groups on Zanzibar) landowning families.[10] According to the Omani historian Saʻid bin Ali al-Mughayri, while most of those who had gone to Zanzibar under the Yaʻariba were wholly integrated into "Swahili" culture, Omanis who followed Sayyid Saʻid bin Sultan in the nineteenth century also became so intermarried that "nobody could tell the difference between an Arab and a Zinji" (1994 [1979]: 189).[11]

With Sayyid Saʻid's death in 1856, succession threatened to destabilize al-Bu Saʻidi rule again.[12] In Zanzibar, a struggle between two of Sayyid Saʻid's sons, Majid and Barghash, ensued and ultimately, with British support, the younger of the two, Majid, was proclaimed the new ruler of Zanzibar. In Muscat, another of the Sultan's sons, Thuwayni (who Sayyid Saʻid left in charge in Muscat during his absences), became the next Sultan there and was appeased by Majid, who agreed to pay an annual fee of MT $40,000. Majid, however, did not have the funds to pay this amount and after several years without payment and with further instigation of their other brother Barghash (who was continuing to plot to take over Zanzibar), Thuwayni went to Zanzibar with an army. When he arrived in Zanzibar, however, the new British consul (the previous one had died a few years earlier), called upon a British warship to intercept the force. And, although British authorities rejected the idea of a partition at first, they subsequently arranged the arbitration between Majid and Thuwayni. After Thuwayni's aborted attack, however, Majid refused to pay again, thus further angering those who opposed Majid already and leading to open rebellion in 1859. The rebellion, which was supported by Barghash, was eventually crushed with the support of the British bombardment of Barghash's plantation house, the Marseilles.[13] In 1861, British authorities established a Muscat-Zanzibar Commission to investigate the incident and report on succession, deciding on the formal partition of Oman into a Sultanate of Muscat and a Sultanate of Zanzibar and for the annual payment, known from then on as the Canning Award, from Zanzibar to Muscat of MT $40,000.[14] The period from the establishment of the Canning Award to the establishment of the British protectorate in 1890 witnessed the cementing of British influence in Zanzibar.[15]

Seven years after the establishment of the British protectorate, with the al-Bu Sa'idi Sultans maintaining nominal sovereignty, an abolition decree for Zanzibar was signed.[16] The British, however, feared that the abolition of slavery on Zanzibar might cause the collapse of the clove plantations and economy. The government therefore decided, as Frederick Cooper has argued, that the "Arab aristocracy must be supported not simply by recognition of its owner-ship of land but by compensation for slaves who were freed" (Cooper 1980: 40). To limit the numbers of slaves being freed at once, obstacles were placed in the process. Specifically, it was made incumbent on slaves to go to court and request freedom. Upon gaining freedom, the slaves would have to pay "rent" (in kind or in labor) for their housing and land, housing in which they had been living and land on which they had been working to raise food for them-selves.[17] A turn to wage labor was the expected and accepted "natural" shift for Zanzibar's former slaves, making them, according to Cooper, an agricultural working class.[18] Cooper has argued that "the colonial state did not simply en-courage monoculture; it helped preserve a particular structure of production . . . [whereby] its policies were intended to perpetuate the dominance of what officials perceived to be an Arab upper class and to link that class to the state" (1980: 135). Thus, despite their decline in terms of their control over slave labor, Arab landowners and planters were able to prosper due to their place in the political and economic hierarchy.

From the establishment of the British protectorate in 1890, and especially from just before World War I until the mid-1920s, the Zanzibar state bureau-cracy expanded, with bureaus for taxing, budget and accounting, medicine and education, and roads and communication. It was often staffed by those who were identified as Arabs. In 1914, the British also established a Protec-torate Council with the Sultan as president, the British political resident as vice president, three other official members, and four representatives of the Arab and Asian communities.[19] In 1926 the Protectorate Council was abol-ished and replaced by a Legislative Council, which, unlike the Protectorate Council, had some law-making authority. The Legislative Council, while going through several permutations in numbers and organization, nonethe-less maintained a majority of British members, followed in number by Arab and then Asian members.[20] "Africans" were not made part of the Legislative Council until 1946, and the first elections for the council were not held until

1957. Until then, the members were nominated by "racial associations" and then approved by the British resident.

Arabs were not only privileged in the political and administrative arenas. By 1925, clove prices, which had previously been quite high, began to drop, and planters began to turn to growing coconuts.[21] Since Zanzibar was only one of many places producing coconuts, the price of coconuts was not determined by Zanzibar alone. While more Arabs were investing in coconuts, the colonial state continued to push, through economic and political incentives, for the production of cloves and the maintenance of an "Arab" elite.[22] With the economic depression of the early 1930s, however, clove prices plummeted from twenty to twenty-three rupees per ton in the late 1920s to six to seven rupees per ton, and Arab clove plantation owners became further indebted to Asian merchants. Nevertheless, with the establishment and reorganization of the Clove Growers Association as well as schemes to plant more cloves and provide loans for landowners to hire laborers, the protectorate administration continued to support the Arab landowners, many of whose properties had been mortgaged to Indians.[23] As the Zanzibar attorney general made abundantly clear: "This is an Arab state. It is the duty of the protecting government to assist the protected people. It is impossible for us to stand by and take the risk of the expropriation of His Highness' people" (quoted in Lofchie 1965: 116).

Despite the collapse of the clove market, Omanis were increasingly attempting to make the voyage to Zanzibar. It should be remembered that in Oman at this time the 1913 Imamate rebellion had forged deep divisions between the Sultanate of Muscat on the coast and a new Imamate administration and territory in the interior.[24] Fighting between the supporters of the newly reestablished Imamate and its adversaries—either the Sultanate in Muscat, the oil companies that were looking (especially starting around 1925) to begin exploration in the region, or local tribal and town rulers who did not support or want to succumb to the taxes, power, and hierarchies of the Imamate administration—made travel to Zanzibar tempting. Compared to the fruits of Zanzibari trade and the East African economy more generally, Oman was considered destitute. And, although the British imposed travel restrictions during World War II, Zanzibar's status as a British protectorate that "protected" the "Arab state" also encouraged migration, especially during periods of drought in Oman.[25] Thus, despite the economic downturn in the 1930s Omanis—including Bahlawis—continued to look to East Africa as the main site of potential prosperity.

The early part of the twentieth century, therefore, marks the third major wave of travel by Omanis to Zanzibar. Between 1924 and 1931, the number and percentage of "Arabs" in Zanzibar increased from almost 19,000 (8.7% of the population) to about 33,500 (14.2% of the population). By 1948 (after the period of rations and "control" that I described in Chapters 2 and 3), there were about 44,500 Arabs in Zanzibar, making up 16.9% of the population. While most of this increase was probably due to migration from Oman, some may also have been due to a shift in the ways people were identifying themselves.[26]

The descendants of earlier periods of migration then, first during the height of the Omani Ya'ariba dynasty in the mid-seventeenth century and then during the move of the Omani capital from Muscat to Zanzibar in the mid-nineteenth century under the rule of Seyyed Sa'id bin Sultan al-Bu Sa'id, were confronted with a new group that became known derogatorily as "Manga." The new group was increasingly from al-Dakhiliya and was poorer than the established, plantation-owning elite of the previous generations. Antagonism between various groups from the Arabian Peninsula even manifested itself in riots in 1928 and then in 1936.[27] And, although difficult to justify politically to the Arab Association in Zanzibar, British policy even actively prevented Manga Arabs from entering Zanzibar from 1939 through the end of the war, and beyond (Zanzibar National Archives [ZNA], archive number DO 40/52). Thus, while Arabs were, for the most part, considered by British protectorate authorities as the Zanzibari aristocracy and while some did in fact own the largest plantations and hold important seats in local government, many, especially those who arrived in the first half of the twentieth century, were petty shopkeepers, small landowners, and laborers in the shops and farms of other Arabs. Indeed, many of these people were not even considered Arabs in Oman, but rather servants.

After a short-lived upturn during World War II, in the post-war period the clove harvest took another downturn (this time from disease) and tensions between Arabs, Aslans, and Africans (both Shirazis / Hadimu and mainlanders) intensified.[28] The British colonial administration created a new governmental structure, again dominated by Arabs, fueling further tensions that culminated in a general strike in 1948. The strike, which began as a demand by porters at the Zanzibar port for a pay increase, soon spread to other sectors, including the government's own labor force, and became openly anti-Arab and anti-British. In the 1950s, Zanzibar witnessed the rise of nationalist sentiment and rhetoric, by both Arab and non-Arab groups. And, although the clove harvest proved to be relatively good (at least in the 1950s), tensions between Arabs,

Asians, Africans, and the British were increasing. After the arrest of a group of Arabs for their nationalist and anti-colonial activities, supporters responded, in 1955, by establishing the Zanzibar Nationalist Party. Although the ZNP claimed to be inclusive (and in opposition to British colonialism), the party was also increasingly espousing anti-mainlander (and thus, anti-"African") rhetoric.

In 1956, the British finally instituted constitutional reforms meant to establish an elected legislature. Over the course of the next seven years, party politics solidified tensions between the racialized groups, groups that were assigned varying numbers in the government body.[29] The 1963 elections, meant to establish independence from Britain, highlighted as well, for the newly established Afro-Shirazi party, the aim of "Arabs" to maintain the status quo on the island. To make matters worse, between 1960 and 1964, two Sultans died. Sultan Khalifa, who had been quite popular, died in 1960 and his successor, Sultan Abdullah, died soon after. Sultan Abdullah and his young son Sultan Jamshid were not only less popular, they were also both ZNP supporters. A month after the 1963 elections and the establishment of independence, a revolution overthrew the new government and thousands of Arabs were killed or deported.

Although by the early 1960s it seemed increasingly likely that oil would be produced in Oman, in 1964 commercial amounts had not yet been discovered, or at least nothing was announced publicly. Therefore, although the Imamate rebellion had been quelled and peace seemed to prevail in northern Oman, few Zanzibari-Omani-Arabs would have chosen to return to Oman in the 1960s. "Going back" was considered a return to poverty and disease. At the same time, Sultan Sa'id bin Taymur was not eager to welcome people who themselves were not "really" Omanis, who had not supported the state and who could pose a threat to his rule. Therefore, many of the elite Zanzibari-Omani-Arabs went instead to Mombasa; others went to Dubai, others to Cairo, and still others managed to remain in Zanzibar—preferring that to a return to a destitute country they had never known. For the newer group of Omani immigrants, return was much easier: their ties to Oman were more recent.

In 1970, upon ousting his father, Sultan Qaboos bin Sa'id immediately passed a decree inviting "Omanis" back from Zanzibar and abroad. Estimates of the number of people who "returned" to Oman after the 1964 revolution and the 1970 coup d'état vary from a few thousand to the tens of thousands. According to Anthony Clayton, by the end of 1964 the numbers of Arabs in Zanzibar were reduced by between twelve and fifteen thousand, either by death, deportation or departure (Clayton 1981: 98–99). Whatever the exact figures, many of the returning soon formed a new, distinct Omani elite.[30] The new post-coup state relied on this community, with the expectation that as an educated elite already, they would be in the best position to help build the quickly expanding Omani bureaucracy. At the same time, pressures to make Oman an "Arab" nation increased.

Tensions between relying on Oman's "Zanzibari" elite as its intelligentsia and emphasizing Oman's pure "Arab" pedigree, between celebrating Oman's empire in East Africa and denying its historical involvement in slavery and the slave trade, had, by the late 1990s, become critical axes around which social life was practiced and understood in Bahla. National representations of Omani history since the 1970s, and its growing connections with the rest of the Arabian Peninsula (through its inclusion in the Gulf Cooperation Council, for example) have helped define Oman as an Arab nation, further fueling these tensions. Underlying these tensions, however, was yet another set of opposing ideologies. On the one hand, being "Arab" had, especially over the course of the nineteenth and twentieth centuries, been understood as a caste or class category (even though in Zanzibar British colonial policies considered Arab to be an ethnic or racial category). On the other hand, as Oman became tied to the politics of the Arab world, "Arabness" increasingly became understood as an ethnic or racial category in Oman as well. It is in the context of this particular tension between opposing ideologies of class or caste and race or ethnicity that Bahlawi sociality—and histories of marriage—must be understood.

The Problem of Genealogy

While British policy in Zanzibar established an administrative hierarchy based on what officials variously understood to be racial distinctions between Arabs, Indians, and Africans, it also acknowledged (although did not consider "true") Arab practices of patrilineal genealogy that conferred the identity of the father to the children of "mixed" marriages.[31] Although distinct, these two theories of and approaches to identity—race and patrilineal genealogy—in the context of colonial Zanzibar did not for the most part disrupt the administrative hierarchies on the island.[32] Indeed, these concepts seemed to fuse quite easily, at least in practice, such that the British protectorate could consider Arabs as upper-class, Indians as middle-class, and Africans as lower-class.[33] "Arabs" could thereby maintain themselves as the island's elite.

At the same time, racial theories, even with their shifting meanings over the course of the nineteenth century, were not the same as patrilineal models, and each could reveal the contradictions of the other. Just as genealogical models of male descent could reveal how people's identities were not a matter of mixed male and female biologies, notions about racial mixing could destabilize the practice of recognizing only men as conferring identity to children. While the two ideologies tended to collude in the ruling practices of the protectorate, as more and more non-elite Omanis traveled to Zanzibar at the beginning of the twentieth century, this collusion became increasingly difficult to maintain.[34] Race served as the basis of rule in colonial Zanzibar, but as lower-caste and lower-class Omanis migrated to Zanzibar—many of whom were not considered Arab by other Omanis—British officials scrambled to explain why they were preventing people they considered Arab from entering the island during World War II.

In colonial Zanzibar, British officials recognized "traditional" practices of patrilineal genealogy (even though such practices seemed to them to be anachronistic). In contemporary Oman, official interpretations of the relations between "Omani-Arabs" and "Africans" have not only presented the relationship as peaceful and as part of a civilizing process, but also have maintained patrilineal genealogy (and not race) as the sole structure through which identities were understood.[35] Although by the late twentieth century, while I was in Bahla, a racialized notion of Arabness seemed increasingly important, in the early and mid-twentieth century, Arabness was still a caste or class notion, reproduced through patrilineal genealogy. The introduction to the standard Omani text on the history of Omanis in Zanzibar, al-Mughayri's *Juhaynat al-Akhbār fī Tārīkh Zinjibār*, originally published in 1979, is an excellent example:

> The Arab-Omanis intermixed (*imtazaja*) with the local population (*al-sukkān al-waṭanīyīn*) in the provinces (*al-jihāt*) and they and the African sultans were entangled (*in'aqadat*) in ties of friendship (*ṣilāt mawadda*) and good neighborliness. And the Arab-Omanis left for these kings and sultans their authority (*nufūdhuhum*) over their subjects (*muwāṭinīhum*) as well as the existent laws over their subjects (*ra'āyāhum*) and slaves (*mamālik*). [This is] because the Ibadi madhhab and the Omani soul (*rūḥ*) does not know prejudice (*tafāḍulān*) for race (*jins*) or religion.[36] . . . The Arab-Omanis never interfered with the local population either by coercion or pain. They did not impose humiliation (*dhullan*) or shame (*hawān*) and enslavement (*isti'bād*). On the contrary,

they worked hard to save them from the tyranny from their own kind (*ibna' jinsuhum*) who enslaved them (*istaraqqhum*) and herded them like sheep or made them stray from the path. So they taught them handicrafts and farming and they shared with them everything in life. They gave them property and farms so they could sell or inherit in complete freedom. [. . .] So, they obtained them from their owners. [. . .] They were exhibited to be sold, starving and naked, and they offered them to live among them and they cultured them (*thaqqafhum*) and taught them manners and the religion of Islam and they knew that they had God who created them and he is the one they should worship, and this after they had known nothing. [. . .] And they married from among them. So some of their women became the mothers of noble Arabs. And, they became, thank God, brothers of the Arabs. And among them, there were agents, governors, and managers of the properties of the rulers. And some of them become captains in the armies and a number of the "Zinji" became partners of Arabs through inheritance and a number of "Zinji" became models (*qudwa*) for the Arabs in matters of life and religion.

According to this standard account of Omanis in Africa, Arab-Omani men married non-Arab-Omani women and created through their unions Arab children. Simultaneously, there were those Arab-Omani men who did not marry non-Arab-Omani women, but instead expended their efforts on converting the women and men to Islam, "teaching them culture." And yet Arabs remain distinct from "Zinjis" here. The relationship between the two groups is conceived as brotherly and "neighborly," yet clearly hierarchical. Through the paternalizing and patronizing care of the Arab-Omanis, the "Zinjis" could become brothers; brothers, however, who would never be allowed to forget that they had been slaves, that they had known nothing, and that they had had to be cultured.

While I was in Oman, members of the Swahili-speaking elite often denied "intermarriage" (*imtazaja*). Certainly, the marriage practices of "Omanis" who lived in East Africa shifted over the years. Perhaps like the experience of the Dutch in Batavia (J. G. Taylor 1983), marriage practices that might have been acceptable and even encouraged at one time became by the early twentieth century less common (except perhaps during the depression years of the 1930s when Arab landowners began selling parts of their farms). The disjuncture between actual marriage practices and what some "Zanzibari" men, in particular, claimed to me about the histories of their descent line's conjugal affairs is hardly surprising given contemporary tendencies in Oman to insist on the nation's Arabness and to associate with the other Persian Gulf Arab states.[37] Since by the twentieth century a Swahili-speaking "Arab" creole elite was already firmly entrenched in Zanzibari life, it was also likely that marriages were often arranged from within this already elite creole community.

The notion of patrilineal genealogy that the standard Omani text presents as fundamental to Omani relations in East Africa, however, also suggests the coupling of Omani-Arab charity with Ibadism. As I have mentioned elsewhere in this book, Ibadism often provides the basis for Omani distinctiveness. In this passage, Ibadism becomes both proof and reason for Omani practices of not discriminating in marriage. Ibadis theoretically accept as Imam any free man ("even an Abyssinian" as the common retort goes) who is the most just, wise, and pious (rather than someone who necessarily must be a descendant of the Prophet or of the Prophet's tribe). So, among Ibadis, the essential status (*dhātī*) of the Prophet's descendants does not provide the same force for distinguishing between people as it does among other branches and schools of Islam.

The notion of patrilineal genealogy that the text presents as paramount to Omani practices of equality and nondiscrimination also presupposes (although does not mention directly) the concept of "sufficiency in marriage" (*kafā'a*).[38] The importance of and criteria for sufficiency, which posits that a man of higher status can marry a woman of lower status, but a woman of higher status cannot marry a man of lower status, is, like other ideologies of identity, context dependent. Therefore, discourses about sufficiency provide a particularly interesting site for understanding shifting notions about hierarchies and identities. At the beginning of the twentieth century, Nur al-Din al-Salimi addressed the issue directly in his *Jawhar al-Niẓām* (1989 [n.d.]: vol. 2, 250):[39]

> Therefore the one responsible for a woman should not (*lam yilzam*) marry her [off] if he [the potential groom] is not satisfactory (*mardhīyan*).
> Such as a grocer, a coppersmith, a tailor or servant (*mawla*) in Islam and others.
> Each of them has his position (*'akfa*), until they attain quality in their "*nasab*" and "*ḥasab*" and state.

Here, grocers, coppersmiths, tailors, and servants have their positions—positions that are determined by their occupations and by their "genealogies" (*nasab*).[40] Neither race nor religion is mentioned. I suspect that while religion is so taken for granted that there is no need to mention it, race, on the other hand, does not "officially" matter.

At the same time, although Nur al-Din suggests that it would be possible for a woman to marry once the status of the groom changes, in practice and among current Omani scholars, unions between men from servant families and women from "Arab" families are considered forbidden.[41] During my fieldwork, for example, my landlady Zaynab's niece in Muscat almost "accidentally" married a man of a servant family, a neighbor's friend who had originally come from a different town. After the two young people announced their engagement—with the blessing of Ahmad (the grandfather)—a man from the groom's town traveled to Muscat and informed the bride's family about the groom's true identity and state. The young girl consulted her grandfather and he declared that it was forbidden for them to marry and that the impending wedding should be canceled. Ghania (Zaynab's mother) explained to me that she felt bad for the young man, that he was a good person, educated, and seemed to be a good worker: "How can you tell who is a *khādim* and who is an Arab?" But, she said, there was nothing they could do, it was forbidden. Ghania acknowledged both the uncertainty of these categories and the necessity of applying them. Ghania also pointed out that one would not be able to tell the difference, just by "looking" at him. Clearly, here, the young man could not change his "state," making, as Nur al-Din had written, such a marriage possible.

Although Ghania was adamant that one could not "see" status, others in Bahla would often tell me that you could in fact see differences, especially in terms of skin color. These distinctions, I should note, were not visible to me. Therefore, while official Omani discourses on patrilineal genealogy and sufficiency, not to mention general Ibadi charity, maintain that rigid class and race separations are antithetical to Omani history and Ibadism, in practice, some notion of race, especially in reference to color, mattered. This coloring of the world—a racializing gesture—would also appear in referring to the traces of the mothers that were being erased in ideologies of patrilineal genealogy: I was often told that a "white man" and a "black woman" would have "red children."

Ghania and Fatima, as well as many others in Bahla who lived in, were born in, or who grew up in Zanzibar, would not describe themselves as Zanzibari. They were not elite nor had they migrated to East Africa in the eighteenth or nineteenth centuries. Nonetheless, their histories must be understood in this context.

Ghania was born in Bahla but never, despite her years in Zanzibar, learned Swahili. And, Fatima, from Bar Nyamwezi, on the African mainland, never spent much time in Zanzibar itself. Others in Bahla, however, who grew up on Zanzibar and as children spoke Swahili as a first language, were quickly pressured to speak Arabic and rid themselves of their identification with the island. While identities are certainly contextual, and how someone would be described in one moment might be different in another, in Bahla itself, the tendency was to reserve the category of *Zanzibari* for—once again—the elite Swahili-speakers, now in Muscat.

The complexities of Arabness become evident in the women's stories. The naturalizing collapse of *Omani* and *Arab* in the introduction to al-Mughayri's history is less apparent in the women's stories, both of whom are aware of how the terms contain within them hierarchies of gender and class. The term *Arab* is often used in Oman both in contrast to servant (rather than to Zanzibari) and to refer to a man as opposed to a woman. The asymmetrical relationship between "Arabs" and others once again plays out in this context. The fathering of "Arabs," in many ways, works towards the exclusion both of women and *akhdām*.

The life histories also reveal the ways that an ethic of productive work and neighborly responsibilities help structure people's memories, even of violent revolutions.

I. Ghania

Ghania was born to a family of "Arabs" (that is, not of *akhdām* [servants]), probably in the early 1940s. When I met her, she was a grandmother and most of her children and grandchildren were living in the lower-middle-class area of Muscat called al-Khodh. One of her daughters was living in Bahla, Ghania's natal home town. For the most part, Ghania stayed in Muscat with one of her other daughters, but she would come to visit Bahla occasionally, either during the holidays or when her daughter needed extra help around the house. Ghania's husband Ahmad lived in a large house in the more wealthy area of al-Ruwi with his second wife, their children, and some of their grandchildren. Ahmad was both a businessman and a respected and well-connected religious scholar: he was the imam of a mosque in his neighborhood and knew the Grand Mufti of Oman (also originally of a family from Bahla and also someone who grew up in Zanzibar).

Every time Ghania would come to Bahla, she and I would sit and talk. She loved to tell and I loved to hear stories of the spirits, black magic, and scholars for which Bahla is famous. She also would, from time to time, speak of her own life: what it was like in Bahla when she was young, her marriage, her time in Zanzibar, and her return to Oman. When her grandchildren asked her how old she was then or how old she was when she went to a certain place, she often replied "What do I know?" One of her earliest memories though, she said, was of Shaykh Abu Zayd, the famous Bahlawi governor from 1916–1945, who used to patrol the streets of the town at night listening for unusual noises. She remembered how she used to be terrified of him, with his long hair and ability to call upon the spirits. She also remembered how as a little girl during Abu Zayd's time, she would go to the prison in the fort, bringing food for a family member who was being punished.

One evening, Ghania, her daughter Zaynab, her grandsons Sa'id and Sayf, and I were sitting in the family room when I asked whether Ghania would speak about when she was in Zanzibar. I brought the tape player down, a practice she had gotten used to since I had, by then, recorded many of her stories of spirits. She began her story:

> Many years ago, before I was born but when my father was alive, there was a terrible drought (*maḥl*) and our family (*hayyannā*) all traveled from Bahla, some going to Khaburah, some to Zanzibar, and some to Hamra. And, there was no one of our family left here.

Traveling to Khaburah 150 miles away was likened to traveling to Zanzibar 2200 miles away and likened to traveling to Hamra 30 miles away. Ghania made no categorical distinction of different spatial or political boundaries.

> We had been living in the neighborhood [in Bahla] (Ḥārat al-'Aqur) and my father worked as a porter. There were no jobs then; he had a donkey and would ride it, carrying with him water, dirt, and manure (*samād*). He couldn't work with heavy things, but he had a donkey. When my father died, they said: "it is better if she marries her cousin (the son of her paternal uncle)." I did not have a brother. So, four months after my father's death, they sold our house, and he took me.

This must have been in the early 1950s.

> We stayed in Bahla at first, farming alfalfa (*qat*), indigo (*nīl*), chick peas (*dengiū*), onions (*baṣal*), and sesame (*simsim*). Within the year, he came to me and said Zanzibar is nice, let's go to Zanzibar. Most people would go to Zanzibar when there was fighting (*ma'ārik*) or drought, but there wasn't either when we went.

They just told us it was nice (*zayna*). So, we went to Zanzibar, together (*irbāʿa*), and opened a store. We lived in a village where there were plantations (*shanba*, plural *shawānib*), outside of Zanzibar town. When Ahmad [her husband] would go to the town (*al-balad*) [Zanzibar town], I would stay in the store and I would buy and sell. Ahmad's brother Abdullah was there too, and also opened a store. His wife Salma would run his store. In our store we sold whatever people wanted: groceries (*samān*), sugar, rice (*aysh*). I would make *mandāzī* [a type of fried bread] and sell it.

They also had coconuts, she explained:

Do you know what we did with the coconuts? We would break the coconuts in half and use an iron stick, a *shanga*, that's what they would call it, to skewer the coconuts, and we'd put the coconuts above a fire. I would add to the fire, and when it would go down, I would add more, and then, when they were cooked, they would be ready. We would use them to make bags and would sell them. Abu Hilal [the overseer of the laborers on their farm] would bring the coconuts.

The process of preparing the coconut husks for drying, a process foreign to those in northern Oman and foreign to me, fascinated her, and my own inexperience provided an occasion to describe it.

And then there was the clove season. There, we knew people from the neighborhood (*al-ḥāra*), and the town too. There were many from the town that we got to know. They would work with us during the clove season. They would put the seed on one side, and would put, what do they call it? "maqoni," or "makroni," on the other side. And then they would come and we'd weigh by the kilo, on the scale, and give them money at the price of the kilo, and then we'd give them their pay (*igārathum*). And I was in the store.

When I asked who worked for them, Ghania said:

They were all Omanis; they would work (*yishtighilū*), sometimes five or six people.

Sayf, her grandson, needing clarification, asked: "You would rent them (*tistagirhum*), the workers, or were they servants (*akhdām*) that you had (*'an andkum*)?" And, the following exchange ensued:

Ghania: They were workers (*'ummāl*), workers. They worked (*yishtighilū*). Workers.

Sayf: From there? You would find them there?

Ghania: No, not from there, they were all Omanis all of them. There was Su'ud bin Ali, he worked. And, there was Hashu, you know him, the one who used to work at the hospital, at the doors. Then, Muhsin bin Shaykhan worked with us (*ma'nā*), and Muhammad bin Khamis.

Sayf: And you'd pay them money (*ma'āsh*)?

Ghania: What's wrong? Yes, we'd give them money.

Sayf: So, they weren't servants, they would work?

Ghania: We'd give them money. One would carry (*yisuq*) coconuts, one would pick up (*yaṭla'*) coconuts, one would go to the town also, taking and bringing wood. And Su'ud, do you know Su'ud who now fertilizes your father's date palms? Well, him. He was young when he came to us. He was young, like your brother Nasr when he came to Zanzibar, he worked. First he worked in the store and then he sold wood, he'd go to the town, inside the neighborhood (*jiwār*).

For Sayf, *work* not only meant getting paid, it also meant not being a servant. Ghania, though, does not answer Sayf's questions directly, saying instead that they were paid and that they were "Omani." Ghania, here, is eliding the question of how people of the servant class, although engaged in wage labor, continued to be servants: Omanis, but not Arabs. As it was clear that Ghania was adamant about maintaining the workers' Omaniness although not their Arabness, I turned to another set of questions, about what was going on in Bahla while she was in Zanzibar.

> When I was in Zanzibar, my mother died in Bahla. Someone brought the news in a letter, as there weren't telephones (*tilifūnāt*) in those days.

Ghania spoke about these events in her life without mentioning her distress, at her father's death, at being "taken" after her father's death, or at her mother's death.

> People would come from Oman with letters. And, the war in Oman too, we heard from people who came. We were in Zanzibar then, but we heard about it. We heard that they bombed the fort.[42] When my mother died, they tricked my sister and sold our house behind her back (*khafūhā*).

Ghania's natal home is now in ruins, but it is as much what happened to the house as its state of ruin that makes her angry—"behind her back," she insisted. Earlier she had stated that they sold the house after her father had died, but it later became clear that after her father died, her mother continued living there, and it was after she had died that they sold it. Then, there was the revolution in Zanzibar.[43]

At first we began to hear of people getting killed. When they would go to the plantations and other villages, they would be kidnapped and killed. We heard of injuries. Then, one day, they attacked the store. I was not in the store that day, but Ahmad's niece was there. They came in and started cutting everything and they cut her and she jumped under the table and they were going to kill her, but they thought she was already dead. They said "she's already dead, let's go." She still has a scar, but they sewed her up. I could not find two of my children or husband for three days. There were places where there were schools (*madāris*), schools (*skūlāt*), that's what they called them. I don't know. They'd put them there. And the women, also, they would take them. I spent the next three days with my neighbors. We tried to escape (*shardīn*), first to a place called Bunda near the water. There, a group of men saw us and asked what we were doing. We explained to the men that we needed to save our children. Then, we went to a place called Bikunguna and I went to speak to the head of the neighborhood who was from there (*bū hunāk*) and who was a friend of Ahmad's.[44] The head of the neighborhood told me that they would look for the children, but I protested, the children are young and if they see your men, they'll be scared, they won't come out. The next day, the head of the neighborhood sent one or two men, *Gumma'*, whatever they were called in those days, and my neighbors and I went out into the plantations to look for coconuts and bananas to eat.

Sayf turned to me, translating *Gumma'*—but with uncertainty—as "police" (*shurṭa*). Ghania relates her search for her children and her escape with her neighbors; the administrative structure of the neighborhood also translated for Ghania: she went to the head of the neighborhood who was "from there" to ask for help. It seems that in Zanzibar too, Ghania's neighbors and the neighborhood played a central role in her life.

The men said that they found my children, in Mtuni, Maqumbira. So I went there where the plantations were like prisons, and found my children and took them. Then Ahmad returned. His hand had been cut and he had been beaten up. He hadn't gone to one of the prisons because he was in the hospital. We still, however, hadn't found Ahmad's brother Abdullah. Finally they tracked him down, hiding in a neighborhood mosque. We decided that it would be best to go to the town, where there was a hospital and where we could go to the association house, Bayt Gammʻiya.[45] Ahmad and his brother Abdullah went first and returned the next day. When Ahmad started to cover us up, I asked what he was doing and he said: "Do you want to be killed?" I then said I wasn't going to go without my neighbors (gīrān): I would not leave my neighbors! Ahmad said that he wouldn't come back the next day to get us, but would send a driver. So, the next day, a car came and took my children, a neighbor, and me, and then another car took the other neighbors and we went to the town, to the association house.

Ghania insists on her responsibilities to her neighbors. Ahmad, seemingly less concerned, arranges for a car to pick her up. But, she insists, I will not leave without my neighbors! She demands that he send cars for everyone.

We stayed there for a bit, but then decided to take [rent] a house in town. They came and said that it was safe now, whoever wanted to return to their houses could go, but we were afraid that we would be killed, so we stayed in town and rented a house. We would get some money from someone who would come from our farms, but he wouldn't give us everything, just a little bit, just enough to eat and drink. For three months, we lived off our farms in the village. Ahmad then heard that a travel ban might be imposed from Zanzibar so it would be better if we signed up to get our papers to go. I was not sure about going back to Oman though. What would I have there? I didn't have a father, or mother, or brother. I didn't have anything. So, I said to Ahmad, give me the farms, and I will stay here with my children.

Ahmad had, several years before, married another woman, the woman he now lives with in Muscat, and it was perhaps with her that Ahmad lived when he would go to town, leaving Ghania to manage the store. Although her husband had not divorced her—probably from his own devoutness and pity—she knew that she actually had "no one." But, Ghania explained,

I realized that in fact I would not receive enough money from the farms to provide for my children. What could I do? I delayed. But, in the end I signed our names and we boarded the ship, the "mail," and went to Oman.

Saʻid, another of Ghania's grandsons, then asked where she had learned Swahili. Ghania responded emphatically that she never knew Swahili.

When I was there no one taught me. There were, though, people who would speak everything: Hindi, English, and Swahili. I would go to the doctor and he would only speak English so he never understood what I was saying and I never understood what he was saying. Sometimes there would be someone there to translate.

Since Ghania's return to Oman, she has been moving back and forth from Muscat to Bahla. She once explained that when they got to Muscat, her husband at first wanted to return to Bahla. "I should not have returned, but what would I do? So I went. I did not have anyone there." In the end, though, they went back to Muscat where her husband bought apartments and started a small-scale construction company. Ghania continues to travel back and forth from Muscat to Bahla, her natal home, to which she was—since her first departure to Zanzibar—always reluctant to return.

II. Fatima

Fatima, who was about ten years older than Ghania, lived across the street from Ghania's daughter Zaynab. She lived in a house with her son, her daughter, and their families. Unlike most households in Bahla in the late 1990s, Fatima's consisted of several generations. I had asked earlier whether I could come and talk to her about Africa, and Fatima said, "Of course, come, I don't know anything, but you can come." So, one day I took my tape recorder and talked to her about her life in East Africa and arrival in Bahla.

I came to Bahla long before Ghania's family ever went to Zanzibar. My father was from Hawia.

Hawia is a neighborhood in Bahla next to the Ḥārat al-'Aqur, where Ghania's family was from. Unlike Ḥārat al-'Aqur, in which "Arabs" resided, Hawia was predominantly populated with *akhdām*, servant families.

My father traveled to Africa a long, long time ago. He went when the government in Africa was German and before, even, the German and the English fought the war. He was very young and there was no work in Bahla, so in those days people would travel (*yisāfir*). My father did not stay long in Zanzibar, but went to Bar Nyamwezi, in Africa. He stayed there for a long time and he farmed, and he had a store. He took my mother from there, from among the Sudānī and they had three children: Sa'id, Salim, and me. I was the oldest, but when I was very young, so young that I never knew my father, he died. Sa'id was still crawling and Salim was not even born yet, still in his mother's stomach. My mother didn't have anyone. When my father died, my mother's family, Africans, said that they didn't want the children of an Arab, they didn't want an Arab in their family. "They would grow up and be our uncles." They wanted Sudānīs. So my mother went to a man and to the government for food. She would ask them for help and say "I am a Sudānīya, my husband died, and I have these children." We were living in Mwanza [a city in what is western Tanzania today] then and my mother would sometimes also tell people that our father had gone to Oman, that her children were still very young. It was a mess (*fawḍa*).

Fatima asked, as though in her mother's voice,

"Who would want these children, they don't have anyone, the children whose father was Omani?" A man, though, then came and said that he wanted us. The man, Abdullah Amin, took us and raised us with his family, saying that he would keep us until our Omani father's family came, until they decided they wanted us. And the daughter, he said, he would marry her off. And so my brothers and I stayed in his house for ten years.

I asked her if she saw her mother again.

Yes, she would come and stay sometimes, but not for long. They would not let her stay for very long and besides, she had taken another husband. But, when she would come, she would give us a little something. She did not have much but she would give us a bit. My father's brother and his family never came. But, eventually, a man did arrive and he took me. He was from Oman, from Mustāḥ [another neighborhood in Bahla made up of both *akhdām* and Arabs]. He had gone to Africa for work, with his brother and family.

As she and Ghania had often repeated, there was no work in Oman and so people would go to Zanzibar.

They said, "her family is from Oman, we are similar (*shibh*), we'll take this girl" The man, though, also said that if I wanted to go with my family, he wouldn't take me. I was young when I got married; I had reached maturity (*bulūgha*) only one month before. And, soon, I had a daughter and when she had just started walking, my husband consulted me, saying that he wanted to go back to Oman, but was wondering whether I wanted to go as well. Everyone else said that I should not go: "Don't go to Oman, it's difficult there, you'll have to work so hard, they don't have anything there." But, I said, my family is from Oman. And, if I stay here, with whom will I go? I was young when he took me, that man, Abdullah Amin. He raised us and now I had a child, I wouldn't have the strength to do anything, to go some place without a man, someone would have to give me another husband, if this man goes to Oman. So, I decided to go to Oman. I didn't care if it would be difficult or tiring.

Was it a long trip?

The distance from Mwanza to Bahla was very far. It took me three days from Bar Sudani to Zanzibar by ferry, and then from Zanzibar to Matrah by dhow (*khashba*). The mail ship at that time was not running to Matrah, only from Dar al-Salam to Zanzibar. There weren't airplanes then. I can't remember how long the trip from Zanzibar to Matrah was, but I know that if the wind was blowing hard, it would take about fifteen or twenty days, but if the wind died, the boat would just sit there in the sea and it might take a month: that was our life years ago. The ships would leave Zanzibar during the monsoon, the time of the date harvest.

Were there a lot of people on the boat?

There were more than fifty people on the boat with us, but there were only ten women. Women didn't want to go to Oman in those days. It was hard. You would have to collect wood. No one wanted to go.

Was anyone else going to Bahla?

Of the ten women on the boat with us, one other was going to Bahla and we traveled together in a caravan, on camels (*bawsh*). The other woman had two daughters with her, but one died on the way, it was hot. I didn't know how to ride a camel. It took us seven days to get from Matrah to Bahla. I had my daughter and I cried almost the entire way. We moved to Mustāḥ, where my husband's parents were living. When I first came to Bahla, I couldn't speak Arabic and people would laugh at me. Even now I don't speak it very well. The old people would say that it was disgraceful (*'ayb*) to speak Swahili. They said that it wasn't good that Omani children would speak only Swahili, forgetting all their Arabic. Now, though, it is fine to speak Swahili. When I went to Bahla, women used to wear their clothes open at the neck, not like in Africa, among the Arabs. In Zanzibar, the Arab women would always wear the *buī-buī* [complete black cover], which I also wore. When I went to Bahla, I left it behind. I lived there, in the neighborhood of Mustah, for fifty years and then, several years ago, went to Africa, to visit my brother. But this time I took an airplane. No, actually, I took six planes: first from Muscat to Bandar Salam and then another one to Mwanza and then another one to Kindani, where my brother was living. I wanted to go, but when I got there I didn't like it. There were too many thieves. It's funny, it used to be that Oman was poor and Africa was rich, now it is the other way around and everyone wants to come here. Who would have ever guessed?!

Arab, But Not Quite

In some ways, the two women's stories conform to the standard, officially sanctioned narratives of the experiences of Omanis in East Africa. In other ways they reveal that these experiences were much more varied and complex than the formulaic narratives suggest. The certainty in the construction of Arabness in the standard Omani history of Zanzibar becomes much less stable in Fatima's story. From the perspective of al-Mughayri's introduction (not to mention British colonial policies), she is Arab—born of an Arab-Omani father. Indeed, through their father's own Arab-Omaniness both Ghania and Fatima could work towards establishing and maintaining, in their stories, their Arab identities. At the same time, however, Fatima was born of a *khādim* who had married a Sudānīya. Fatima was aware of the multiple meanings of the term *Arab*, and she and Ghania both used the term selectively in their stories. Fatima used it when she was quoting her mother's families' objections to taking care of the children: "They would grow up and be our uncles." *They* here referred to the three children. The use of *uncles*, though, highlights that Fatima was a female in a collective with men (necessitating the use of the masculine plural), but also touches on the fact that her own "Arabness" would not be able to be passed on to her children. So her presence in her Sudānīya family might not have been as threatening as that of her brothers, who would eventually, according to patrilineal ideology, pass their tainted Omaniness and Arabness on to their children. Fatima was aware of the use of *Arab* as opposed to *servant*, and she used the category *Omani* when she spoke of herself and about one who was similar (*shibh*) to the family of her soon-to-be husband. Here, she did not use the term *Arab*, reserving it for the language of her Sudānī family. Similarly, Ghania did not use the term *Arab* when describing the people, presumably of the servant class from Bahla, who worked for them. Rather, she referred to them as Omanis.

The genealogies that connected these women to Oman and to being, partially in Fatima's case, Arab, however, were not only comprised of a list of names, but also seemed to provide, in part, the structure for their memories.[46] For example, with the death of their fathers, the two women found themselves in situations in which it seemed they were adrift. The image of being adrift is not one that the women used, but one that suggests the sense of no longer being connected to their natal homes. Their fathers had been the anchors in their lives, creating stability and maintaining who they were and how they fit in the world. For Fatima, in particular, her father was the one who anchored her to an Omaniness and an ambiguous Arabness, an Arabness that her mother's "Sudānī" family rejected, as well as one that her "Omani" family could not fully accept: they never came to get her. For Fatima, the figure of Abdullah Amin became her surrogate father until her husband found her. The women's stability was predicated on the life of their fathers and then, to a certain extent, on their husbands.

When their fathers died, the two women found themselves searching and being considered for marriage. Ghania speaks of how, after the death of her father, their house was sold—a statement she later corrects by saying that it was really after her mother's death that some people tricked her sister into selling the house. Ghania conflates the loss of her father with the loss of her home. Collapsing the selling of the house, which marked a permanent rupture with her natal home, with the timing of her father's death suggests both how the absolute loss of one came to mean the loss of the other and the extent to which the narrative of the father as home so powerfully worked to help shape her memories.

Fatima also describes how the loss of her father meant the loss of home. In Fatima's account, her mother goes on an almost desperate search for charity, from individual and government sources. The sense of movement—of this woman traveling with her three children to beg for pity from the charitable man and the government—defines her first memories. She does not actually remember her father, but knows that before his death, they must have been living in some kind of stable place, a situation unlike what they found themselves in after his death.

In contrast to the stories of their fathers, their mothers, although with them much longer, somehow fade away. Their mothers were unable to maintain the stability that would allow them to provide their daughters with a home or allow them to continue living in the homes where they had been. In their stories, their mothers are both responsible and ultimately not capable of taking responsibility for their children. Without their husbands, their mothers lost their homes and were forced to find someone to take their children. For Ghania, it is not even her mother who looks for a husband for her daughter. Her mother simply is told that it would be better if her daughter were married:

"It is better if she marries her cousin." For Fatima, the death of her father is the beginning of her life journey, which she describes as though plotting a series of points on a trail, moving from one place to the next.

A similar story is repeated for their own children and for their relationships with their husbands. Their own dilemmas mirror their mothers': as adults they equally become the product of genealogical structures and of complex status hierarchies. The moments in which they have to decide whether to go to Oman are fraught with the necessity of taking care of their children: they articulate the same dilemma, what would they do for and with their children if their husbands left? They would be stuck there, alone, with no one, and their children would not be fed, they too would be adrift. While Fatima says that she would have to go back to Abdullah Amin and would have to ask him to give her another husband, Ghania does not even seem to consider that possibility. They were different ages when they were faced with this decision, and it happened in different contexts: Fatima was leaving in a time of peace, when it may have been possible to marry other men, while Ghania was thinking about staying on after the revolution, when potential husbands were presumably fleeing the island.

This more-or-less shared narrative illustrates the ways that, in the stories, the figure of the father is emblematic of a time of security and is seen as the (incomplete) conferrer of identity. Once he is gone, the women must somehow try to create a new form of security, whether they are the ones able to create it or, because of their conditions, must ultimately rely on their husbands. Divorcing their husbands, though, is different from the loss of their fathers, since losing their husbands would mean the creation of a new basis, a new foundation: it is possible to think about their lives without their husbands even if they ultimately remain married. Fatima would get another husband and Ghania would run the farms. Without their fathers, whose deaths they had no control over, they were instead at a loss: they were given husbands, they were dragged to charities.

In some ways, both women were continuously "not home," especially from the time their fathers die. While one can be at home being "in between" as much as in any other place (Cooper 1994: 1539), the uneasiness with which these women speak of their movements and of their anxieties about where they are going suggests that for them this state is not a state of "home." Their fathers' deaths reveal the extent to which they have never fully been at home, since home is predicated on their fathers' bestowal of stability. For Ghania, her "home" is lost when her father dies. Although she goes to Zanzibar for some time and then returns to her natal town, by then the man that she had been married to had remarried and she no longer had a place of her own, either with him or anyone else. She again follows him to Muscat and occasionally returns to Bahla to visit her daughter. Fatima, who left her mother and her brothers as well as the family of Abdullah Amin, was also not home. Even though they did not come to get her, her own family (on her father's side) was in Bahla, in Hawia. Her decision to go to Bahla was formed, as she describes it, in a way that almost suggested she was returning to her family. It was her only option, it seems, to recover a sense of belonging.

Through their stories, partly organized around the figures of their fathers,[47] both Ghania and Fatima also construct what it means to be Arab and what it means to be Omani. Their stories, however, simultaneously reveal how unstable these categories of Omani and Arab are. Although Ghania's Arabness is not so much in doubt, she continues to construct her identity through her own and her father's natal home, securing herself through his life. Fatima, on the other hand, reveals the instability of her position through her insistences on her Omaniness. While her Arabness is seen through the eyes of the Sudānī family who reject her, she is less willing to define herself as Arab. Thus, as Fatima was establishing her Omaniness through her father's family, she was also being confronted with the institution and history of servitude in Bahla, a hierarchical structure that has strictly limited intermarriage between the two groups and that posits the khādim population as not Arab. These stories and memories described by both women work to reinforce the father's place and the father's family in the construction of their ideal stability, that moment before they were adrift, before they became dependent on a husband to support their children. In the case of Fatima, despite her mother's erasure from the explicit telling of the stories, she continues to leave a trace in Fatima's ambiguous racial identity.

Fatima's ambiguous Arabness is not only revealed in her story about her mother and her paternal uncles, but also in her references to her flawed Arabic. Fatima's description of people laughing at her inability to speak Arabic predates the 1964 revolution and the 1970 coup d'état, and shows that markers such as language have long been significant in defining Arab identity in Oman. But, the importance placed in maintaining Arabness and Omaniness in contemporary Oman must be read through these political histories. With these two events (the 1964 revolution and the 1970 coup d'état), establishing Arabness and

Omaniness became a priority. After the 1964 revolution, those who could claim descent from an "originary" Arab male could then also claim Omaniness. From the perspective of post-1964 revolution and of post-1970 coup d'état, if a man claimed Arab-Omani descent, his offspring could claim Arab-Omani identity and nationality, leaving Zanzibar and moving to a soon-to-be oil-rich state. It was important at this juncture to maintain and support Arab-Omaniness and to forget the Zanzibari identity that so many had claimed in the 1958 census.[48] Fatima's own accent, therefore, would theoretically not matter in the genealogical structure in producing Arabs. Yet it does.

Being Bahlawi

While being Omani and being Arab were the main categories through which the two women constructed their identities in the stories, in many ways it was through their relations with Bahla that they negotiated their unstable sense of belonging. Ghania was already and would always be Bahlawi: both her mother and father were Bahlawi, she was born there, her first language was Arabic, and she came from a prominent family. Fatima, on the other hand, was connected to Bahla first genealogically through her father and his family who never came to get her and then through her husband. The certainties of the genealogical structure that provided her these affiliations were also destabilized by the semi-erased traces of her mother in her "redness," her accent, and the history of servitude in Bahla. She had to establish her sense of belonging through other means.

Both women constructed their relations to these categories through the figures of their fathers. On the one hand, the uncontested figure of the father is the bearer of identity. He appears in the stories as the ground of stability, as home, and as the link to Arabness, to Oman, and to Bahla, all distinct from East Africa. From the perspective of post-1964 revolution Zanzibar and post-1970 coup d'état Oman, the importance of maintaining this descent and this identity has become critical: no matter how long his descent had been in East Africa and who his wives and partners were, his children would be Arab. In many ways, this construction of identity provides the basis for eliding concepts of race: genealogy provides the basis of identity. At the same time, clearly, this genealogical model did not fully allow for the complexities in the ways that these two women constructed their understandings of being Arab, Omani, and especially Bahlawi. Not only do the hierarchies embedded in the genealogical model that they use to describe their life histories produce discordance with the model itself, but the hierarchies of gender and of ambiguous racialized status simultaneously become mutually entangled.

In the end, despite Ghania's status and race, it was, ironically perhaps, Fatima who was more comfortably Bahlawi in the late 1990s. This was not only because she was the one who lived there permanently, but also because she had made it her place, partly through her rejection of "returning" to Africa and partly through her accepted participation in appropriate and regular visiting. Ghania, instead, the one who was born in Bahla and whose parents were both from prominent families, was the one who remained the more ambivalent of the two about being there, both as a result of her relationship with her husband and as a result of no longer having her own "group" to visit. She was always hesitant about going to Bahla. Fatima, on the other hand, was very much in place in Bahla, even when all the structures and discourses of language, genealogy, race, class, and gender were conspiring against her. Irrespective of all the genealogical structuring that might be expected to have firmly reestablished Ghania's place in her father's—and her mother's—Arab town, Fatima was the one who created this place as her place, and herself as Bahlawi.

Fatima had to work to become Bahlawi, not only because of genealogical structures that led her toward marriage with another Bahlawi, but also because her Sudānī family rejected her.[49] She had to work to become Bahlawi despite the power of the genealogical model that deemed her "not quite" Arab. Ghania on the other hand, whose own status would suggest a comfort with expressing her "Bahlawiness" through her presence in Bahla, was reluctant to go to Bahla. Despite Fatima's in-betweenness, and despite her initial rejection at the hands of people in Bahla who said it was shameful to speak Swahili, she eventually managed to create—most likely by appropriately participating in neighborly groups—a sense of belonging in Bahla, a sense that perhaps Ghania could afford not to be as concerned about.

Conclusion

Both Ghania and Fatima's stories not only reveal the complex ways that Omani notions and categories of belonging shape people's memories, but also speak to the prevalence of work and neighbors in these memories. The past and the present in these life stories are structured both through the narrative of family trajectories and through a discourse about work. Ghania, in particular, often spoke of how she used to run the store and how she would make the coconut fiber bags, how she would pay the workers and help weigh the cloves. Her descriptions of these activities come together in a narrative about her productivity. Her time in Zanzibar was marked not only by the violence of the revolution, but also by her activities selling and making. Producing and trading, rather than consuming, are the traits that marked her memory of Zanzibar. Even in describing her life before she moved to Zanzibar, she recounts what she and her husband cultivated: chickpeas and sesame.

In addition to work and productivity, Ghania reminded her listeners that in Zanzibar she was particularly concerned about her neighbors' well-being, that she would not leave the plantation without them, even though her husband seemed less concerned and even though her family faced certain danger. Her insistence on expressing these obligations and responsibilities towards her neighbors in Zanzibar would make sense to me in Bahla. Obligations to neighbors, like productive "work," are what, in part, made a good Bahlawi woman.

Fatima, instead, was less focused on her neighbors and less nostalgic about her time either in Africa as a child or about her travels to Bahla. Nevertheless, her account of her decision to go to Bahla revolves around her defiance of advice from other women about the hard life in Oman. Other women, she emphasized, had said that she should not go to Oman because life was much more difficult there than it was in Africa. Why would anyone have wanted to go to Oman? Women especially, Fatima pointed out, were unwilling to leave the relative security of Africa for the hardships of Oman. She, however, did not mind the impending work, and besides, what other choice would she really have.

The opposition between hardship and ease, between the past and the present, also has a spatial dimension in Oman—one predicated on the separation between Oman and Africa. Whereas "there" had been a land of relative economic ease, "here" had been a place of hardship. A strange twist of fate suddenly made Oman wealthy and Africa poor. This strange twist of fate, however, not only seems to have coincided with a need to insist on the "Arabness" of the Omani population today, but also reveals that strange twists of fate can occur, and could even reverse. The emergence of "modern" Oman, then, was not simply a step of development, but was also a strange twist of fate.

7 Perhaps He Has a Son
Succession, Depletion, and the Uncertain Future

ONE DAY AFTER I HAD BEEN IN BAHLA FOR NEARLY A YEAR, Zaynab and I went to visit a *gīrān* that gathered down the road from ours. We had not visited this group for several months and Zaynab thought we should. This *gīrān* was quite different from ours, partly because it was half *akhdām* and half Arab, but also because one of the members of the group owned a satellite dish. No one in our group had one and to our unaccustomed eyes and ears it seemed to be a pretty glamorous possession. I include myself here because after a year of nearly complete separation from media besides official Omani sources (and BBC radio), the production value of satellite television seemed overwhelmingly and mesmerizingly sophisticated. At first we watched a French station and then turned to a more appropriate Sudanese station broadcasting a religious game show. The women were particularly giddy and nervous that day, but their mood had less to do with the satellite television than it might at first have seemed. It was instead the fact that as we were sitting and drinking our coffee, eating our dates, and exchanging news of the town, one of the women of the group took a Qur'an from a shelf above us and began to open it randomly, reciting a passage she was able to recognize. I knew immediately what she was doing. In my Iranian family, a similar form of fortune-telling was possible through random openings of the *Dīvān-e Ḥāfez*, compilations of the poetry of the fourteenth-century poet Hafez. Sometimes such readings were made in response to specific questions, but this day the woman was interpreting and reading in the context of open questions about what might happen in the near future.

The nervous energy in the room was palpable. While some of the women encouraged her, others began insisting that fortune-telling was not good and that she put the Qur'an away. This anxiety was, of course, partly due to my presence. Two of the women who were insisting that the fortune-teller stop threw me furtive glances trying to judge my reaction. While some people I had come to know in Bahla were very comfortable speaking to me about the occult, others were reluctant. Those who were reluctant often maintained that practices of establishing relations with spirits through occult knowledge or of attaining occult knowledge at all reflected badly on local practices and reaffirmed Bahla's reputation as a center of (black) magic. And, as I had not spent much time with this particular neighborly group, some in the group were, not surprisingly, worried about my presence. But, it was not simply my presence that made these women anxious. Or, rather, it may have been a combination of my presence and the particular *kind* of occult knowledge that this woman was claiming. In Bahla, there were many different forms of occult knowledge, from amulet writing to burnt offerings and possession rituals.[1]

What made these women nervous was making claims about the future at all. "Only God knows the future," my landlord insisted a month earlier after he described how he had received, partly read, and then discarded a book about dream interpretation and prediction. "It's bad, it's *harām*. I did not like it. I only read a little bit," he said.[2] The discomfort displayed by these women and by my landlord stemmed not from doubts about the possibility or veracity of fortune-telling, but rather from the belief that fortune-telling infringed too closely on God's unique qualities and abilities. Besides, such knowledge was often uncontrollable by humans, and anyone who made claims to such knowledge could easily become a victim of the powerful spirits who helped him or her attain such knowledge. Or, even worse, someone might use such knowledge to harm others. Only a great scholar, if any human at all, could and should safely and properly pursue and dispense such knowledge. Furthermore, because Bahla was so well known for activities associated with occult knowledge, many people were particularly sensitive to this kind of activity. A reluctance to try to manipulate, or even make claims, about the future, however, was not limited to the particulars of everyday life in Bahla: what would happen in the *nation's* future, only God could know.

The coup d'état of 1970 and the oil economy that accompanied the post-coup regime inaugurated a new era in Oman, an era of flawless asphalt roads and shiny banks with marble floors and gold doors, an era of piped water, "modern" schools, and abundant coffee. Along with these changes came a sense, shaped by different branches of the Omani state, that the past had both traditions that should be preserved as well as beliefs and practices that were better left aside and forgotten. As I have described in this book, such memories from before the era of "the renaissance" and from before the oil boom, often surfaced to disrupt life in Bahla. From new systems of governance to coffee consumption, education, water sharing, and affiliations of belonging, Bahlawis continually compared the past and the present. Women's sociality in particular straddled divergent views of the past, revealing how moral questions—what it meant to be a good person, what it meant to be human at all, and how one was to relate to God—stood as tense markers of shifting ideologies and senses of the past.

But it was not just the past that was in contention in these perceptions of what it meant to inhabit the present or to be a good person. The politics of the past, of tradition and memories, was certainly critical for national and personal understandings of political and moral legitimacy in Oman, but perhaps even more important was the future. The past assumed the particular salience that it did precisely because of people's questions about the future. The question of the future in Oman permeated both official and unofficial discussions of the country's previous traditions and post-1970 transformations, as well as the current state of its economy and moral life.

As I described at the beginning of this book, three factors have intersected to make the future a matter of paramount concern in Oman. First, the Sultan is generally understood to have no heir. The recognition that the leader, who the state has presented as the driving force of Oman's great transformation, is both mortal and has no obvious successor has helped shape an atmosphere of grave concern about Oman's future political stability. What will happen once the country's founding father, the one who produced such staggering development, is no longer? Anxiety about the Sultan's mortality was heightened after 1995 when he was in a near-fatal automobile accident. Second, Oman's oil reserves are understood to be severely limited, especially in comparison to other GCC states. The limit of Oman's supplies, as various branches of the Omani state remind citizens, is a constantly threatening, albeit deferred, horizon. While Oman's supplies are more modest than those of its neighbors, it is the continual twenty-year deferral that is even more noteworthy. The end of Oman's oil is a future that will happen soon, but not too soon. Finally, interpretations of Oman's Ibadi doctrine leave open and make easily available the possibility of the reestablishment of a theocratic state, a state that is within the living memory of many older Omanis. While I was in Bahla, some people

openly expressed the desire for such a future, though most were less enthusi-
astic. In either case, many Omanis understand another theocratic state to be a
possibility, whether in the distant or near future. But, as they would say, "only
God knows the future."

Oil Futures and Deferrals

While oil appears tangential to narratives about the establishment of modern
Oman, in my conversations in Oman from my first trip in 1994 to my last visit
in 2002, and in long-distance conversations since then, many people, from older
women in Bahla to oil industry managers and religious scholars in Muscat, mentioned that the country had only twenty more years of oil. For example, in a much
publicized statement, on October 19, 2002, the *Times of Oman* reported: "At the
current proven reserves and rate of production, Oman's oil reserves are expected
to last for 20 years, Ahmed bin Abdulnabi Macki, minister of national economy
and deputy chairman of the Financial Affairs and Energy Resources Council,
told the Times of Oman." Over and over again, I heard this projection. Given that
the official Omani press also consistently projected that the country had twenty
years of oil remaining (with some occasional variation, of course), it was not entirely surprising that people I spoke to used the same time frame. What is striking
is that the Omani state has been projecting the twenty-year end of oil for nearly
four decades. The future was not only disturbingly bleak, but also deferred.

To be sure, official declarations on national television and radio and in state-
run newspapers in Oman about the limits of oil have also been accompanied by
emphasis on economic diversification through the development of LNG (lique-
fied natural gas) projects, aluminum smelters, tourism, real estate, and fertilizer
and petrochemical plants, as well as by growing national proclamations and local
incentives about saving water, learning to sew, and accepting manual labor. On
the one hand, these calls may be interpreted as continued faith in the teleological
model whereby "modernization" could be said to be attainable and sustainable
through diversification and a neoliberal shift to increased economic privatization. Rather than producing a sense of security about future prosperity, however,
statements about diversification and privatization seem to have produced, among
many Omanis at least, the opposite: either the expectation of poverty or the assumption that the future is unknowable.[3] Indeed, date production and sewing,
while examples of diversification, could hardly substitute for the oil economy.

While the twenty-year projection of remaining oil has been remarkably
consistent over the years, some variation has, of course, existed in official and

nonofficial statements about oil reserves and oil production, not to mention production expectations. For example, in 2003, the Omani Ministry of Information and Ministry of Oil and Gas announced that Oman produced 956,000 bpd in 2001 and 898,000 bpd in 2002.[4] The same year, the *Middle East Economic Survey* instead estimated that Oman produced 830,000 bpd in 2001 and 770,000 in 2002 (MEES 2003). Figures for 2003 also vary. The *Times of Oman* announced 835,000 bpd in May and 750,000–800,000 in August, compared to 702,000 announced for 2003 by the *Oil and Gas Journal* the next year (*Oil and Gas Journal* 2004). Similarly, a December 20, 2004 *Times of Oman* article quoted PDO's daily production to be at 702,000 for 2003 (affirming the *Oil and Gas Journal*'s numbers) and at 660,000 in 2004.[5]

This variation is not limited to the 2000s. In 1980, for example, a Japanese newspaper reported that, according to Omani government officials, daily output was 350,000 bpd (Associated Press, February 26, 1980), while other official documents reported that in 1980 daily output was 282,000 bpd (al-Yousef 1995: 50).[6] The year before, in 1979, the Minister of Petroleum and Minerals Saʿid bin Ahmad al-Shanfari predicted that with the discovery of new fields in the south of Oman, oil production would soon reach 800,000 bpd (*Al-Usrah* and *Gulf News*, December 4, 1979). It would in fact take until the mid-1990s for national production levels to reach 800,000 bpd (al-Yousef 1995; PDO Annual Report for 1996). Such discrepancies have not gone unnoticed. An April 8, 2004 *New York Times* article pointed out that two reports by officials from PDO give different numbers for production from the Yibal oil fields. One states that there was a decline from 251,592 bpd in 1997 to 88,057 in 2004, while the other states that there was a decline from 225,000 in 1997 to 95,000 in 2004.

Despite these discrepancies, however, the most cited source for calculating and determining national projections is PDO. And, PDO's projections are strikingly consistent. It should be noted that projection calculations that focus exclusively on quantity of oil assume that the quality of the oil in the proven reserves, the ease of extraction, and consumption are all steady, which they decidedly are not. Such variations would, of course, affect the amount of oil that could be available for export and for sale. Indeed, conversations with engineers and management at PDO (as well as articles in trade journals) often focus on the fact that, as one friend at PDO put it: "Oman has very bad and difficult rock structure."[7] It should also be noted that "years remaining" is not a category in PDO annual reports. It is generally calculated by dividing PDO statements about proven reserves by daily production (and then again by 365).

According to al-Yousef's (1995) and my own simple calculations of the PDO figures for each year from 1970 to 2000,[8] the number of projected years of remaining oil in Oman ranged from about 12 in 1970 to 24 in 1980, 17 in 1990, and 18 in 2000. The largest difference was between 1977 (11 years) and 1984 (25). Besides the jump between 1978 (13 years) and 1979 (23 years), which is attributed to a number of major discoveries in southern Oman, and the decreases earlier in the 1970s, which are attributed to the Dhofar war in southern Oman, the number of years of oil remaining in Oman has been remarkably consistent, hovering around twenty years. In other words, as proven reserves have increased, production has also increased at a rate steady enough to maintain the twenty-year projection.

The possibility that there would be more years of oil predicted every year is not particularly surprising: the discovery of new fields and improving technologies of extraction continue to allow for the deferral of the end. Horizontal drilling and other Enhanced Oil Recovery (EOR) techniques such as pumping steam, other gasses, or chemicals into the reservoirs have enabled engineers to continue to extract oil from what are called "maturing fields" as well as from the difficult rock structure in Oman. A *Washington Post* article from August 12, 2008 describes how Oman had already invested $4–$6 billion on EOR projects hoping that more oil could be extracted. But, even with EOR, a petroleum geologist is reported to have said, "It's just a case of people catching on to the buzzword that this is going to fix it, and we're going to get a whole lot out of it. And it doesn't quite do that." Even John Malcolm, who has been managing director of PDO since 2002, described Oman's pursuit of EOR as follows: "When you come to a cliff, you've got two choices. You can walk away from the edge, or you can fall off the edge." But a technical advisor to Oman's Ministry of Oil and Gas, also cited in the *Washington Post* article, may have explained the situation most clearly: "Without enhanced recovery, Oman could expect to run out of gas within 15 years. With it, Oman hopes for forty."

This 2008 mention of forty years refers to a possible new state policy that seems to have begun in 2005. Indeed, in a surprise statement in January 2005, with the renewing of the nation's primary oil concession, the minister of oil suddenly announced that there were "forty years of oil" (Oman Renews 2005). This sudden doubling of the lifespan of Oman's oil production was so unexpected that discussions about its feasibility, implications, and the motivation for the announcement were rampant both on internet chat sites and among oil industry engineers and managers. A young man who I knew from fieldwork wrote me after the announcement and suggested two reasons for the shift: the need for Shell to explain its concession renewal with PDO (which had been renegotiated in December 2004 for another forty years); and the desire of the government to encourage the sense of *stability* for investment.

Whatever the most dire predictions (fifteen years) or the most "hopeful" (forty), it is the twenty-year time frame that most observers (at least foreign ones) still cite as a reasonable estimate of Oman's remaining oil supply. In April 2005, for example, a Bloomberg News article noted simply: "Oman's oil may be exhausted within 20 years."[9] Similarly, on April 10, 2008, the *Business Times of Singapore* noted: "From a high of close to one million barrels a day in 2001, Oman's oil production has dropped by an average 6.5 per cent to 743,000 barrels a day in 2006. If this persists—and no major new reserves are discovered— the country will no longer be a significant oil exporter in less than 20 years." And, indeed, as noted in the first chapter of this book, even the US Department of Energy in 2005 predicted that Oman had about twenty years of oil remaining (US Energy Information Administration 2005).

Twenty years is soon, but not too soon. Twenty years is something one should worry about, but is distant enough so as not to cause panic. Or perhaps, as the shift in state policy suggests, it is not quite distant enough. As the Sultan ages, might twenty years of oil appear just too unstable? Is it unstable enough to warrant the doubling of oil's life expectancy?

Palm-Frond Huts

Given the consistency with which news reports within and about Oman fixate on its depleting oil supplies, it is not surprising that popular notions and expectations of the future are also structured around depletion, whether the end of oil is projected at fifteen, twenty, or forty years. Indeed, expectations of the end of oil and a return to poverty exist across all sectors in society, from poor older women in Bahla to elite businessmen in Muscat.

On my first visit to Oman in 1995, I had the occasion to meet, through an especially helpful military historian living and conducting research in Muscat, an outspoken, engaged, and distinguished businessman, Mr. Sultan. The military historian directed me to him not only because Mr. Sultan was a thoughtful, unofficial spokesman of an important Shi'ite community in the capital who might be able to arrange a visit to the community's walled and self-regulated neighborhood, but also because he was deeply interested in Oman's history. While Mr. Sultan did not question the official representations of Oman's "renaissance," he was very much interested in drawing attention to Oman's "true" history—a history that could not ignore the three wars of the second half of the twentieth century. These wars accompanied, although did not parallel, transformations in rule and were, to varying degrees, about establishing national boundaries and control over oil territory. For Mr. Sultan, however, history was less about exploring these turbulent pasts than about tracing more distant dynasties, as well as the migrations, economic endeavors, and social lives of Oman's cosmopolitan communities.

When I returned to Oman to conduct fieldwork for my dissertation in 1996 and 1997, I went to visit Mr. Sultan again. This time, we had a longer conversation. As we sat in one of the beautifully and elaborately decorated rooms of the wood-engraved, silently air-conditioned, and marble-laden mansion (of a style that one might associate more with India than with the Arabian Peninsula) that overlooked a lush garden, a servant brought us piles of fresh fruit. We began talking. Mr. Sultan hailed from a family of merchants who had made their fortune in a trading firm in the nineteenth century. The firm's partners had included an American, a Scot, and an Indian Omani. The firm imported kerosene to Oman and exported dates to the United States, and dried fish and pomegranates to India. At the beginning of the twentieth century, the Omani partner bought his partners' shares. As Oman's fortunes declined in comparison to other Persian Gulf states, Mr. Sultan's family—like other merchant families— solidified its businesses in Kuwait. Drawing on family connections throughout the region, in the pattern of successful merchant families throughout the Gulf, they took advantage of shortages and surpluses to build the firm into one of the most important in Oman. The family, although not wealthy by today's standards, was certainly well off with respect to the rest of the Gulf and especially Oman. They lived in the walled Shi'ite neighborhood of the commercial capital, in coral and gypsum buildings, and had maintained themselves since at least the nineteenth century as one of the most important business families in Oman.

As I pressed him for details about his family history, which at the time I thought was the most valuable information I would glean from him, Mr. Sultan insisted on returning our conversation to the problems of the country's young people, their ignorance of the past, and the country's dangerous lack of economic diversification. This discussion was one I had become familiar with during my time in Oman and seemed to me to be a repetition of commonly held notions. Since my first visit in 1995, I had engaged in many conversations about Oman's youth, their disrespect for and ignorance of the difficulties of the past, and their inability to grasp the threats of the future. I therefore attempted to change the topic of our discussion back to his family's history. Besides some basic facts about his family and the history of his business, however, Mr. Sultan would not give way and again returned to the subject of Oman's youths and the uncertainties about the future. With little choice but to yield to his insistence on returning to these issues, I soon came to understand the degree to which the past and questions surrounding it were intensely resonant for Mr. Sultan, as well as the ways they suggested a complicated relationship to the notions of development and progress.

Indeed, as we continued talking, Mr. Sultan's commitment to the legacies and fate of his country became more evident. As president of the Omani Historical Association, he was obviously deeply interested in Oman's past and believed that an understanding of it was critical for the present. Catering primarily to English-speaking expatriates (with a nostalgic love for Oman's rugged beauty) and "Zanzibaris" (Oman's Swahili-speaking, cosmopolitan intelligentsia with historic connections to East Africa), the association brought together visiting scholars, local history buffs, and, less often, university professors. Similarly, Mr. Sultan authored a number of editorials published in both English- and Arabic-language newspapers about problems he saw with the national education system, students' lack of knowledge about their past, and the possibility of mass tourism eroding Oman's unique and pristine historic sites. As the public expression of discontent in Oman is often either highly restrained or only implicit, these editorials were particularly strong statements of doubt.

In addition to his interest in the past and outspoken concerns about the future, Mr. Sultan made another powerful, symbolic statement about Oman's fate: he had had a palm-frond hut, known as a *barasti*, built in his lush backyard. *Barastis*, which thirty years earlier could be found all over coastal Oman, were by then rare. If not happily forgotten as markers of Oman's past poverty, they were beginning to become incorporated into Oman's growing heritage industry. What struck me about this rebuilt *barasti*, however, was not so much Mr. Sultan's keen attention to national traditions, as he had already demonstrated, but his conscious claim about the future and his own family's place within it. He had the structure built because, as he told a mutual friend, "That is where we came from, and where we will be returning."[10]

Surrounded by the marble, wood paneling, and flowing bougainvillea of his mansion, Mr. Sultan's *barasti* stood in stark contrast to these comforts and luxury. The past ("this is where we came from") was simple, earthy, and rugged, while the present was sumptuous if not opulent. This contrast between the *barasti* and the marble mansion, however, was not only one of before and after. According to Mr. Sultan, it was also one of now and after. The *now* in this logic is the temporary and anomalous state of wealth between eras of poverty.

Perhaps He Has a Son

While the question of the number of years of oil remaining has been a persistent source of uncertainty in Oman and expectations of the country's future poverty seemed to be so widespread that Mr. Sultan could build a *barasti* hut in his backyard, questions about Sultan Qaboos's heir have also been legion and remain unanswered. This issue too may have motivated the shift in the state's declaration about oil reserves. As I noted earlier, in September 1995, just after my first trip to Oman, Sultan Qaboos was in a serious car accident. One of his closest advisers, Qais bin Abdul Munim al-Zawawi, died in the accident, and another British companion, Air Marshal Sir Erik Bennett, received minor injuries.[11] As was his custom at the time, and in a public display of self-reliance reminiscent of King Hussein of Jordan's propensity to fly jets, Sultan Qaboos drove his own car rather than relying on a driver. Sultan Qaboos's survival sparked some demonstrations in his support, but also, it was rumored, some in celebration of the adviser's demise. This near-fatal car accident, however, was also an all-too-real reminder of the Sultan's mortality and, it is generally assumed, lack of an heir. It was as a result of this accident that the government issued the constitution that outlined the measures for the period after the Sultan's demise; and the announcement of that constitution propelled Majid, one of my landlord's grown sons, to race from his house in one of Bahla's suburbs to his father's house within the old walls.

After the anxiety about a potential coup d'état subsided, Majid and the family began to discuss the details of the constitution.[12] The constitution was going to be called, the newscaster on the day of the announcement declared, the white book, and would be made available to the public the next day. But, when the national newspapers printed articles about the white book the following day, the mystery of the future was only partially resolved. Although the constitution consists of eighty-one articles in seven chapters, covering topics from "Principles Guiding State Policy" and "Public Rights and Duties" to the Oman Council and the judiciary, it was on the particular question of succession—article 5—that many conversations in Bahla focused.

According to the constitution, the future Sultan had to be a male descendant of Sayyid Turki bin Sa'id (r. 1871–1888), effectively disqualifying the descendants of both the Zanzibari branch and any Imamate lineage of the al-Bu Sa'idi dynasty. At the same time, it was announced that the Sultan had enclosed the name of his intended successor in a sealed envelope, to be opened only at the time of his death. The successor would also have to be approved by the Council of Ministers, an appointed advisory body to the Sultan, thereby introducing another layer of uncertainty. In the eventuality that an agreement among the ministers could not be reached, the military would take control of the government until consensus could be reached. Thus, on the one hand, the line of succession was clarified at least in theory. On the other hand, the name of the future Sultan, hidden in a sealed and secret envelope, fueled further mysteries and, not surprisingly, speculation.

One evening, a week after the constitution was made public, as I was sitting in the family room with my hosts after dinner, we began discussing the provisions for the future as laid out by the new constitution. It was during this conversation that my landlord said, "Only God knows what will happen. Maybe Qaboos has a son. We did not know that his father, Sultan Sa'id bin Taymur, had a son. So perhaps Qaboos bin Sa'id also has a son too." On the one hand, this comment was one of the more hopeful speculations I had heard over the previous week. The words pointed to a desire for continuity, despite the fact that there was no evidence that the Sultan did in fact have an heir. On the other hand, the comment demonstrated a ready acceptance of the inevitable mystery, surprise, and uncertainty of the future. Omanis had not known that Sultan Sa'id bin Taymur had a son, so it was possible that they did not know whether Sultan Qaboos bin Sa'id had a son. One of the continuities between the past and the present was a continuation of mystery. Instead of lamenting the state-sanctioned mystery of the secret-envelope succession policy, my landlord was introducing a new mystery of his own: a secret son.

My landlord, it should be noted, was extremely loyal to and supportive of Sultan Qaboos, but he was also distinctly of the Imamate era and, like most people in Bahla of his generation, had supported the theocratic administration. Most Bahlawis I knew would not have actively supported a returned Imamate in the near term, but depending on conditions, they and other Omanis could see it as one possibility for the future. My landlord's comment, therefore, rather than signaling his confidence in a secret son, indicated his uncertainty. "Only God knows what will happen," he had said, suggesting too that the future might hold a variety of possibilities. There was no expectation that the present state of affairs would continue indefinitely.

Thinking Back

Throughout this book, I have illustrated the complex and divergent ways that the past—in discursive, material, and embodied forms—was salient to the present of late-1990s Bahla. The past was evident both as people distinguished their lives from Oman's former conditions and as they harkened back to it. *The past*, of course, also meant different things to different generations. To some people, it could be retold through accounts of great leaders and origins, while for others through personal memories and local events. To some, it was conceived of as an age of great engineering and scholarly glories, while for others a time of simple wells and everyday embodied piety. To some, it signified authenticity, to others human fallibility. For some, it was a "monumental time," for others a "social time," as Michael Herzfeld (1991) put it.

Such differing conceptions of the past, as this book has illustrated, were evident in Ghania and her grandchildren's visit to the Jabrin fort, in accounts of coffee consumption and everyday visiting, in nostalgia about religious education and old-style wells, and finally in Fatima's memories of her early years in East Africa and her move to the land of her father. Bound up in many people's conceptions of the past was an understanding that trajectories of change are unpredictable. Fatima put it best when she noted at the end of her account of moving as a young bride from the relative comfort of East Africa to the hardships of Oman: "Who would have ever guessed that one day Oman would be rich and Africa would be poor?" My landlord similarly implied that one never knows what might happen in the future: "Sultan Qaboos may have a son." And, indeed, as the anxiety over the women's fortune-telling revealed, predictions of the future could, in any event, infringe on God's unique abilities.

This view of the unknowability of the future did not mean, however, that some possibilities did not loom larger in people's imaginations than others. Some people (though few) were even taking some steps to prepare for some of the alternatives. As I learned on my trips to Zanzibar in 2002 and 2005, many Omanis were traveling there in search of property, sometimes to recover what had once belonged to their families. One young man from al-Dakhiliya, who I met on a visit I made to the Zanzibari town of Mwera (which had been a center for Omani Arabs—indeed Ghania's family had lived in Mwera, and I happened to meet people who had known them), explained why he was in Zanzibar. He had gone to Zanzibar, he said, "because conditions in Oman were bad, really bad. And, you might as well have some property in Zanzibar." What this young man meant by "really bad," he did not say; he could have meant anything from economic circumstances to moral corruption. Though the economy may have been his concern, his long beard and short dish-dasha also signaled his piety and his possible distaste for what he saw as Oman's moral corruption. In either case, as he suggested to me, he made this trip precisely because the situation in Oman was "not good," and, it seems, it was not going to get any better.

For others, the reestablishment of an Imamate was a redemptive possibility (imagining that Oman could enter another "way of religion" was not lost on most Bahlawis). But there was no consensus on what such a change might look like. If the difference between Ghania and her grandchildren's perspectives on the fort or Aisha's views on "traditional" education and proper sociality are any indication, then for many younger people, the future could be much grander and purer that that imagined by Ghania. Similarly, there was no consensus on how everyday social life might be transformed. Would Zaynab's visiting disappear, either because there would, again, be no time or because it would be considered useless? Would such sociality be replaced by women's study circles? No one knows. However it might be transformed, new conditions would undoubtedly alter the form as well as the content of social relations.

At the same time, others, like Mr. Sultan, seemed to have specific expectations of the nation's future: it would be poor again. Focused as he was on Oman's difficulty in reshaping itself to cope with the impending end of oil, Mr. Sultan convinced himself that Oman's future would resemble its past. Though his family, given its means, was not likely to face the prospect of a descent into poverty, his construction of the simple palm-frond dwelling in his garden was a clear statement of his expectations for the nation as a whole. In this case, Oman's recent past, its "renaissance," would have indeed been just a dream.

Notes

Chapter 1

Material in this chapter reprinted by permission from *Timely Assests: The Politics of Resources and Their Temporalities*, edited by Elizabeth Emma Ferry and Mandana E. Limbert. Copyright ©2008 by the School for Advanced Research, Santa Fe, New Mexico.

1. Though I returned to Bahla in 2002 and have remained in touch with friends there since, my references to the "present" must be understood to refer to the period from 1970 to the late 1990s.

2. This year is often given in the Gregorian calendar (1970) rather than the Ḥijrī Islamic calendar (1390). The Gregorian calendar, popularly called the "English" calendar, has become an increasingly standard way of marking time in Oman.

3. The theocratic Imamate state of the interior did not always exist, nor was it always unified. One Imamate administration lasted from 1868 to 1871 (though scholarly discussion of reestablishing the Imamate can be traced to the early nineteenth century) and another from 1913 to 1955. In the interim, local rulers in Oman, who were at times allied with each other and at other times independent, controlled the towns and villages of the area.

4. The notion that the interior was completely separate from the coast is somewhat misleading. Although the distinction between interior Imamate Oman and coastal Sultanate Muscat may be useful shorthand, it simplifies familial networks, trade routes, and political allegiances. The town of Rustaq, for example, which sits on the eastern coastal slope of the Jebel Akhdar mountains, was long a center of Ibadi political life. Similarly, it was not until 1920 that the Imam and the Sultan signed an agreement, the Treaty of Sib, that recognized two distinct polities, something that had not been officially acknowledged previously by either side (or by British officials, who

were the de facto colonial rulers of Muscat). Rather, local rulers of interior Oman and around Rustaq rarely pledged allegiance to the al-Bu Saʻidi dynasty, especially since the eighteenth century when the ruling family ceased using the title *Imam* in favor of *Sultan*, emphasizing the family's legitimacy beyond a purely scholarly and Ibadi one.

5. Although Oman was not officially a British colony or protectorate, Sultans from the late eighteenth century had signed treaties with the British ensuring that they approve all decisions regarding foreign affairs. Indeed, the foreign minister of Oman from 1953 to 1958 was a Briton. At various periods, British officials also discussed whether Oman should formally become a protectorate. The reason it never did so, according to British records, was that the British had in 1862 signed a treaty with France stipulating that neither would attempt to make Oman a colony, and it seems that ignoring the treaty was not worth the potential international discord. Besides, as several nineteenth-century and early twentieth-century officials openly declared, Oman was, in effect, a British protectorate anyway. See, for example, Lorimer (1915) and Curzon (1966 [1892]). For accounts of the British in the Persian Gulf, see, for example, Busch (1968), Kelly (1968), Smith (2004), and Onley (2008).

6. The details of the coup, and especially the degree of British involvement, have remained obscure. For the most detailed account of the coup, in either Arabic or English, see Peterson (2007: 238–243).

7. For a discussion of the expenditures of the early state, see Skeet (1992) and Townsend (1977).

8. For an early critique of the state's discourse of successful modernization, see Pridham (1986). While much contemporary discussion about Oman tends to blame Sultan Saʻid bin Taymur for the stagnation of the Omani economy and the closedness of the society, Pridham argues that the accusations against the former Sultan are either exaggerated or false. Pridham instead blames the Imamate tradition of the interior.

9. This particular term was not used immediately. In the first years of his rule, Sultan Qaboos called the time after the coup "the new era." He first referred to the post-coup era as *al-nahḍa* in a speech on the fourth National Day (the annual celebration of the post-coup era), on November 18, 1974.

10. For a discussion of "awakening" in Indonesian nationalist discourse, see Anderson (1990: 241–270).

11. Salafiya revival movements emerged in the nineteenth century, particularly in Egypt and Saudi Arabia. Salafiya derives from the word *salaf* meaning "ancestors of Islam."

12. Sultan Barghash's (r. 1870–1888) Zanzibar Press helped this process of synthesis and explication. Scholars began publishing commentaries, in particular on "classic" Ibadi texts as well as encyclopedic compendia, the most famous of which is the *Kitāb al-Nīl* by the North African scholar ʻAbd al-Aziz bin Ibrahim al-Thamini (d. 1808). The *Kitāb al-Nīl* was popular in Bahla in the late 1990s.

13. For accounts of the history of oil exploration in Oman, see Hughes (1987) and al-Yousef (1995). See *Oil and Gas Journal*, November 5, 2007 for a basic chronology of oil exploration by Petroleum Development Oman (PDO, Oman's semi-national oil company). Also see D. Eickelman (1983) for a brief but elegant analysis of "the meaning of oil" for another Omani village.

14. The question of Muscat's boundaries was raised with regard to possible oil exploration in 1934. In a message from Major C. E. U. Bremner, political agent in Muscat, to the British political resident in Bushire (Iran), Bremner expressed concern about oil concessions and therefore where to draw boundaries between states and tribal areas. In 1936 British diplomats disagreed over what towns were included in Muscat territory. The political agent in Muscat, Major R. P. Watts, stated that Muscat also included the area between Musandam at the Straits of Hormuz and Sohar on the coast, two hundred and forty kilometers north of Muscat—that is, Khor Fakkan and Fujairah, two towns in what has become the United Arab Emirates. Tom Hickinbotham, who served as British political agent in Bahrain, consul in Muscat, political agent in Kuwait, and governor of Aden from the 1930s to the 1950s, disagreed and drew the boundaries as they are today (India Office Records [IOR], archive number R/15/6/185 and IOR, R/15/6/186).

15. Prior to 1957 Sultan Sa'id bin Taymur had already discussed with British diplomats taking control of Imamate territory in order to have access to potential oil fields. In 1946 when rumors reached Muscat that Imam Muhammad bin Abdullah al-Khalili, who was Imam from 1920 to 1954, was seriously ill, Sultan Sa'id bin Taymur and British diplomats considered attacking the area. In a telegram from the government of India at New Delhi to the secretary of state for India in London on March 10, 1946, the political resident wrote: "Access to Oman hinterland has been denied for too long and opportunity of opening it for development of oil and other resources which extension of Sultan's control would provide is too good to be missed. We therefore support proposal to supply Sultan with 1000 rifles (and ammunition), six point 3 inch mortars and four machine guns." These British officials clearly did not expect that it would require much weaponry to take control of the interior (IOR, R/15/6/242).

16. For a superb account of the Jebel Akhdar and Dhofar wars, see Peterson (2007). There are also a number of memoirs written by former British military officers who participated in these (and the Bureimi) conflicts. See, for example, Shepherd (1961), Smiley (1975), and Thwaites (1995). For an account of the Bureimi conflict, see Kelly (1964).

17. The four ways of religion, or stages of a community's relationship with religious law, are: manifestation, defense, sacrifice, and secrecy. For some excellent English language studies on Ibadism, see Crone and Zimmermann (2001), Ennami (1972), Hoffman (2004), Lewicki (1971), al-Maamiry (1989), and Wilkinson (1982, 1985,

1987). Wilkinson (1987) has argued that the pattern of the establishment and collapse of Imamate administrations, throughout Omani Islamic history, overlaps with the propensity, noted by Ibn Khaldun (the medieval North African scholar), of tribal societies in the Middle East to rise and fall. For Ibn Khaldun, cycles of history in the Middle East are due to the pattern of tribes to begin pure and cohesive in opposition and become corrupt and fragmented once they come to power and settle. Wilkinson calls this pattern in Omani history "the Imamate Cycle," echoing a once common trope in Islamic historiography to describe Islamic history as structured around such cycles. For one of the more fascinating theorizations of cylical time in an Islamic tradition, see Corbin (1983). My view is that the concept of four "ways of religion," though a characterstic of Ibadism, becomes important and is called upon at particular moments in history. It should not be understood as an unchanging feature of lived Ibadi temporal consciousness.

18. Although the thirty-one people who were arrested were found guilty and sentenced to prison terms ranging from ten to thirty years, the Sultan pardoned them, and they were freed (*Times of Oman*, April 20, 2005; *Times of Oman*, April 21, 2005; *Times of Oman*, April 25, 2005; *Oman Observer*, May 5, 2005; *Agence France Presse*, June 9, 2005).

19. Associated Press, December 1, 1985, "Oman Rushing into Modern Times before Oil Money Runs Out." In this article, the years of oil reserves available is, unusually, said to be "50 years." It is unclear how this calculation was made since daily production was also said to be 500,000–550,000 bpd (barrels per day), and the amount of reserves was not given. According to Petroleum Development Oman and Oman's statistical year book, the amount of proven reserves at the time was nearly four billion barrels (al-Yousef 1995).

20. See Anderson (2003) for his reflections on what would happen to nationalism with a shift from optimism to pessimism.

21. It seems to me that this twenty-year deferral is similar to the kind of forecasting that might be considered a "near future," a temporal frame that Jane Guyer (2007) associates mostly with developmentalist five-year plans and that she has argued has been evacuated in recent years. The near future, Guyer argues, has been replaced by a focus (in macroeconomic and evangelical discourse as well as in anthropology and public rhetoric) on either the immediate or the long term.

22. The term "dreamtime" is also used in the venerable literature on Australian aboriginal societies. In the Australian context, dreamtime, as Eric Silverman describes it, is "a prehuman yet atemporal era in which ancestor spirits, anthropomorphic or otherwise, created the cosmos by shaping the landscape during migrations and formulating the moral rules that govern social life" (1997: 114). I use the term in a completely different context and to signify a different sensibility. For Walter Benjamin's notion of dreamworlds, see also Buck-Morss (1989, 2000).

23. As Ann Stoler and Karen Strassler (2000) artfully demonstrated, the anthropological desire to find breaks and fissures in colonial and state narratives has often over-determined the presence of such disruptive memories in people's personal accounts of their lives.

24. In anthropological literature, one of the key features of modernity is often taken to be the temporal consciousness of rupture. Indeed, as Mary Steedly has noted, the notion of a "modern moment" is a "way of thinking about time that is predicated on the idea of historical rupture and steeped in the consequent inevitability of loss" (Steedly 2000: 815). While Omani historiography, in the form of chronologies of scholars and dynastic rule, has long revealed a temporal consciousness that marks rupture but certainly not sentimental loss, there is nevertheless a particularity to the sense of rupture centered on the 1970 coup d'état made possible by the power, politics, and economic conditions of the oil state.

25. As I discuss more fully in Chapter 3, there is an excellent literature that examines women's sociality in the Middle East (see, for example, Deeb 2006, C. Eickelman 1984, H. Geertz 1979, Hoodfar 1997, Joseph 1983, Meneley 1996, and Singerman 1995). My work draws from this work, but emphasizes the historically constituted dimensions of social life. C. Eickelman's ethnography (1984) of Hamra, a town thirty kilometers from Bahla, describes the forms and practices of sociality there in the late 1970s. Though many women in Bahla explained to me that such sociality did not take place in "the past," it is certainly evident that similar forms did take place in the late 1970s.

26. Saba Mahmood (2005), Marilyn Strathern (1988), and many others have noted the false dichotomy between individual and society in liberal and some anthropological thought. Mahmood, however, makes a further political argument noting how scholars such as Charles Taylor (1989), Jürgen Habermas (1991), and Seyla Benhabib (1992) have nevertheless valorized such selves (however socially constituted) against the presumed impositions and constraints of society as the correct vehicle for attaining individual freedom or communitarian good. She highlights the ways that the women of the mosque movement in Cairo with whom she worked emphasized instead the individual voluntary submission to social conventions in the interest of cultivating "spontaneous" and "free" *conformity*. I am less concerned with the relationship between individual freedom and social authority than I am with historically constituted notions of self and the social. For a history of the notion of the self in European thought, see Seigel (2005). Similarly, the different notions of personhood I analyze are not either liberal-nationalist or traditional Islamic ones, as Mahmood discusses. Not only are liberal-nationalist perspectives not as relevant in Oman as they might be elsewhere, but I am also less inclined to consider contemporary religious movements in the Middle East as principally reflecting "historically sedimented discourses" (Mahmood 2005: 115). Although such movements do engage with canonical texts, I consider them products of modern education as much as carriers of "traditions."

27. The notion that "uselessness" is sinful has more to do with Ibadi religious doctrine than it does with twentieth-century development discourses. The medieval scholar Qadi 'Abd al-Jabbar (d. 1025), a major religious authority in Ibadism and Oman, wrote about the "evil" of "uselessness." For a brief discussion on Abd al-Jabbar and uselessness, see Leaman (1980).

28. This book is indebted to the extensive literature on gender and Islam (see, for example, Abu-Lughod 1998, Ahmed 1992, Badran 1995, Deeb 2006, Gole 1996, Haddad and Esposito 1998, Kamalkhani 1998, Kandiyoti 1991, Mahmood 2005, and Metcalf 1984). Rather than outlining the multiple religio-legal precepts (such as inheritance and divorce or veiling and sex segregation) that impact gendered lives, this book examines how Islam is transforming in Bahla and finding expression through concerns about women's homo-social comportment and productivity. I am interested both in the ways that appropriate religiosity defines gender as well as the ways that debates about gendered practices are helping to define appropriate religiosity.

Chapter 2

Material in this chapter was adapted from "In the Ruins of Bahla: Reconstructed Forts and Crumbling Walls in an Omani Town" by Mandana E. Limbert. 2008. *Social Text* 95 26(2): 83–103. Permission courtesy of *Social Text*, Columbia University.

1. The fort and the wall have not been white for as long as anyone I spoke to could remember, though some mosques had been. The whiteness that Miles noted was from the gypsum used to plaster the walls of buildings.

2. The beige color of most government buildings in Oman has been highly regulated, and not only by Omanis. Indeed, on a trip to see ancient rock art in the eastern region of Oman, a British man working in Oman's Ministry of the Environment and Regional Municipalities (who accompanied me and an American historian) had us make a detour so he could inspect the paint of a new school to make sure that it was the correct shade of beige, a color that he had chosen. The management of Oman's architectural landscape to keep it as "pristine" as possible was clearly of interest to a number of British expatriates working in the Omani government.

3. Classic studies of "Islamic cities" from W. Marçais (1928) to von Grunebaum (1955) and Berque (1958) illustrated the centrality of activities surrounding Friday mosques and markets to the organization of Middle Eastern cities. Later in the twentieth century, research on Iran highlighted the important relationship between the religious world and the bazaar in the making of the Islamic revolution of 1979 (see, for example, Amanat 1988). As J. Abu-Lughod (1987) argued, however, most of these descriptions of Islamic cities focused either on North African cities or on Damascus and Aleppo (Syria) and generalized from these examples to suggest that cities throughout the Islamic world have, over the centuries, followed the same basic patterns, both in terms of physical structure and governance. Although Abu-Lughod disputed the

generalizations and functionalist approach of the earlier studies, she nevertheless maintained that there is something particular about cities in Islamic contexts. She suggested several characteristics of cities in the Middle East that are roughly shaped by religious forces: the relationships of different communities to the community of believers (*umma*), reflected in or resulting in spatial segregation; gender segregation that is encouraged by a set of architectural imperatives; and property laws that privilege individual over collective use and ownership. These three features, which have shifted in their degrees and practice over time and from place to place, together, for Abu-Lughod, produced the particularities of cities in the Islamic world; religious and political conceptions and exigencies of social control and defense work together to form particular characteristics of cities in the Middle East. However, the work of cultural ecologists has raised questions about whether factors such as weather might have had a greater influence on urban form than sex-segregation (high walls and twisting alleys provide shade in ways that low or no walls, and straight streets do not). Further, Paul Wheatley's monumental book (2000) illustrates how scholars should focus on the particular changes in cities born from or influenced by Islam, rather than attempt to generalize and speculate about the reasons for the structures of such urban sites.

4. I use the terms *restoration* and *reconstruction* almost interchangeably here since much of the work on the forts has not only been to repair the forts, but to rebuild them, although not always according to their original or most recent architectural features and plans. In fact, I heard that during a trip to Oman in the late 1990s, UNESCO representatives warned the architects working in Bahla that in their reconstruction they were straying from the original plan.

5. In these accounts, the destruction of the fort took place during fighting between the Bani Hinai tribe (with the aid of the *amīr* of Sumayil, Shaykh Umayr bin Himyar and the *amīr* of Dar Sayt, Sayf bin Muhammad al-Hinai) and the supporters of Sulayman bin Muḍaffar al-Nabhani, one of the last Nabhani *amīrs* (al-Ma'wali n.d.: 88; Sirhan bin Sa'id 1984: 39; A. H. al-Salimi n.d. [1927]: I, 394; Wilkinson 1987: 217). A. H. al-Salimi's account of the fighting in Bahla at this time is almost exactly the same as the accounts in Sirhan bin Sa'id's *Kashf al-Ghumma* and al-Ma'wali's *Qiṣaṣ wa Akhbār*. However, while *Qiṣaṣ wa Akhbār* puts the date of the destruction of the fort at AH 1024 (1615–1616 CE), the *Kashf al-Ghumma* puts the date at AH 1019 (1610–1611 CE). A. H. al-Salimi follows the *Qiṣaṣ wa Akhbār* date.

6. Most Omani histories maintain that the Nabhani (also referred to as the Bani Nabhan) ruled Oman continuously from the thirteenth through the seventeenth centuries. Wilkinson (1987), however, argues that there were three different Nabhani families in three different areas of present-day northern Oman, and that since there are so few textual sources for about 250 of those years, it is impossible to conclude that the Nabhani ruled continuously throughout that time. Furthermore, in the mid-fifteenth century, at least, Omani scholars elected Imams to rival the power of the Nabhani.

From the mid-fifteenth to the early seventeenth centuries, supporters of these Imams and other local leaders were able to undermine the control of the Nabhani in various areas of Oman, including Bahla. For an interesting debate about whether the powerful Bahraini Jabri tribe (Banū Jabr or al-Jubūr) supported the Imam or the Bani Nabhan in the fifteenth century, see Abu 'Ezzah (1995). For a study of the references to the Bani Nabhan in Omani historiography, see al-Naboodah (1997).

7. Although the main written histories of Oman do not refer to the rebuilding of the Bahla fort specifically, it is generally assumed that it was rebuilt and / or expanded during the period of Imam Nasr bin Murshid al-Ya'arubi (d. 1649). Imam Nasr bin Murshid appointed his cousin Sultan bin Sayf al-Ya'arubi (d. 1680) to be *walī* (governor) of Bahla (Wilkinson 1987: 351 n. 31). An inscription above one of the doors of a house in the fort, I was told, notes that the house was built under Sultan bin Sayf. Sultan bin Sayf succeeded Nasr bin Murshid as Imam.

8. In 1957, Sharjah was a town within what was known, depending on the source, as the Trucial Coast, Trucial States, or Trucial Oman, a British protectorate comprised of many of the shaykhdoms of the Persian Gulf. After gaining independence from Britain in 1971, and with the exception of Qatar and Bahrain, which became their own independent states, seven of these states formed the United Arab Emirates. Sharjah is the largest town of the emirate with the same name. The other emirates are: Abu Dhabi, Dubai, Ajman, Fujairah, Ras al-Khaimah, and Umm al-Quwain. See, for example, Heard-Bey (2004) for a history of the United Arab Emirates.

9. The main exception to this rule is the Tanuf fort, which was completely destroyed in 1957. For a description of the destruction of the Tanuf fort, see Shepherd (1961: 47–48).

10. In Oman, Jabrin is sometimes called a *ḥiṣn* (fort), sometimes a *qal'a* (fort) and sometimes a *qaṣr* (palace). Jabrin tended to be used as a house, but it was also fortified. Furthermore, depending on who was living there or controlling it, it was used for different purposes. For simplicity's sake, I will use the term *palace* to describe Jabrin in order to maintain its distinction from the Bahla fort.

11. For more on the history and architecture of the Jabrin palace, see Baldisira (1994) and Galdieri (1975). According to Galdieri, there is an inscription in the room known as the Sun and the Moon Room that states that ". . . the houses which rise up towards the sky are one, but this one of the *Qal'a* of Bahla surpasses all of them." In other words, the palace was considered part of Bahla when it was built. Baldisira, who has documented the inscriptions of the Jabrin fort, does not mention the inscription that Galdieri notes.

12. Miles (1910) states that when Rashid bin Humayd died, his son Humayd bin Rashid became Amir of Jabrin and Bahla. A. H. al-Salimi (n.d. [1927]), instead notes that Humayd bin Rashid died before his father.

13. Over the centuries, Iranians have attacked Bahla several times. The eighteenth-

century historian Abu Sulayman Muhammad al-Ma'wali mentions in his *Qiṣaṣ wa Akhbār* an incident that occurred in 1265 CE when an army from Shiraz reached Nizwa and then Bahla, blockading it for four months (n.d.). Abdullah bin Humayd al-Salimi relates the same event, putting the date at 1277 CE (n.d. [1927]: I, 353–354) while the *Kashf al-Ghumma* by Sirhan bin Sa'id mentions that in 1279 CE, a Fakhr el-Din Ahmad-bin al-Dayah and Shihab el-Din from Shiraz occupied Nizwa for four months, but were unable to take Bahla (1984: 31). None of these accounts, however, mentions a wall.

The most notable attack of *'ajam* against Bahla took place in 1737–1738 at the end of the Ya'ariba dynasty during Nadir Shah's time (Lorimer 1915: I, 406–407). Rivalries among the Ya'ariba had led to the intervention of Nadir Shah's army, which was in Oman notionally aiding Sayf bin Sultan II against his cousins Bal'arab bin Himyar and Ya'rab bin Bal'arab. Although Imam Ahmad bin Sa'id al-Bu Sa'id was able to expel Nadir Shah's troops, which effectively led to the end of the Ya'ariba dynasty, Omanis continued to pay a tribute to Nadir Shah until 1747 (Lorimer 1915: I, 411).

My landlord's account suggests that the Iranian's arrival was not a singular attack, but part of a more organized tribute-collecting procedure; so this eighteenth-century expedition could be the time of the wall's construction. However, the eighteenth century is too late. The main histories of Oman mention the walls when describing the end of the Nabhani dynasty in the seventeenth century. In the events leading to the destruction of the fort, supporters of the Bani Hinai are said to have scaled the walls of the town and moved to control most of its quarters (al-Ma'wali n.d.: 86; Sirhan 1984: 38; A. H. al-Salimi n.d. [1927]: I, 392).

14. God's punishment was due to Bahla's support for or at least acquiescence to the ruler Nassir bin Humayd, as well as opposition to the Imamate of Salim bin Rashid al-Kharusi.

15. Although histories of Oman tend to associate Bahla with the other towns in the region, it is clear that, with the exception of Bahla and Jabrin's connection, at least in the nineteenth century many of the region's towns were independent of each other politically. The high point of political unification in nineteenth-century Oman was during the brief Imamate of Azzan bin Qays (1868–1871). Azzan bin Qays appointed a *wali* from outside who administered the *bayt al-mal* (state-owned religious endowment or state-appropriated) lands as well as collected *zakat* (religious tax). While the *waqf* (local religious endowments belonging to local mosques and Qur'anic schools) for water, date palms, and land would continue to be administered by the local *wakīl* (or imam of the mosques) and school teachers, the *bayt al-māl* lands, those lands that belonged to the religious community as a whole, would—during the times of the Imams—be administered by the government.

Imam Azzan bin Qays was the only Ibadi Omani Imam between the death of Imam Ahmad bin Sa'id al-Bu Sa'id in 1783 and the Imamate revival of 1913. During the rest of the nineteenth century, the al-Bu Sa'idi Sultans, who ruled from the coast and even from Zanzibar, were not only unable to administer the interior region physically, but were also unacceptable as *zakat* collectors or *bayt al-māl* administrators. In the twentieth century, with the revival of the Imamate in 1913 until the mid-1950s, the region of the Imamate was once again administratively unified.

16. Different sizes of openings have different names. Generally, *bāb*, or "door," is used for the main entrances of the town. The two main entrances of Bahla before the building of the main highway were the entrance Sīlī, which is also the entrance to the Khaṭwa neighborhood, and the Bāb Bādī, which no longer exists but was where the new highway was built in the west of the town. The path Kadam, which Dawood mentions in relation to Bāb Sīlī, was the main road in the direction of Nizwa. Before the construction of the highway, the two main entrances of the town were accessible from the Bahla riverbed or *wādī*. A smaller door or gate is called *ṣabāḥ* and generally is used for the entrances to the neighborhoods within the walls of the town. But two of the entrances of the walls in Dawood's account are also called *ṣabāḥ*. The first, Ṣabaḥ al-Sharīgāt, is also the entrance into the Bani Ṣalt neighborhood. The second, Ṣabaḥ Gabiyah Magra, is an entrance to the Nadwa neighborhood, though this is not indicated in Dawood's account. A *naqub* is the smallest size of entrance and is more like a "hole" in a wall, small enough for animals and people to slip through. Some of these holes became *ṣabāḥs*. One *naqub*, Naqub al-Sālim, next to Burg al-ʿAqad in Dawood's account, was by the late 1990s called Ṣabaḥ al-Sālim. Other doors or holes have more than one name. For example, what Dawood calls Naqub al-Ḥazāza was most commonly called Naqub al-Baṭḥā or Bāb al-Baṭḥā, and what Dawood calls Naqub al-Ḥaḍārmubiya was also called Bāb al-Khur Zabān.

17. Abu Mu'thir al-Salt bin Khamis al-Kharusi was a great supporter of Imam al-Salt in a ninth-century dispute over the deposing of Imam al-Salt. This dispute led to a civil war between what are called the Nizwa and Rustaq schools and was the subject of debates among theologians for centuries (Wilkinson 1987: 173–174)

18. For a fascinating discussion of *fitna* in Islam, see Pandolfo (1997: 81–103, 156–162, 332–333 n. 12). Following Fischer and Abedi (1990), Pandolfo argues that *fitna* does not simply mean chaos. In fact, she shows that there is much ambivalence about the term and that *fitna* is both "a blessing and a curse." While this may be the case, in Bahla, *fitna* was most commonly used to mean "out of control" and "chaos." Although the condition of being "out of control" might allow for the possibility of being cured (for example, in spirit possession, the person loses control in favor of a spirit who then cures the person the spirit is possessing), a sense of control is ultimately fundamental for peace. It is, in fact, the out-of-control body that needs to be cured in the first place. In Bahla, the world beyond the walls, or the world beyond in general is in a state of immanent chaos.

19. Although the entrance into Bahla via the main highway was not noted verbally or through bodily action, the highway itself was significant for a number of reasons:

in terms of national infrastructure projects and their centrality in representations of Oman's post-1970 renaissance, in terms of Bahla and al-Dakhiliya's political relations with and connections to Muscat, and, finally, in terms of Bahla's structures, experiences, and systems of organization. The road clearly made defunct the old defenses of the wall and altered the ways that the town was divided into upper and lower Bahla. This particular highway, completed in the 1980s—from Muscat to Sumayil to Nizwa, Bahla, Ibri, and Bureimi—is one of the key early construction projects. Road construction is often taken as a hallmark of development and modernity (Khan 2006, Mrázek 2002), and this particular road is no exception.

20. For the younger generation, the neighborhoods of al-Sifāla are Ḥārat al-'Aqur, Ḥārat al-Ḍraḥ, Ḥārat al-Mustāḥ, Ḥārat al-Hawīa, and Ḥārat al-Hadītha. For the older generations, al-Sifāla also includes the Ḥārat al-Rim, Ḥārat al-Furāg, and Ḥārat (or, more commonly known as Būstān) al-Laḥma. In al-Sifāla, when someone said "*the* neighborhood," they were usually referring to the old neighborhood of al-'Aqur next to the fort. The main exception to younger people's north-south dividing line in Bahla was the area in the east-central part of the town near the new hospital. Although below the main road, it tended to be called, even by the young, 'Ālī. This naming, however, was connected to a particular house, Bayt al-Sharq, which was also sometimes called al-'Ālī.

21. In Bahla, west not only points to the place where the sun sets, but the term *gharb* (west) was also, for older Bahlawis especially, another way of saying "Kuwait." In the 1960s, Bahlawis would travel to Kuwait, working for the oil companies or as servants in the homes of newly wealthy Kuwaitis or European and American expatriates.

22. These groupings are not timeless, but emerged at the beginning of the eighteenth century. Furthermore, although these groupings are evident in official lists of tribes in Oman and are continually reiterated as common knowledge in everyday conversations as well as in histories of Oman, it immediately becomes clear that these categories are not fixed and that tribes have occasionally moved from being considered in one grouping to another.

23. One clear division was between the al-'Aqur and Hawia neighborhoods, the former being predominantly an "Arab" neighborhood and the latter being a predominantly servant neighborhood. On the other hand, some servant families lived in al-'Aqur, but they had their own servants.

24. The uncertainty about whether neighborhoods were in al-'Ālī or al-Sifāla is evident in the absence of any mention of this division in the booklet. Instead, the list begins with the most northern neighborhood of al-Khaṭwa and ends with the neighborhood of al-Hadītha in the east of the town. Al-Hadītha, which means "the new one," was built, I was told, in the aftermath of the British destruction of Tanuf, a nearby town that had served as an Imamate stronghold during the 1957 rebellion. The newness of the neighborhood was evident in its structure. Al-Hadītha, unlike the other neighborhoods of Bahla, did not have direct access to a water canal. It also had

a single road running down the middle with houses lining both sides, rather than numerous paths running in a variety of directions.

25. Because not everyone who moved out of the old neighborhoods moved to property that they owned, instead renting land and homes, either from other Bahlawis or from the state on *bayt al-māl*, this movement created a new "mixing" between groups of different statuses. *Bayt al-māl*, although considered government land, is a particular type of government land. It is land that had previously been owned by the Imamate (usually through confiscation) and became Sultanate government land. More than one half of the land in Bahla, including the main market, is *bayt al-māl* land.

26. For example, in al-Sifāla, such neighborhoods would include al-Giṣa, Raḥab al-Fawq, and Raḥab al-Taḥt.

27. It would be misleading, however, to suggest that this practice is completely new. In fact, mayors (*wālis*) and judges (*qāḍīs*), even before Qaboos, tended to come from outside. Now, however, more local administration is organized by officials from other towns and areas. This turn of events was a source of concern for some townspeople, especially those who had controlled local *bayt al-māl* lands and who could have chosen the best plots for themselves. Now, theoretically, there is less favoritism.

28. The term *mufti* is rarely used locally in Oman. Today there is a Grand Mufti, who is the national religious leader, but this particular government role is of recent origin, as many people will point out. The current national Mufti, Ahmad al-Khalili is, I was often told, himself a Bahlawi (who spent many years in Zanzibar) and is highly respected.

29. The following tribes were associated with the following neighborhoods:

Ḥārat al-ʿAqur: al-Qassabi, al-ʿAbri, al-Hashemi; Ḥārat al-Mustāḥ: al-Shukri (Bani Shakayli); Ḥārat al-Ḥadītha: al-Riyami, al-Nabhani; Ḥārat al-Furāg: al-Mufargi; Ḥārat al-Rim: al-Mahruqi; Ḥārat al-Laḥma: al-ʿAlawi, al-Hamimi; Ḥārat al-Khaḍraʿ: al-Wardi, al-Kharusi, al-Zahimi, al-Khalili, al-Niri; Ḥārat al-Ḥadād: al-Shakayli; Ḥārat al-Khaṭwa: al-Yahyai [not on official list: Ḥārat al-Khurm: al-Hitali].

30. For an excellent study of this mosque, see Monique Kervran (1996). Although her work focuses on sixteenth-century stuccowork, she has dated the mosque, from an inscription inside, to 1494. One Bahlawi scholar counted eighty-three mosques in all of Bahla. But coming as he did from upper Bahla, he did not count some of the mosques in lower Bahla.

31. In Bahla, the imam and muezzin of each mosque was someone who lived nearby and took on this role by consensus of the attendees. Growing up close to each other, people knew who was qualified to lead the prayer. While there were complaints sometimes, the selection was generally clear cut.

The records of the mosques became divided between the imams and the local office of religious endowments; each mosque had a booklet with a list of who donated what religious endowment. After the Friday mosque, the wealthiest mosque, according to local *waqf* and water records, was the Mahd mosque.

32. I suspect that the regulation of the number of mosques had less to do with minimizing disputes over the numbers of attendees and more to do with controlling the amount of money that would be needed for the upkeep of the mosques, not to mention controlling what went on in mosques.

33. Attendance in Friday prayers for men is a controversial issue in Oman among some Ibadis. They claim that there should be Friday prayers only when there is an Imam. Since there is no Imam now, there should not be Friday prayers. This question was even asked of the national Mufti while I was in Bahla, but he, as a state official, not surprisingly argued that it was mandatory for Muslim men to attend when they could. The Friday prayers are the places where, through officially sanctioned speakers, the state disseminates some of its policies and argues for their religious sanction. This is not to say that all Friday prayer leaders follow each and every state policy. While some "deviations" are themselves sanctioned by the state, as was the case with the Omani government's decision to open and then close an Israeli trade mission, at other times the speakers will carefully allude to their opposition to a particular policy, official, or practice.

34. The bathing rooms are generally small mud-brick rooms sitting over the canals, sometimes with a curved entryway to block the vision of anyone who might want to peek.

35. With the introduction of piped water in the mid-1970s (discussed in Chapter 5), some bathing habits have changed.

36. In addition to the mosques, washrooms, and canals, the town and neighborhoods are divided and categorized by types of land. Land in Bahla is divided into government (*bayt al-māl*), private (*aslī* or *milk*) and religious endowment (*waqf*) land as well as into different types of fields such as *māl* and *'ābīya*. Almost every plot in Bahla, whether owned by the local mosques, by the state as "common" land from a religious endowment (or, more likely, a confiscation), or by individual owners, has a name. The inevitable division and reconfiguration of land through inheritance and trade sometimes creates new names and sometimes does not. During a single interview, one woman listed, from memory, the names of seventy-eight plots of land and houses outside the old main neighborhood of al-'Aqur in al-Sifāla alone.

37. The preference for women to avoid the main market, though certainly not universal, has been noted in many other contexts in the Middle East. In Bahla, as a result, it was men who did most of the food shopping. A secondary more acceptable, yet makeshift, market (where women would put household goods, cloth, and ready-made children's clothes for sale on mats on the ground) began near the entrance to the Bahla hospital. Here, it was mostly women who were the merchants. They would either get their goods from markets in other towns (where the Bahla women might not be known) or have their sons and husbands buy goods in bulk at the main market for

them to sell. Since it was acceptable for women to go to the hospital to visit relatives and neighbors, this was an ideal public space for women to shop. In addition to this makeshift market near the hospital, women would often also purchase cloth or housewares from each other during their neighborly visits. Birth visits were particularly well known for such shopping, and women who had goods to sell would drop off a bag or two of goods with a woman who had given birth so that other women who would come to wish her well could also buy something.

Chapter 3

Material in this chapter was adapted from "The Sacred Date: Gifts of God in an Omani Town" by Mandana E. Limbert. 2008. *Ethnos* 73(3): 361–376. The journal can be accessed at http://www.informaworld.com. Permission courtesy of Taylor & Francis.

1. Although men also partook in visiting practices and were obligated to be hospitable and social, the degree to which women's daily lives were structured around socializing, neighbors, and coffee has helped produce the sense that such practices were largely women's practices.

2. For a discussion of this debate in non-Ibadi sources, see Van Arendonk's *Encyclopedia of Islam* entry, "Kahwa."

3. According to Dale Eickelman (1992) and Gregory Starrett (1998), modern mass education in particular has helped produce the objectification and functionalization of Islam. See Saba Mahmood (2001) for a critique of this thesis on objectification and Charles Hirschkind (2006) for a discussion of the (continued) embodied qualities of religious experience in contemporary Egypt. My own view is that, in Oman in particular, while religious experience may indeed often be embodied—and not *always* objectified—the generational shift I witnessed certainly supported the notion that younger generations, much more than older ones, were concerned with determining what was "religion" and what was not, what was Islam and what was not, what was Ibadi Islam and what was not. For the older women I knew, being "good" simply implied being devout. It was precisely in these debates about sociality that these differences between generations became particularly apparent.

4. Whether one was supposed to drink the coffee before eating the dates was a matter of some debate and although most of the women I spent time with ate the dates first, this was not uniform. Discussions with people visiting from other towns and discussions with men in the family drew out distinctions of what was "better" practice. Usually it was older men who would prefer to drink coffee first and then eat dates.

5. Women who had given birth would not serve coffee for the time of their "rest," which lasted forty days. They would allow someone else in the family or in the neighborly group to do the serving.

6. Both former servants and "Arabs" would comment on this practice. Former servants might openly point out how this humiliation would no longer be tolerated,

while "Arabs" would reestablish their claimed superiority by reminding everyone who was who.

7. Daily average temperature in Bahla is about 45°C (113°F) in the summer.

8. Wikan (1982) noted how women in Bahla were louder and more vivacious than in Sohar, the coastal town where she conducted most of her fieldwork. It is, of course, possible that the relative "silence" of the Sohari women was due to the women's reluctance to speak in front of the visiting anthropologist.

9. The neighbor also figures prominently in Jewish legal hermeneutics, as the commandment "love thy neighbor as thyself" testifies. From a psychoanalytic perspective, both Freud and Lacan also discuss the topos of the neighbor. For a discussion of Freud and Lacan on the neighbor, see Reinhard (1997).

10. Maliki law is one of the four schools of Islamic law. Barbier (1900–1901) and Brunschvig (1947) have also examined and translated Maliki law (from Arabic to French) on neighborly relations, rights, and building guidelines. All three, Barbier, Brunschvig, and Hakim, have focused on the work of Isa ben Mousa (d. AH 386 [996 CE]) and/or Ibn al-Rami (d. AH 734 [1334 CE]). Brunschvig and Hakim have noted the remarkable similarity between the two medieval scholars, despite their separation by almost 350 years.

11. Interestingly, according to Hakim, the fourteenth-century Tunisian scholar Ibn al-Rami notes that garment-beating and wheat-grinding are two frequently mentioned offensive sounds. Clearly, which sounds are considered offensive and which are inscribed as nostalgic or beautiful is historically and culturally coded. I will return to a discussion of sound and nostalgia in Chapter 5.

12. The transformation in the language about neighbors and neighborly actions from one of "nuisance" to one of "rights" marks a particular turning point in the construction of the figure of the neighbor as a purveyor of neighborhood structure and organization.

13. In her ethnography of local complaints and the production of subjects, Yngvesson (1993) raises the question of the place of the neighborhood as the site of legal complaint, and yet she elides the difference between "member of the neighborhood" and "citizen." This difference, in terms of the perspective from which one issues a complaint and that from which an individual is expected to enact his or her obligations, is my interest here.

14. The book was clearly published in the post-1970 era by the Ministry of National Heritage and Culture, but there is no date on the publication. From the typesetting, it seems to have been one of the earlier books printed following the coup. Clearly, the motivations behind publishing books or chapters which emphasized "good neighborly relations" as religious obligation can be read not only as unthreatening to the Omani state (which heavily controls what is published and allowed into Oman), but also as supporting a peaceful and harmonious society. My point in bringing these texts to

bear is not, however, to question the motivations for their publication, but to emphasize how the neighbor as a legal and moral figure holds a particular position in everyday life. These texts, although embedded in a history of state censorship, nevertheless testify to the particular place of the neighbor in questions of dispute.

15. Hadith are the sayings and doings of the Prophet Muhammad, which form, along with the Qur'an, one of the primary sources of Islamic law.

16. The *majlis al-shūrā* is the Omani "parliament."

17. By the early 1990s, Oman was importing over 10 million Omani rials worth of coffee, tea, and cocoa, or about 11 thousand tons. From Costa Rica, Oman was importing about 750 thousand Omani rials worth of goods and from Brazil over 1 million rials worth. Excluding the United States, Oman was importing about 9 million Omani rials worth of commodities from the Americas. Oman's population at the time was about 2.5 million. These figures are all from the Development Council's *Statistical Yearbook* (Sultanate of Oman 1992). In the late 1990s, many families consumed one to two kilograms of coffee in one or two weeks.

18. While I was in Bahla most people preferred Brazilian coffee to coffee from Costa Rica, India, or the US. Coffee types were distinguished by their size, color, and smell, and those that were considered the best were those that were large, green, and smelled "like saffron."

19. This brief account of coffee in Oman is not meant to suggest that these are the only factors that give coffee its cultural value. Nevertheless, the effect of the dichotomy between import and export (consumption and production) is important, since Bahlawis themselves are exceedingly conscious of products as falling into the categories: Omani (from Oman) or *baḥrī* (from the sea, that is, brought over the sea). I raise this point again (discussing both coffee and dates) in Note 45 of this chapter.

20. Robert Landen has noted that while the Muscat port was in decline after the middle of the nineteenth century, when an Imamate revolt rocked the stability of the area, in the eighteenth century, Muscat was very active and "monopolized the lucrative coffee trade into Iran and Iraq" (Landen 1967: 61). M. Reda Bhacker writes that in the 1790s, Muscati merchants, who handled the Yemen-Persian Gulf coffee trade, witnessed a doubling in the amount of coffee shipped towards the Gulf (Bhacker 1992: 26).

21. A kind of sailing ship no longer used.

22. Under Sayyid Sultan and "in the last decade of the eighteenth century the proportion of the trade of the Persian Gulf that passed through Masqat was about five-eighths of the whole or one crore of rupees per annum; and almost every line of business there was represented. The principal exports . . . to places in the Persian Gulf were Yaman coffee and European and Indian stuffs. . . . The leading import from the Red Sea was one of coffee, representing, it was supposed, half the entire produce of Yaman, and fully providing the countries of the Middle East as well as, to some extent, Russia, Germany and other European States" (Lorimer 1915: I, 436). While in the eighteenth cen-

tury and the beginning of the nineteenth century, it seems that much of the coffee passing through Oman came from al-Hudaydah in Yemen (via the port of Mocha), in the nineteenth and twentieth centuries coffee also came from Africa. Bhacker notes that by 1811, coffee was also grown in Zanzibar (Bhacker 1992: 126). Abdul Sheriff quotes an American trader to Zanzibar in 1828 who wrote that the government of Zanzibar "for some time past have turned their attention to the cultivation of spices, the sugar cane, coffee, etc. all of which . . . will shortly be articles of export" (Sheriff 1987: 50).

23. An eighteenth-century traveler to Muscat also mentions locally grown coffee in the market there (Ward 1987: 9).

24. In his biography of Shaykh Abu Zayd, the *qāḍī* Dawood also writes of the control era saying that Abu Zayd refused to allow control, creating a system instead where wheat would be sold at auction every day in the market. He would give the poor and servants one *qursh* (the local term for a Maria Theresa dollar) to pay for their wheat. Dawood does not indicate, however, where the wheat came from, who instigated the control restrictions, for what reasons, or to what effects. The important point in Dawood's account is that Abu Zayd refused to implement an order that clearly would have been harmful to the townspeople. The goods that Dawood mentions as being under restrictions are rice, sugar, and textiles. He does not mention coffee, the import of which was clearly not critical for the survival of the community.

25. Interestingly, the first head of the Control Department was Sayyid Abdul Barri al Zawawi, who was replaced the following year due to complaints against him (see Annual Administration Report, 1946). The Zawawi family has continued to play an important role in government finances to the present day. The death of Qais bin Abdul Munim al-Zawawi (who was deputy prime minister and minister for financial and economic affairs) in a car accident in September 1995 in which the Sultan, although not injured, could have died as well, sparked off a double "celebration" in Oman. The celebrations for the Sultan's survival hardly masked a simultaneous celebration for Zawawi's demise.

26. The regulations of the Control Department call for "the personal control of the Sultan of all sales to the interior, the appointment of Agents at each town on the Butinah coast and of inspectors who are to carry out regular tours and to submit reports, the establishment of a price committee, and the introduction of ration cards in Muscat and Matrah for certain commodities" (IOR, L/PS/12/2972, Muscat News and Intelligence Summaries, July 31, 1945). The rest of this note reads: "For the present it can be said the situation has been much improved and that public approval of these measures is widespread. Queues at the Control shops have disappeared and many of the officials responsible for the more serious abuses of this branch of the administration have been dismissed."

27. Muhammad bin Sa'id bin Abdullah al-Qassabi, one of the main coffee merchants in Bahla in the first half of the twentieth century, brought coffee from Zanzibar.

His son Abdullah then took over the business. Other merchants in Bahla included the Qur'anic teacher Sulayman bin Nassir al-Mahruqi, who was a very old man during my fieldwork, Salmin bin Salih al-Gadidi, Sulayim bin Salim al-Gadidi, Muhammad bin Sulayman al-Hashimi, and his son Sayf.

28. Sometimes families would sell, through an auction, any surplus of coffee given to them on these occasions.

29. The Maria Theresa dollar ($MT) was the standard currency in Oman in the nineteenth and much of the twentieth centuries. In Oman it is called *qursh fransī* or *qursh*.

30. Debates about the legality and dangers of coffee in the eighteenth, nineteenth, and twentieth centuries were not isolated to Oman. Similar debates were taking place in other places in the Middle East and Europe. Ralph Hattox (1985) has argued that opposition to coffee in the Middle East first emerged in early sixteenth-century Mecca, but more from opposition to coffeehouses than to coffee itself. Hattox also illustrates how within the Sunni schools of legal thought there have been different interpretations of hadith about wine and whether coffee relates to those hadith. Generally, for the Shafi'i, Maliki, and Hanbali schools all intoxicants are forbidden and therefore wine, by definition, is forbidden. For some Hanafis, instead, it is not the essence of the intoxicant, but the intoxication or the intoxicating effects of wine that is forbidden. In this understanding, small non-intoxicating quantities of wine are not forbidden. The hadith in question is one from Ibn Qutayba "*kull muskir khamr wa kull muskir ḥarām.*"

31. I wish to thank Abdulrahman al-Salimi for pointing this out to me.

32. Al-Salimi here seems to be suggesting that being "permissible" is not enough and that for coffee to be acceptable for some people it must fall under the legal categories of recommended (*mandūb*) or obligatory (*wājib*).

33. It is interesting that al-Abri refers to the pourer as *sāqī*, a figure generally associated with the "wineserver."

34. The "book" is the Qur'an.

35. Fire could also be said to purify substances.

36. This is a rhetorical question.

37. The name of a river in paradise.

38. Sacred places of the Hajj pilgrimage.

39. Al-Nubi refers to a slave.

40. Two other short poems are:

Rashid bin Aziz al-Khusaybi (d. AH 1347 [1928-1929 CE])

Bring me and pour me the husk coffee, which is even better than the first wine,
    and delight the cups for me (*al-fanājīnā*)
It summons what life gives, it summons what causes annihilation, we come
    (*al-finā jīnā*)

If one thousand kneeled in its fields seeking protection, you will see one thousand saved (*al-'alf nājīnā*)

Oh God of Beauty, give us your protection, if we ask, be generous and if we call,
respond to us (*fanājīnā*)

This poem is particularly witty: each line ends with a different version of the combination of the letters f-a-n-ā-j-ī-n-ā, sometimes as one word and sometimes divided
into two. Each version has a different meaning.

Darwish bin Juma'a al-Mahruqi

It is roasted for us as husk and brought to us with the fragrance of musk, and the
color of ink

Like pure milk in its taste, the only difference being its black color

41. For a summary of different types of metaphors, see George Lakoff and Mark
Johnson (1980).

42. For a description of "traditional" practices of hospitality in Oman, see al-
'Ansi's (1991) chapter *Tabādul al-Ziyārāt wa Ākrām al-Ḍaif* (The Exchange of Visits
and Respect for the Guest).

43. As in many societies, foods in Bahla were divided between hot and cold. To
maintain good health, people had to maintain a balance in their bodies. Some dates,
however, were considered more "hot" or more "cold" than others. This distinction
among dates became clear to me early in my stay in Bahla when someone, who had just
performed a branding on my landlady to cure a skin rash on her hands, instructed my
landlady to eat hot dates, such as *khalāṣ*, and not cold dates, like *khusayib*. Nevertheless, while some dates are hotter or colder, in general and in relation to coffee, dates
are considered hot.

44. As indicated in note 19, in Bahla, imports are referred to as *baḥrī*, from the
"sea," whereas locally produced goods are called Omani.

45. This is not to argue that the date's position as an export necessarily helps construct it as "local." As Fernando Ortiz (1995 [1947]) beautifully illustrated, different
types of "exports" can have distinct significances. As Ortiz noted there is something
special about tobacco that distinguishes it from Cuba's other main export, sugar. For
Ortiz, "Tobacco is born, sugar is made" (1995 [1947]: 8).

46. In the early 1990s, dates (both fresh and dried) brought about 500,000 Omani
rials per annum. See the Omani Development Council's *Statistical Yearbook* (Sultanate of Oman 1992).

47. For an extended discussion of dates as sacred, see Limbert (2008b).

48. Such early European travelers include Alfonso d'Alboquerque (Portuguese) in
1507, Sir Thomas Herbert (English) in 1617, Pietro della Valle (Italian) in 1625, Jean-
Baptiste Tavernier (French) in the 1660s, Jan Struys (Dutch) in 1672, and Engelbert
Kaempfer (German) in 1688.

49. For a fascinating discussion of trade in the Indian Ocean at the beginning of the nineteenth century, see John H. Reinoehl's (1959) publication and annotation of an 1806 report from the shipping captain (and congressman) Jacob Crowinshield to Secretary of State James Madison. Although dates are not mentioned in this report, it supplies a particularly interesting perspective on shipping rivalries between Americans and the British in the area. The *Sultanah*, the ship the Omani Sultan Sayyid Saʿid bin Sultan sent to New York in 1840 as the first visit by an Arab ambassador, also carried dates.

50. The W. J. Towell Company has continued to play a crucial role in Oman. Although it is now completely Omani owned, it has retained the name of one of its original founders.

51. On his Sur trip, Cole wrote of Nizwa as suffering from a five-year drought, visible in the condition of some of the date groves. Although the date groves "extend in every direction," some of the palms were also withering away (Ward 1987: 163). The dollar was devalued at the end of the nineteenth century. The value of the Maria Theresa dollar, about 80% silver, often fluctuated. Although continuously keeping the Maria Theresa name (although in Oman it is called *qursh fransī* or *qursh*) and being minted with a 1780 date, the currency was not confined to being minted in Austria. In 1935, in a pact between Mussolini and Hitler, the dollar also began to be minted in Rome. At the same time, Britain began to mint the currency in London and then in Bombay. After World War II, minting ended in Bombay, returning to London (until 1962), Rome (until 1960), and Vienna, where it continues (Bailey 1988).

52. This "export tax" was first mentioned in 1879 (actually first described as a tax on imports from interior to coast). Lorimer notes: "By 1886 the rate of this tax, originally lower, had been enhanced to 5 per cent, and the tax had virtually assumed the form of an impost on dates exported from the coast of Oman to places abroad and was represented as a substitute for one of the ordinary taxes on agricultural produce which the Sultan was unable to collect from growers in the far interior" (Lorimer 1915: I, 524).

53. A large amount of land was confiscated at this time in Bahla as well, but these confiscations were not of Sultanate lands. Instead, they were of lands that had been owned or confiscated earlier by the ruler Nassir bin Humayd or by his main local agent, Sulayman bin Abdullah al-Mahruqi. These lands in Bahla were not returned to their original owners with the Treaty of Sib in 1920, but remained as *bayt al-māl* lands. More than half of the land in Bahla is *bayt al-māl*.

54. Several years before, the Sultan had also attempted a similar punishment by raising the tax to 10%, but as this had been done in the middle of the date season, the date merchants in Muscat (who were mainly British subjects) suffered, and the British pushed the Sultan to rescind his declaration. In 1920, however, the Sultan made the announcement several months before the date season and the merchants, it was argued, could plan ahead (IOR, R/15/6/337).

55. The financial situation of the Imamate administration was quite dire and Imam Muhammad bin Abdullah al-Khalili began selling *bayt al-māl* lands and water shares.

56. The year 1932 was important for the finances of the Muscat government. The British political agent at the time, Colonel Alban, had come to replace Bertram Thomas, who after sending false reports to the political resident in Bushire "disappeared" into the Rub al-Khali desert. In 1932, Alban had begun to clean up the "mess" left behind by Thomas. One of his first jobs was to assess the amount of tax that was to be paid by the districts on the Batina coast. The fact that this annual state-imposed tax was called *zakat*, and that Alban wrote that previous to his assessment, *zakat* had been imposed on communities at odd times and under varying circumstances, indicates a significant shift towards a growing state bureaucratization of a religious obligation (IOR, L/PS/12/2971, August 1932, December 1932). Debate about Alban's tax was not confined to Oman: a newspaper in Baghdad heard about what was going on and complained (IOR, L/PS/12/2971, January 1933). How much of the discussion of Alban's *zakat* taxes in 1932 and 1933 affected the discussion of the date tax in Sur in 1936, I cannot say. What seems clear, however, is that the date trade was important both for the place of production, that is, Oman and Batina, and for the Sultanate for the taxes.

57. The international market was often tied to political relations and situations. In May 1940, for example, the government of India prohibited the importation of Omani dates (IOR, L/PS/12/2972, Muscat Diaries: News and Intelligence Summaries, May 12 31, 1940). For an example of price fluctuations, in the early 1940s, the exports of dried dates to India rose from 1,642,642 rupees in 1941–1942 to 3,052,235 in 1942–1943 to 4,371,459 in 1943–1944. The increase was due was to the increase in the price of dates in Oman: the prices more than doubled between 1942–1943 and 1943–1944 (Muscat Trade Report 1946a, 1946b). In 1947, the government of India placed a temporary embargo on the import of dates, affecting merchants in Oman. In the 1950s, the majority of the dates were going to India again, although even then there were fluctuations from one year to the next. For example, between 1958–1959 and 1959–1960, the amount of dry dates being exported decreased from 4,254,285 rupees to 2,367,180, with each bag of dates costing about 125 rupees.

58. When I was conducting fieldwork, several agriculturalists were using that money, as well as money collected from honey producers, to pay for the capture and destruction of a particular type of bee known as the *dabı habayn*. It was generally children who would kill and collect bees.

59. As with the auctioning of user rights of dates, mosques, the government, and individuals could auction user rights for water.

60. The beginning of the date harvest was announced in Bahla with the voice of an auctioneer who walked through the streets yelling "*gamlow, gamlow*"—words that were understood to mean, "come here, come here" in Bahlawi, but that were used specifically for the date harvest. The auctioneer, the scribe, the money collector, and

the group of people interested in buying user rights to a tree for the season, would meet in the market and then walk towards one area of town and focus on one or two types of dates, depending on what was ripening. The auctions, which lasted several hours, could not cover all the date palms in season, so the same process was repeated the next day, until all the date palms in season in an area were auctioned. The auctioneer and the group would move from individual tree to tree, knowing beforehand which mosque the tree belonged to and what kind of dates it had. As the auctioneer yelled out prices, the crowd inspected, and when someone wanted user rights for the season at the price that the auctioneer announced, he would yell, "I want" (*bāghī*). The auctioneer then moved up about half a rial (about one US dollar), trying to pull in another bidder. When the bid remained firm for about a minute, the auctioneer would yell out the name of the man who made the last bid, the name of his father, sometimes the name of his grandfather, and the tribe. The scribe would write down the name, the amount, and the mosque to which the funds would go. Most often the person would pay immediately, but at times the bidder would pay later. During my fieldwork, many of the date palms went for about five rials (thirteen US dollars) for the season. That time, however, was a time of plenty (*khaṣab* in Bahlawi)—that is, not a time of drought—so the prices were quite low.

61. Dates ripen in the following order: *naghāl, qash swayh, miznāg, khalāṣ, khanayzī, hilālī, zabad, kaṣāb,* and *farḍ.*

62. Date palms really begin producing after about ten years of life and then stop producing after about forty-five or fifty years: many people said that after they get too tall, it is difficult to harvest so they are cut after about thirty or forty years.

63. Similarly, in English, one could use the verb *digest* to mean "understand," or the expression *he ate his words*, not only to mean that he mumbled, but also to mean that he performed a faux pas. For a discussion of "digested words" in a different context, see Erik Mueggler (2001).

64. Work on the relationship between words and gendered bodies, such as Fedwa Malti-Douglas's *Woman's Body, Woman's Word* (1991), or Saddeka Arebi's *Women and Words in Saudi Arabia* (1994), has focused less on the materiality of words and their effects on the body, and more on representations and constructions of gender in Arabo-Islamic literature or on discourses about writing and literary expression.

65. As Irvine summarized, "Thus, linguistic forms have relevance for the social scientist not only as part of a world of ideas, but also as part of a world of objects, economic transactions, and political interests. The verbal sign, I have argued, relates to a political economy in many ways: by denoting it; by indexing part of it; by depicting it . . . and by taking part in it as an object of exchange. These multiple functions may all co-occur, because they merely reflect the multifunctionality of language in general" (1989: 263). My own point is not to argue that language be considered either material or symbolic, but rather to recognize the ways that language is both and to focus,

here, on the *kind* of materiality. Just as coffee and dates are kinds of objects—drink and fruit—with specific symbolic values tied to their places in worlds of consumption and worlds of production, words could also be seen to be ingested, and also as having specific symbolic values. Attending to the *kind* of object words are in the context of neighborly social relations puts their exchange within this social world in perspective. While they relate to the material world by creating context (as does the presence of coffee and dates), words also relate to the material world by being *of* that world of exchange and, in particular, being an ingestible gift.

Chapter 4

Material in this chapter was adapted from *Monarchies and Nations: Globalization and Identity in the Arab States of the Gulf*, edited by Paul Dresch and James Piscatori. 2005. Permission courtesy of I. B. Tauris Publishers.

1. Although early Ibadi scholars were influenced by Mu'tazilism, a theological perspective that opposed the anthropomorphisizing of God and emphasized rationalism, they also differed from Mu'tazilites in the degree to which hadith should be consulted. While Mu'tazilites are understood to have had little regard for hadith, relying on rational methods almost exclusively, Ibadi scholars did not rely solely on reason, especially when hadith were available (Ennami 1972: 143). Nevertheless, Mu'tazilism has had a significant influence on Ibadism. The work of the medieval Mu'tazilite scholar and theologian 'Abd al-Jabbar was cited to me in Oman as particularly significant for understanding Ibadi notions of morality, God-human relations, and knowledge. On 'Abd al-Jabbar, see, for example, Peters (1976) and Reynolds (2004, 2005). Some Muslim scholars outside the Ibadi tradition have, in the late twentieth century, also been drawn to Mu'tazilite thinking (see Martin, Woodward, and Atmaja 1997), just as some Ibadis have turned away from Mu'tazilism.

2. The approach, or "school" of law, that is considered the most literalist is the Hanbali school. There are four major schools (*madhāhib* [singular *madhhab*]) of Islamic law in Sunnism, each of which is based on the teachings of a particular scholar: Abu Hanifa (d. AH 150 [767 CE]), Malik bin Anas (d. AH 179 [795 CE]), Muhammad ibn Idris al-Shafi'i (d. AH 204 [819 CE]), and Ahmad bin Hanbal (d. AH 241 [855 CE]). These schools have historically been influenced by different theological (*kalām*) perspectives, which are distinct from the schools of law per se, usually divided between Mu'tazilites and Asharites. Different regions, peoples, and states throughout the Islamic world follow one of these four schools, one of the Shi'ite schools or, much less commonly, Ibadism. For excellent accounts in English of the emergence of the schools of law in Islam, see Calder (1993), Coulson (1964), Hallaq (1997, 2005), Schacht (1964), and Weiss (1998).

3. Of course, in practice, literalism can also make it less incumbent on laypeople to rely on scholarly (and external) interpretations.

4. Mahmood (2005) illustrates how, among the women's mosque movement in Cairo, everyday moral and ethical actions are understood to create desires, which in turn make rituals easier and habitual. This is a reversal, as Mahmood points out, of liberal assumptions that desire and will are both natural and antecedents to moral action. Mahmood describes how the mosque movement's emphasis on learned will and desire also contrasts with Pierre Bourdieu's (1977) notion of *habitus*, in that the former highlights the conscious pedagogy of will and bodily habits, while Bourdieu focuses on the unconscious learning of bodily habits and social (and class) position. Mahmood, however, also suggests that the cultivation of desire happens through formalized study groups, pointing to the work of al-Miskawaih (a tenth-century Baghdadi philosopher) who wrote in his *Tahdhīb al-akhlāq* that the good life flows from the cultivation of a pure soul. According to Lapidus, whose work on al-Miskawaih Mahmood draws from, such cultivation is manifest, in part, in bodily activities and friendship and is incompatible with asceticism and withdrawal from society (1984: 45). Such an emphasis on cultivation through bodily activities and friendship (rather than classes) would make perfect sense to the older Bahlawi women and men I knew.

5. For a sustained critique of Omani propaganda on education, among other popular themes, see Pridham (1986). For a more detailed examination of the history of "modern" education in Oman, see Mohammed Hafied al-Dhahab's (1987) PhD dissertation "The Historical Development of Education in Oman." Al-Dhahab documents the changes in the curriculum of the schools over the century, the types of building that were used, how the classes were set up, and who the teachers were. It becomes clear that what is considered to be "modern" education has shifted over the century.

6. Between 1970 and 1980, for example, the number of modern state schools increased from 3 to 363.

7. Most work on gender and modern education has focused on the relationship among nationalism, education, and domesticity. Najmabadi (1998), for example, has traced discourses involved in the production of educated housewives as fundamental to the formation and foundation of nation-states in the Middle East.

8. The government closed all these schools in the wake of the arrests in 1995 of about two hundred government officials, university professors, and students who were accused of plotting against the government and spreading "fundamentalist" literature. While I was there, the school's sign was still up on the Friday mosque in Bahla where the school had been, but it was taken down during the summer of 1997. The Bahla school had six subjects: Islamic studies, English, Arabic, Mathematics, Science, and Social Studies, which included Geography and History. Egyptians and a Tunisian taught all the subjects except English, which was taught by my landlord's son Ibrahim and Islamic studies, which was taught by my landlord's son by a first marriage and Gamal (Aisha and Zuwayna's father). Unlike at the "regular" schools, each of the five main Islamic studies subjects (Qur'an, jurisprudence (fiqh), exegesis (tafsīr), prophetic biography (sīra),

and hadith) had its own textbook. The three groups of students were taught simultane-ously in different corners of the mosque, each group facing in a different direction. The students sat at desks, in straight lines, like in the regular schools and unlike the more advanced religious classes in the days before the introduction of mass state education.

9. At the time of my fieldwork, there were 126 schools and approximately 73,000 students in the interior region of Oman. The Aisha Riyamia school in Bahla had 196 students: 100 in the humanities and 96 in the science section. The principal of the school predicted that about half of the students in the science division would attend the university, a teacher training college, or the medical college. There were 41 teach-ers, only 8 of whom were Omanis. The other teachers were Egyptians, Jordanians, and Sri Lankans.

10. One of the main concerns of educators in Bahla was the teacher-to-student ratio. Because of the lack of space and teachers in relation to the number of students, some of the schools would teach two sessions: one in the mornings and one in the afternoons. There were some teachers who would teach both sessions, either in the same school or in different schools. Some teachers pointed out that it was unlikely that the government was going to build any new schools soon. Although there was pub-lic discussion about this teacher-student ratio and of the double schedules, it seemed that unless the government built new schools, the structure would be very difficult to change. At the time of my fieldwork, there was also discussion about whether there was going to be an annual fee for schooling. Many women I spoke to said that although it might help the Ministry of Education, they were afraid that if such a fee were imple-mented, their daughters would not be sent to school.

11. For further description of the reforms, see Ministry of Education (2001) and Rassekh (2004).

12. El-Shibiny (1997) notes that "traditionally" in Oman, *sablas* were used for teaching young children. While this might have been the case in other parts of Oman, in Bahla, classes were held either in or adjacent to mosques. In addition, *sablas* were not built in Bahla until the first half of the twentieth century.

13. A similar spatial disjuncture between the mosque and the school occurred in Ottoman Yemen in the 1860s and 1870s (Messick 1993: 104).

14. By August 1997, the library was moved to a larger house in another neigh-borhood. Women were still only allowed to use the library on Friday mornings. A few things did change with the move, however. Before, the system for checking out books was self-organized: whoever wanted to check out a book would write his or her name, the title of the book, the author, and the date he or she borrowed the book in a notebook. In the new house, a man sat at the entrance and checked people and books in and out.

15. *Abayas* are long, black, silky coverings worn over clothes and are somewhat different from the *chadors* worn by some women in Iran. While *abayas* are usually

cut as loose-fitting robes that rest on a woman's shoulders, *chadors* are less robelike and rest on the top of a woman's head. In neither case is the woman's face covered. Face coverings, when used, are separate articles of clothing from the *abayas* or *chadors*.

16. In a similar example, Bayly (1986) describes how in mid-nineteenth-century India, certain cloth and colors did not symbolize particular things, but *were* those things.

17. The low dividing wall was also used in the Qur'anic schools for young children, to divide them between boys and girls. This way, the young boys and girls could be in the same classroom, and yet still be somewhat separated.

18. The debates between Oman's national Mufti, Ahmad al-Khalili, and the late Saudi Mufti Bin Bazz became a source of discussion over who Ibadis are and how they differ from other groups. For Ahmad al-Khalili's response to Wahhabism, see his *al-Ḥaqq al-Dāmigh* (AH 1409). For more on these debates, see D. Eickelman (1989).

19. The school for boys rivaled the Qur'anic school twenty-five meters away. This rivalry between the state-sponsored Qur'anic school and Ibrahim's private religious studies classes points to a tension between the state and many people's understandings of religious knowledge as well as a tension between religion learnt through basic Qur'anic teaching and religion learnt through defined precepts. Ibrahim had received official permission to open this school that provided Qur'anic and hadith instruction to boys either before or after school depending on the students' schedules. Ibrahim hired a Tunisian Ibadi to teach the students.

20. Interestingly, even the entry on "Halka" in the *Encyclopedia of Islam* was written by Tadeusz Lewicki, a scholar of Ibadism.

21. According to Ennami (1972: 62–64), there were three different kinds of gatherings or *majālis* in the eighth century: those of the shaykhs, or leading scholars and political planners, who would plan the organization of the community; those of the entire community to address questions to the shaykhs; and finally the study groups.

22. Ibadis consider their first Imam to be Jabir bin Zayd, who also lived in Basra. There is, however, some discussion as to whether he considered himself to be an Ibadi (Ennami 1972: 40–44).

23. For more on the Ibadi movement in Basra, see Wilkinson (1982).

24. For example, chapter 8 of the main textbook for the history of Islam in Oman at Sultan Qaboos University, College of Literature, *'Umān wa al-Ḥaḍārat al-Islāmiyya*, (Oman and the Islamic Civilization) sketches the role of the *ḥalqa* in Islamic education among Ibadis of North Africa.

25. Bin Bakr's rules are found in al-Darjini's thirteenth-century CE work, *Kitāb Ṭabaqāt al-Mashāyikh*. The fifteenth-century CE scholar al-Barradi wrote an almost identical book of rules as part of his *Kitāb al-Jawāhir*. For a comparison of the two versions, see Rubinacci (1961). In his translation of Bin Bakr's rules as found in al-Darjini,

Rubinacci carefully notes how al-Barradi's version is almost identical to Bin Bakr's four centuries earlier. Although al-Barradi changed some of the phrases, he was careful to maintain the same regulations that Bin Bakr had established.

26. Interestingly, besides the discussion of the Qur'anic classes, Bin Bakr only refers to the Qur'an once near the end of the rules. He makes no reference to the Prophet, either in terms of what kind of lifestyle he approved of, ascetic or not, or in terms of his approach to knowledge.

27. The hostels were also places for the sick, the elderly, and for men and boys with physical and mental disabilities. These men and boys had particular rules and were obliged, if physically able, to serve meals to the rest of the recluses.

28. In his introduction to Bin Bakr's rules, al-Darjini defines the *halqa* as "the name for the group that gathers around the Shaykh who teaches them (*yu'allimuhum*) knowledge and instructs them (*yulaqqinuhum*) on observance and informs them (*yubassiruhum*) on the religion depending on what God opens for each one of them" (al-Darjini n.d.: vol. 1, 4). For al-Darjini, then, the term *halqa* refers both to the individual study-circles that gather around the shaykh and to the group of students and scholars who live and study at the refuge. In his rules, on the other hand, Bin Bakr uses the term more exclusively for the hostel in general, referring, instead, to the gatherings of students and teachers in meetings and Qur'anic recitations as *majālis* and the lessons themselves as *dars*: "and the students take from him [the shaykh of the *halqa*] lessons" (Rubinacci 1961: 61). For al-Kafi's rules, see Warjalani (1878: 254–257). For a study of al-Darjini, see Lewicki (1936).

29. While Rubinacci suggests that al-Kafi's rules reflect an "evolution" towards a political and religious role for the *halqas* by the twelfth century CE (1961: 57), Lewicki insists that the political *halqas* really became important after the fifteenth century CE, particularly in the Mzab (1965: 97).

30. The age of secrecy is one of the four states of Ibadi communities; the other three stages of the religion (*masālik al-dīn*) are manifestation (*zuhūr*), defense (*difā'*), and martyrdom (*shirā'*). According to Ennami, these stages were defined very early (Ennami 1972: 229).

31. Although, according to Lewicki, the political power of the *azzabas* diminished during French rule (Lewicki 1965: 98), these ethnographies indicate that the *azzabas* did maintain some political influence in the towns of the Mzab.

32. Abdulrahman al-Salimi, through a personal communication, has pointed out to me how in the classic Omani works such as *Kitāb al-Muṣannaf* by Ahmad bin Abdullah al-Kindi (d. 1162), *Kitāb al-Ḍiyā'* by Salma bin Muslim al-Awtabi (d. early twelfth century), *Bayān al-Shar'* by Muhammad bin Ibrahim al-Kindi (d. 1115), and the much later *Qāmūs al-Sharī'a* by Jumayyil bin Khamis al-Sadi (d. first half of the nineteenth century), the authors focus on the categories of *zuhūr* and *difā'* and hardly discuss the state of *kitmān*.

33. See Harith Ghassany's (1995) doctoral dissertation *"Kitman and Renaissance: Domination and the Limits of Development."*

34. On Sulayman al-Baruni, see J. Peterson (1987); L. Veccia Vaglieri (1934); and Abi al-Yaqzan al-Hajj Ibrahim (1956). On Muhammad Atfayesh, see P. Cuperly (1972).

35. It is interesting to note which texts became emblematic of Ibadi law for colonial officials. Imbert (1903) points out how the Germans in East Africa were basing their study of Ibadi law on work by the orientalist Eduard Sachau (1894), who had one copy of al-Bisyawi's *Mukhtaṣar*, which was reprinted in Zanzibar in 1886. Al-Bisyawi was Ibn Baraka's student in Bahla in the eleventh century CE. Imbert's disparaging tone towards Sachau's limited access to Ibadi law seems to indicate a rivalry between the scholars as well as the colonial powers (Imbert 1903).

36. See Abi Yaqzan al-Hajj Ibrahim (1956: 17–18).

37. A few months before the start of Aisha's summer classes, the difficulty in judging people's responses to a lecture from within the class became clear to me when I went with a friend to a lecture by a male religious scholar. On that occasion, my friend wore a *chador* style cover and was very serious during the entire lecture. As she sat down, she wrapped her *abaya* around her so that even her feet were covered and then stared down at the ground in front of her for the entire hour-and-a-half lecture. One might assume that she, with her "serious" *abaya* and stern face, would agree with the strict prescriptions that the scholar was demanding of the women and girls in the room. As we left the room, however, she turned to me and said: "Can you believe that? What was he saying? I can't even the shake the hand of my daughter's husband?!! That is ridiculous. The question about shaking hands is if there is a chance that there is a [sexual] relationship. If I don't even consider that there could be a relationship, then there is no problem."

38. In the class, Aisha and Mawza not only spoke about women's responsibilities in terms of strengthening the Islamic world, but also in terms of their bodies. Aisha's admonition of women and girls who "go out" stands less on the assumption that they might be attracted to men, however, but rather that men might see them and attempt to make advances. Women who "go out" then, are enticing men, but are not themselves attracted. The passive construction of their sexuality, in this context, neither suggests a similar possibility with other women nor allows a sense of sexual pleasure. Instead, women may flirt and attract, but the object of that flirtation is the allure, not intimacy or pleasure. Women are not only responsible for studying and being aware of their attractiveness to men, they also bleed, signaling their gender and by assumption their sexuality. On July 9, 1997, for example, Aisha gave a lecture on bleeding. Aisha's style was matter-of-fact: she was discussing a biological topic with serious implications for religious practice. Aisha spoke about types of blood, from women's monthly cycles to bleeding after giving birth, as well as about the different consistencies of blood and the way blood smells. This taxonomic and legalistic style of speaking about women's bodies was markedly different from the way older women in everyday neigh-

borly coffee groups spoke. While knowledge about sex and sexualized bodies were transmitted and constructed through teasing and jokes in the coffee groups, in the class, the women's bodies were made biologic. While women in the neighborly coffee groups would sometimes tell each other what to do, what was appropriate in terms of religious norms, for the most part, these reflections on appropriate practice were restricted to the bare essentials. In the study group, instead, bodies became objects of wonder where "blood descends from her" (*dim yanzil minhā*). For Aisha and the class, bodies were not agents that bleed, but objects of biologic fascination that needed to be regulated and categorized to maintain religious and ritual purity.

39. The ambiguous place of "home" in this discourse touches on a tension in feminist scholarship. "House" and "home," as Iris Young (2000) has written, are certainly deeply ambivalent values, especially for feminist scholars: on the one hand, they are associated with patriarchy, domesticity, and repression. On the other, they are also productive spaces and might, at least in their ideal construction, provide security.

40. For a discussion of the medieval scholar 'Abd al-Jabbar (d. 1025 CE) and his notions of uselessness and evil, see Leaman (1980). For an account of 'Abd al-Jabbar's life and theological influence, see Frank (1971), Martin, Woodward, and Atmaja (1997), Peters (1976), and Reynolds (2004, 2005).

Chapter 5

Material in this chapter was adapted from "The Senses of Water in an Omani Town" by Mandana E. Limbert. 2001. *Social Text* 19(3): 35–55. Permission courtesy of *Social Text*, Columbia University.

1. This is not to say, of course, that the system of water distribution has been the same since the seventh century CE. Rather, I wish simply to note that the origins of these canals probably date to this early time. See Wilkinson (1983).

2. These trade figures are from the *Middle East Economic Digest*, July 20, 1973.

3. In the late 1990s, water management fell under three administrative units: the Ministry of Water Resources (MWR) was in charge of water resources assessment, while the Ministry of Agriculture and Fisheries (MAF) was in charge of irrigation, and the Ministry of Housing, Electricity and Water (MHEW) was responsible for providing desalinated water. There have been numerous ministry restructurings since the late 1990s. In 2001, the MWR was reorganized as the Ministry of Regional Municipalities, Environment and Water Resources. In 2007, The MAF was divided into two ministries and the Ministry of Regional Municipalities, Environment and Water Resources lost the "Environment" subsection. In 2007, a new Public Authority was established: the Public Authority for Electricity and Water, which developed out of the former MHEW, which simply became the Ministry of Housing. The relationship among the Public Authority for Electricity and Water, the Ministry of Regional Municipalities and Water Resources, and the MAF has not been completely clear. The

establishment of the new Public Authority, however, has further enabled the privatization of utilities in Oman, a privatization that was clearly beginning while I was conducting research, but which was fully implemented in 2004, with the Sector Law (Royal Decree 78/2004).

4. For a quantitative study of *falaj* water use in Oman that argues against the assumption of unnecessarily high water loss in surface irrigation, see Norman, Shayya, al-Ghafri, and McCann (1998).

5. For more details on the recommended and suggested water privatization policies, see, for example, the *Letters of Intent* and *Memoranda of Economic and Financial Policies* for the following countries: Angola, Benin, Guinea-Bissau, Honduras, Nicaragua, Niger, Panama, Rwanda, Sao Tome and Principe, Senegal, Tanzania, and Yemen (International Monetary Fund 2000a, 2000b).

6. Wilkinson (1980) argues that the change since the early 1970s from *falaj* to wells for irrigations marks a shift from communal to private ownership and practices. Rodionov (1999) makes a similar argument for Yemen. One complication with Wilkinson's conclusion is that in Oman wells have long been used to irrigate lands that were not connected to the underground canal system: rather than being pumped, the water was pulled by animals.

7. On Islamic water law, see, among other studies, Caponera (1978), Sonnier (1933), Wilkinson (1977, 1978, 1990), Salameh (1999), and al-Salimi (1989 [n.d.]).

8. Although my research focuses on Bahla, this system of water distribution from canals is similar in other towns of Oman as well as in other areas of the Middle East. For an analysis of distribution in Morocco, for example, see Hammoudi (1985); for Tunisia, see Attia (1985).

9. Most ethnographic studies on water focus on the relationship between social structure and water-rights. For a review of some of this literature, see Mabry (1996).

10. As I noted in Chapter 3, in his 1978 article on Bahla, Fredrik Barth argued that produce from Bahla, such as dates, cannot be sold for profit in Bahla. While it is possible that this ethic was practiced in the late 1970s, all those that I asked claimed that there were never restrictions on selling produce from Bahla in Bahla. If it were the case that individuals could not make a profit on selling dates in the town, perhaps one could make the argument that one should not purchase or rent water-time for irrigating the date palms that would then be sold.

11. Islamic law recognizes five "principles" (*aḥkām*) or categories of action: those actions that are required (*farḍ* or *wājib*), recommended (*mandūb*), indifferent (*jā'iz* or *mubāh*), disapproved (*makrūh*), and forbidden (*ḥarām*).

Chapter 6

1. For the purposes of this chapter, I will outline only some of the major figures and shifts in the history of Omanis in Zanzibar. For information about the early links

between Oman and Zanzibar, see Hourani (1951), Chittick and Rotberg (1975), and Kirkman (1983). See also extracts from al-Mas'udi (d. 965 CE) and al-Idrisi (d. ca. 1165 CE) in Freeman-Grenville (1962: 14–21). For an excellent account of British involvement in Oman and Zanzibar in the eighteenth and nineteenth centuries, see, in particular, Bhacker (1992). See, as well, Sheriff (1987), Cooper (1980), and al-Mughayri (1994 [1979]).

2. For studies of the Ya'ariba dynasty, see, for example, Bathurst (1967) and Salil ibn Razik (1871). For studies of the Portuguese in Southern Arabia, see Beckingham (1983) and Serjeant (1983 and 1963).

3. Before the increased prevalence of steam ships and the British "mail" ships in the Indian Ocean, Omanis generally traveled from Oman to Zanzibar during the Northeast Monsoon from November to February, and from Zanzibar to Oman during the Southwest Monsoon from April to September.

4. It was not until 1821 that some leading families from Pemba (al-Huthera) asked the Omani al-Bu Sa'idi Sultan of the time, Sayyid Sa'id bin Sultan, for his aid in overthrowing the Mazrui family. Sayyid Sa'id bin Sultan conquered Pemba in 1822 and, after a decade of battles, also conquered Mombasa in 1837 (Middleton and Campbell 1965: 4).

5. Again, for an excellent analysis of this history, see Bhacker (1992).

6. This was not the first time that Sayyid Sa'id bin Sultan visited Zanzibar. He had gone in 1825 and then in 1828, when he had "purchased the surrender of the sovereignty of the Swahili chief" (Gray 1977: 139). The Swahili chief was, himself, an al-Alawi, who traced part of his origins to the Hadramawt.

7. Omani control of the island during Sayyid Sa'id bin Sultan's time was not quite absolute. Until 1865 the leader of the Hadimu (one of the largest "native" and Swahili-speaking groups on Zanzibar, which included migrants from different areas on the mainland)—the *Mwinyi Mkuku* of the time—Sultan Hamadi, continued to administer many towns and villages on the southern part of the island, both on behalf of the Sultan and for himself. This administration mostly meant collecting taxes and supplying forced labor for the growing clove plantations. After Sultan Hamadi's death, however, no one replaced him (the male heir died of smallpox at the age of about twenty-two and the daughters either died young or married into prominent "Arab" families) and the Hadimu shaykhs became answerable to Sayyid Sa'id bin Sultan and then to Sultan Barghash bin Sa'id. Although these shaykhs began to be answerable to the Omani Sultans, the taxes and forced labor ended with Sultan Hamadi's death. For more on the details of the history and relations between the Hadimu leader and the Omani Sultan in the second half of the nineteenth century, see Gray (1977).

8. For lists of some of the tribes, see al-Mughayri (1994 [1979]).

9. The first antislavery treaty between the British and the al-Bu Sa'id was signed in 1822, but it was confined to allowing British fleets to prevent the shipment of slaves

from Zanzibar to Europe. A second, similar treaty was signed in 1840. The 1845 treaty was the first to limit the traffic of slaves to Arabia, Persia, and India. The details of the abolition movement as well as the connection between the changing structures of capitalism and abolition are beyond the scope of this chapter. For more information, see, in particular, Cooper (1980), Sheriff (1987), and Ed Ferguson (1991: 36–78).

10. According to Cooper (1997), this practice of marrying into "native" families was more common on Pemba island than on Zanzibar itself.

11. This is quoted in Bhacker (1992: 68). *Zinji* means "black" in Arabic.

12. When Sayyid Sa'id returned to Oman in 1854, he placed his son Khalid in charge. Khalid, however, died that same year and other Omani families, especially the powerful Barwani family in Zanzibar, began a rebellion. They were resentful of Sayyid Sa'id's submission to the British in outlawing the slave trade with Arabia. Because of this rebellion, Sayyid Sa'id sought to return to Zanzibar, but died on the way. Whether or not he intended to divide Oman and Zanzibar between his sons continues to be debated in Zanzibari-Omani historiography. See, for example, Bhacker (1992), Coupland (1939), Kelly (1968), and Sheriff (1987).

13. The name of the house was of interest to the British authorities since it underlined for them the French involvement in the whole affair.

14. The degree of British involvement in the establishment of the two Sultanates is even evident in the choice of title of the leaders. While Sayyid Sa'id himself had maintained the title Sayyid rather than Sultan, it was the British who insisted on using the title Sultan for both rulers, in Zanzibar and in Muscat: "On the separation of the principalities the Government of Bombay decided that each of the two rulers should in future be styled Sultan, a term by which, from this point onwards, we shall generally describe them" (Lorimer 1915, I: 471). In Oman, the title Sayyid is simply an honorific and does not suggest descent from the Prophet Muhammad.

15. As I have mentioned several times in this book, Oman itself never officially became a protectorate, but debates about whether to do so are evident in many reports and discussions in the records at the India Office, from 1891 onwards. One example of this discussion appears in files from 1891 on whether or how to have the Omani Sultan Faysal bin Turki (1888–1913) promulgate a slavery decree (IOR, R/15/6/20). In the meantime, the newly unified German state was maneuvering to control the mainland of what is now Tanzania. Through an agreement with the British in 1886 and a fifty-year lease of the coastal strip from Sultan Barghash in 1888, the German East Africa Company gained jurisdiction over the mainland. Within a few years, however, the GEAC was near insolvency and the German state took administrative responsibility for the East African territories as well as permanent ownership of the coastal strip. During World War I, Britain occupied German East Africa, renaming it Tanganyika in 1920, and in 1922 the League of Nations consigned Tanganyika to the British Empire.

16. Before abolition, in 1890, the British administration (in the Sultan's name) passed a decree prohibiting the sale of slaves on Zanzibar, allowed slaves to buy their freedom, and permitted only the children of a deceased slave-owner to inherit the slaves (Cooper 1980: 47). For more on the chronology of the legal status of slaves and on the role of missionaries in Zanzibar, see Nwulia (1975).

17. Between 1897 and 1907, almost twelve thousand slaves were freed (Cooper 1997: 73).

18. Within several years, however, many former slaves also moved to Stone Town, where wages were, at first, higher, but where urban employment soon also became scarce.

19. 1914 also marked the year in which Zanzibar affairs were transferred from the Foreign Office to the Colonial Office and when the position of the consul general was replaced by a British resident. The governor of Kenya Colony and Protectorate became the high commissioner to Zanzibar (Lofchie 1965: 58).

20. The first council included: eleven British officials, three Arabs, two Asians, and one European. The British were the "official" members while the others were "unofficial," a distinction which made a difference for voting on policy.

21. For further discussion of clove and coconut production and prices, see Cooper (1997) and Ferguson (1991).

22. For more on the measures taken by the British in maintaining the Omani-Arab status, see Lofchie (1965).

23. The Protectorate was interested in maintaining the solubility of the clove plantations in order to ensure stability on the island. But the Zanzibar custom house was also benefiting from a 25% export tax on cloves. In 1928 the tax was reduced to 20% (Cooper 1997: 137).

24. Alliances between the Imamate rebellion and Omani opposition groups to the Sultanate in Muscat in Zanzibar were not uncommon. Other rebellions against the Sultanate, for example the 1905 brief capture of Muscat, were supported by families in Zanzibar.

25. Blockades of the Imamate territory and travel restrictions did not keep people from migrating later to the newly wealthy oil-states in the Gulf either.

26. According to Cooper (1980), between 1924 and 1931, for example, "Swahili" had assumed a derogatory connotation; and as former slaves gained access to property and established roots in Zanzibar, the percentage of people calling themselves Swahili declined 86% while the numbers of people calling themselves Hadimu increased 69%. And, according to Lofchie (1965), in the 1958 census on Zanzibar, people were asked to indicate their "race" and "nationality, tribe or ancestry." The Zanzibar Nationalist Party, a party mostly of "Arabs," however, instructed its members to classify themselves as Zanzibari and their place of origin as Zanzibar. In the end, the 1958 census divided people into: Afro-Arab, Asian other than Arab, Europeans, and Somali and

other. More than 93% of the population fell into the Afro-Arab group. Sheriff (Sheriff and Ferguson 1991) argues instead that the call for Zanzibari nationalism, rejecting ethnic representation, came from the Shirazi Association ("native" Zanzibaris who claim descent from Shiraz, Iran) and that this was not a clever maneuver by the ZNP. It indicates, for Sheriff, that many of these nationalists viewed the racialized / ethnicized categories of the census and the state as outdated.

27. According to Lofchie, the fighting in 1928 began when someone from the older "Omani" community did not invite someone or some families from the newer Manga community to a wedding. Similarly, the 1936 riot, according to Lofchie, was touched off by Manga Arabs angered by a new policy that they believed was meant to force them out of the coconut industry (1965: 205 n.). While the 1936 riots are well documented in the Zanzibar National Archives, the 1928 fighting over the wedding that Lofchie describes is not.

28. For more on the history of the Shirazi community in East Africa, see, for example, Chittick (1965).

29. At first, the legislature was to be comprised of six constituencies on Pemba and Zanzibar. Elections for the legislature were set for 1957. During the campaign, claiming that the ZNP was simply an "Arab" party after all, an Afro-Shirazi Party (ASP) was established. In 1957 the ASP won everywhere on Zanzibar island except in Stone Town, the main city on the island, where an Asian party won. The ASP also broke into the monopoly of the Zanzibar and Pemba People's Party (ZPPP), a party from Pemba with a reputation for being less adamant about independence. In 1960, the colonial government changed the legislature again and increased the number of members to twenty-two. The 1961 elections, however, divided the legislature into two blocks of eleven seats: ZNP won nine, ASP won ten, and the ZPPP won three. The ZPPP then divided its own votes to give two to the ZNP and one to ASP so that each had eleven seats. The decision to hold a revote, this time with an extra Pemba seat for a total of twenty-three legislative seats, led to a violent and bitter election campaign. In the end, the ZNP, which won ten seats, and the ZPPP, which won three seats, united against the ASP, which had retained ten seats. The ASP refused to enter government and called for elections again in 1963. Soon the ZNP itself divided, with one group establishing the "Umma" Nasserist party. Although 1963 was meant to establish a legislature that would mark the end of the Protectorate, the 1963 elections witnessed the success of the ZNP-ZPPP alliance again and, not surprisingly, many ASP supporters claimed that independence from Britain was for Arabs only (Campbell 1962; Lofchie 1965).

30. This distinction has been maintained through language use. For example, although the children of this Zanzibari intelligentsia have attended national schools that are taught entirely in Arabic, many of these families continue to speak Swahili at home.

31. Ingrams (1967 [1931]) pointed to a question that professional anthropologists themselves began to consider decades later. Marriage itself, as many anthropologists have argued, can hardly be assumed to be the only form of union by which offspring are accepted as legitimate and for whom inheritance is sanctioned. In writing about language, Bakhtin argued that hybrid utterances could both fuse "two speech manners, two styles, two 'languages'" (as in creolization and métissage) as well as be the intersecting of "two contradictory meanings, two accents" whereby one could unmask the other (1981: 304–305). Robert Young (1995) provides an analysis of concepts of race and practices of hybridity in England. For an overview of different phases in racial theories, see Banton (1987).

32. Concerns about the legal status of "mixed" offspring also occupied the Dutch and French in the East Indies. See, for example, Stoler (1992).

33. Zanzibari historiography seems to be divided on the issue of the extent to which the 1964 Zanzibari revolution and antagonisms on Zanzibar were based on race or class. It seems to me that, given Zanzibari history and its racialized politics of classed distinctions (or the other way around), it would be impossible to argue that one factor rather than another led to the revolution of 1964.

34. Ho has illustrated how jurisprudential laws of "sufficiency" (*kafā'a*) (and thus patrilineal genealogy) in Southeast Asia subsumed debates about race: "while explicitly based on a genealogical rather than racial concept, it was inevitable that the idea would be seen as a mirror, within the subject Muslim population, of race hierarchies which organized life under European rule" (2006: 176). I would argue that while concepts of sufficiency and genealogy could and often did collude with the racial hierarchies of European rule, they also contained a contradiction. Whereas patrilineal genealogy assumes identity as derivative of a male line, racial theories—by the end of the nineteenth century—were also focused on determining what kinds of offspring the "mixing" of men *and* women would produce, and it was for this reason that colonial states became so concerned with regulating and limiting the creole population by sending increasing numbers of Dutch women to the Indies (J. G. Taylor 1983). It was the influence of the women that became so important for the colonial state, and it was their activities that, eventually, stood as the ground on which such tensions were played out. It is difficult to know whether there was a parallel concern in Oman over "mixing" in Zanzibar. Nevertheless, increasing numbers of women from Oman did travel to Zanzibar at the beginning of the twentieth century as part of the third wave of migration.

35. Patrilineal genealogy is an ideological construct that not only occludes women, but also that, in practice, people deploy for a variety of reasons and within particular contexts. For other accounts of genealogy as an ideological construct, see Shryock (1997).

36. Understanding the complexity and importance of the history of Zanzibar and East Africa for Omani identities is not only a matter of mapping out the relationship

between the concept of patrilineal genealogical and British colonial notions of race and nation. For example, although the colonial experience in Zanzibar certainly produced shifting knowledges and assumptions about race in the Indian Ocean lands, the history of the concept of *jins* belies a simplistic reading of the colonial restructuring of identity categories. The term *jins*—a word that suggests "type" and refers both to race and sex—has its own trajectory in Arabic. According to Edward Lane (1984 [1863–1893]), *jins*, as "genus," first referred to a generic class or kind such as in the distinction between animals and plants, while *nuw'* referred to the more specific categories such as, within the category of "animal," man, cats, or birds. Scholastic theologians reversed this, so that *jins* became more particular than *nuw'*. Eventually, *jins*, as it is used in the introduction to al-Mughayri and in contemporary Oman, refers to particular types of people—of sexes and races.

37. While histories like al-Mughayri's, and a number of bookstores in Muscat that cater to Swahili speakers, illustrate that the Omani state is not attempting to erase this history (since in many ways it is interpreted as a proud history of Omani maritime strength), the Zanzibari element of Oman's cultural makeup was also, for example, not considered in the 1993 national census, a census that detailed, instead, the numbers of cars and televisions people had.

38. While "sufficiency in marriage" is not as vigorously debated or divisive in contemporary Oman as it was in the turn-of-the-century Dutch East Indies (as described by Ho [2006]), debates nonetheless surface from time to time.

39. The *Jawhar al-Niẓām*, a two-volume compendium of Ibadi laws written in rhymed prose, is the most referenced book in contemporary Oman for matters of religious regulation. In Oman, if Ibadis (and Sunnis, in fact) were to have one book in addition to the Qur'an at home, it would usually be the *Jawhar al-Niẓām*.

40. Pandolfo points to the dialectical relationship between "the *ḥasab* and the *nasab*" (1997: 104–131). Pandolfo's account of the relationship between *ḥasab* and *nasab* points to a partial inversion of understandings of the relationship in other contexts, however. In Oman, for example, someone's *ḥasab* would refer not so much to their naturalized tie to patrilineal genealogies, as Pandolfo describes, but to their acquired position through marriage or their own "work" effort. By the same token, someone's *nasab* would refer not to synchronic acquired relationships, but to their "natural" patrilineal genealogies.

41. The national Omani Mufti issues hundreds of *fatwas* annually; most of these are responses to questions about marriage, prayer, food, and forms of entertainment. He is rigid about maintaining that it is forbidden for women to marry men of lower status, and this includes servant families who might be quite wealthy.

42. As mentioned earlier, the bombing of the Bahla fort in 1957 was part of a campaign by Sultan Sa'id bin Taymur and supported by the British military to oust the Imamate government of Imam Ghalib bin Ali.

43. It was not clear exactly when they left Zanzibar, whether it was in 1964 or later.

44. I have understood this to mean that the head of the neighborhood was not an Omani.

45. Association houses were established by the British protectorate administration along racialized lines.

46. For a similar emphasis on genealogy in the autobiography of a twentieth-century Omani scholar (Shaykh Ibrahim Sa'id al-'Abri), see D. Eickelman (1991).

47. For ethnographic work on the figure of the father in another Middle Eastern context, see Pandolfo (1997), and for a discussion of the place of the "father" as the source of poetic models, see Lucine Taminian's (2001) doctoral dissertation "Playing with Words: The Ethnography of Poetic Genres in Yemen."

48. Despite the historicized centrality of maintaining Arabness through the male lines in Zanzibar at other moments, during the 1958 census most people on Zanzibar wanted to be considered Zanzibari, not Arab or African, not Omani, Tanganikan, or Kenyan. This claim to be Zanzibari and not Arab or African is not surprising given the context of the 1950s in Oman.

49. This rejection by her Sudani family belies assumptions that political and economic status are the principal drives for marriage and that "native" populations necessarily look to the power of elite immigrants and colonial populations as their goals for marriage.

Chapter Seven

Material in this chapter reprinted by permission from *Timely Assests: The Politics of Resources and Their Temporalities*, edited by Elizabeth Emma Ferry and Mandana E. Limbert. Copyright ©2008 by the School for Advanced Research, Santa Fe, New Mexico.

1. There is often a false dichotomy drawn in Islamic studies between a presumed ascetic approach to Islam and a more mystical one. This dichotomy stems from oversimplified distinctions between Sunni (and especially Hanbali) perspectives and Shi'ite views about the relationship between humans and knowledge. Given that many of its great scholars encourage personal and social asceticism as well as engage (and produce) more mystical writings, Ibadism confounds such assumptions.

2. For fascinating work on dream interpretation in Muslim contexts, see Mittermaier (2007) and Lamoreaux (2002).

3. Even an article in the free daily *7Days* (a daily that has become immensely popular in Dubai as an alternative to the more official *Gulf News* and *Khaleej Times*) mentions Oman's diminishing supplies. The article describes the motivation behind plans for a $15 billion tourist resort city in Oman called "The Blue City" as follows: "Worried that oil reserves may one day fail to support its economy and a growing population." It adds, "Until recently, Oman has avoided Dubai's mass tourism pitch, targeting instead

middle- and high-class tourists to try to better stimulate the economy and not offend local sensitivities. But Oman's oil reserves are gradually being depleted, and now the country has little choice but to encourage other forms of revenue." *7Days*, June 9, 2005.

4. Proven reserves, according to these government sources, were 5.5 billion barrels in 2001 and 5.7 billion in 2002. At these estimates, there would be 15.8 years of oil remaining from 2001 and 17.4 from 2002. *Oman National News Agency* (ONA), April 26, 2003 and September 4, 2003.

5. Petroleum Development Oman owns 90% of Oman's oil reserves. The Omani government owns 60% of PDO, while Shell, Total, and Partex Oman own 34%, 4%, and 2%, respectively. Part of the discrepancy in reporting can be explained by the fact that sometimes the numbers refer to PDO's production levels and sometimes the numbers refer to national production levels, including fields operated by Occidental.

6. The discrepancy here may be accounted for by the fact that other oil production firms were also operating, albeit at smaller amounts.

7. Proven reserves is different from percentage recoverable. Throughout the 2000s, percentage recoverable of the proven reserves, according to PDO, hovered around 25%.

8. For Annual Reports from 2000 to 2007, see *http://www.pdo.co.om/pdoweb/tabid/161/Default.aspx*. Last accessed on December 5, 2008. Annual Reports from 1970 to 2000 were available through the PDO website in 2003, but are no longer available there. Hard copies of the annual reports through 2000, however, are still available.

9. Shell to Lose 10% of Oman Oilfield Acreage as Production Falls. *http://www.bloomberg.com/apps/news*.

10. This remark was not made to me directly but reported to me by the American historian who had introduced us. I believe it to be fully accurate and consistent with Mr. Sultan's other oft-stated views.

11. *Sunday Times*, September 17, 1995.

12. For an analysis of the constitution, or "Basic Law," see Siegfried (2000).

Bibliography

Abu 'Ezzah, Abdullah. 1995. Imam Umar b. al-Khattab of Oman and Banu Gabr of al-Hasa. *Proceedings of the Seminar for Arabian Studies* 25:1–13.

Abu-Lughod, Janet. 1987. Islamic City—Historic Myth, Islamic Essence, and Contemporary Relevance. *International Journal of Middle East Studies* 19(2): 155–176.

Abu-Lughod, Lila. 1998. Feminist Longings and Postcolonial Conditions. In *Remaking Women: Feminism and Modernity in the Middle East*, edited by L. Abu-Lughod. Princeton: Princeton University Press.

Ahmed, Leila. 1992. *Women and Gender in Islam*. New Haven: Yale University Press.

Alexander's Gas & Oil Connections. 2005. Oman Renews Oil Concession Pacts with Shell, Total and Partex. *Alexander's Gas & Oil Connections* 10(1). *http://www.gasand oil.com/goc/company/cnm50377.htm*.

Amanat, Abbas. 1988. In Between the Madrasa and the Marketplace: The Designation of Clerical Leadership in Modern Shi'ism. In *Authority and Political Cultural in Shi'ism*, edited by S. A. Arjomand. Albany: State University of New York Press.

Amuzegar, Jahangir. 1982. Oil Wealth: A Very Mixed Blessing. *Foreign Affairs* 60(4): 814–836.

Anderson, Benedict. 1990. A Time of Darkness and a Time of Light: Transposition in Early Indonesian Nationalist Thought. In *Language and Power: Exploring Political Cultures in Indonesia*. Ithaca: Cornell University Press.

Anderson, Benedict. 2003. *www.uvic.ca/~anp/Public.posish_pap.html*. Untitled Position Paper for Asian Nationalisms Project, The University of Victoria.

al-'Ansi, Saud bin Salim. 1991. *al-'Ādat al-'Umānīyya*. Muscat: Ministry of National Heritage and Culture.

Appadurai, Arjun. 1986. Introduction: Commodities and the Politics of Value. In *The Social Life of Things*, edited by A. Appadurai. Cambridge: Cambridge University Press.

Appadurai, Arjun. 1996. *Modernity at Large: Cultural Dimensions of Globalization*. Minneapolis: University of Minnesota Press.

Arebi, Saddeka. 1994. *Women and Words in Saudi Arabia: The Politics of Literary Discourse*. New York: Columbia University Press.

Asad, Talal. 1986. *The Idea of an Anthropology of Islam*. Occasional Papers. Center for Contemporary Arab Studies. Washington, DC: Georgetown University.

Asad, Talal. 1993. *Genealogies of Religion: Discipline and Reasons of Power in Christianity and Islam*. Baltimore: Johns Hopkins University Press.

Ashur, Sa'id Abdulfatah, and Aud Muhammad Khalifat. 1993. *'Umān wa al-Ḥaḍārat al-Islāmiyya*. Muscat: Sultan Qaboos University.

Attia, Habib. 1985. Water-Sharing Rights in the Jerid Oases of Tunisia. In *Property, Social Structure and Law in the Modern Middle East*, edited by A. E. Mayer. Albany: State University of New York Press.

Austen, R. A. 1988. The Nineteenth Century Islamic Slave Trade from East Africa (Swahili and Red Sea Coasts): A Tentative Census. *Slavery and Abolition* 9(3): 21–44.

al-Awtabi, Salma bin Muslim. n.d. *Kitāb al-Ḍiyā'*. Muscat: Ministry of National Heritage and Culture.

Badran, Margot. 1995. *Feminists, Islam and Nation: Gender and the Making of Modern Egypt*. Princeton: Princeton University Press.

Bailey, Ronald W., ed. 1988. *Records of Oman, 1867–1947*. 7 vols. Farnham Common: Archive Editions.

Bakhtin, Mikhail M. 1981. *The Dialogic Imagination*. Translated by Michael Holquist. Austin: University of Texas Press.

Baldisira, Eros. 1994. *Qasr Jabrīn wa Kitābātuhu*. Muscat: Ministry of National Heritage and Culture.

Banton, Michael. 1987. *Racial Theories*. Cambridge: Cambridge University Press.

Barbier de Meynard, Charles. 1900–1901. Des Droits et Obligations entre Proprietaires: D'Heritages Voisins. *Revue Algerienne et Tunisienne de Legislation et de Jurisprudence* 16:9–144; 17:65–84, 89–108.

al-Barradi, Abu al-Qasim. 1885. *Kitāb al-Jawāhir*. Cairo: Baruni Press.

Barth, Fredrik. 1978. Factors of Production, Economic Circulation and Inequality in Inner Arabia. *Research in Economic Anthropology* 1:53–72.

Bathurst, R. D. 1967. *The Ya'rubi Dynasty of Oman*. D. Phil., University of Oxford.

Baudrillard, Jean. 1994. *The Illusion of the End*. Palo Alto: Stanford University Press.

Bayly, C. A. 1986. The Origins of Swadeshi (Home Industry): Cloth and Indian Society, 1700–1930. In *The Social Life of Things: Commodities in Cultural Perspective*, edited by A. Appadurai. Cambridge: Cambridge University Press.

Beckingham, C. F. 1983. Some Notes on the Portuguese in Oman. *Journal of Oman Studies* 6:13–20.

Beinin, Joel, and Joe Stork, eds. 1997. *Political Islam*. Berkeley: University of California Press.

Benhabib, Seyla. 1992. *Situating the Self: Gender, Community and Postmodernism in Contemporary Ethics*. New York: Routledge.

Benjamin, Walter. 1969. *Illuminations*. New York: Schocken Books.

Benjamin, Walter. 1983. *Charles Baudelaire*. London: Verso.

Benjamin, Walter. 1986. *Reflections*. New York: Schocken Books.

Berlant, Lauren. 1996. The Face of America and the State of Emergency. In *Disciplinarity and Dissent in Cultural Studies*, edited by C. Nelson and D. Parameshwar Gaonkar. New York: Routledge.

Berque, Jacque. 1958. Medinas, Villesneuves et Bidonvilles. *Les Cahiers de Tunisie* 6:5–42.

Bhacker, M. Reda. 1992. *Trade and Empire in Muscat and Zanzibar: Roots of British Domination*. London: Routledge.

al-Bimani, Ahmed bin Nassir. 1990. *Sirat Abi Zayd: al-Sheikh al-'Ulama*. Bahla.

Birenbaum-Carmeli, Daphna. 1999. Love Thy Neighbor: Sociability and Instrumentality among Israeli Neighbors. *Human Organization* 58(1): 82–93.

al-Bisyawi, Abu al-Hasan. n.d. *Mukhtaṣar al-Bisyawi*. Muscat: Ministry of National Heritage and Culture.

Bourdieu, Pierre. 1977. *Outline of a Theory of Practice*. Cambridge: Cambridge University Press.

Boyarin, Jonathan. 1994. Space, Time and the Politics of Memory. In *Remapping Memory: The Politics of Timespace*, edited by J. Boyarin. Minneapolis: University of Minnesota Press.

Brenner, Suzanne April. 1998. *The Domestication of Desire: Women, Wealth and Modernity in Java*. Princeton: Princeton University Press.

Brunschvig, Robert. 1947. Urbanisme Medieval et Droit Musulman. *Revue des Etudes Islamiques* 15:127–155.

Buck-Morss, Susan. 1989. *The Dialectics of Seeing: Walter Benjamin and the Arcades Project*. Cambridge: MIT Press.

Buck-Morss, Susan. 2000. *Dreamworld and Catastrophe: The Passing of Mass Utopia in East and West*. Cambridge: MIT Press.

Busch, Briton Cooper. 1968. *Britain and the Persian Gulf, 1894–1914*. Berkeley: University of California Press.

Calder, Norman. 1993. *Studies in Early Muslim Jurisprudence*. Oxford: Oxford University Press.

Campbell, Jane. 1962. Multiracialism and Politics in Zanzibar. *Political Science Quarterly*, 77(1): 72–87.

Caponera, Dante Augusto. 1978. *Water Laws in Moslem Countries*. Rome: Food and Agricultural Organization of the United Nations.

Chakrabarty, Dipesh. 1997 [1994]. The Difference-Deferral of a Colonial Modernity: Public Debates on Domesticity in British Bengal. In *Tensions of Empire: Colonial Cultures in a Bourgeois World*, edited by F. Cooper and Ann L. Stoler. Berkeley: University of California Press.

Chakrabarty, Dipesh. 2000. *Adda*: A History of Sociality. In *Provincializing Europe: Postcolonial Thought and Historical Difference*. Princeton: Princeton University Press.

Chatterjee, Indrani. 1999. *Gender, Slavery and Law in Colonial India*. New Delhi: Oxford University Press.

Chatterjee, Partha. 1989. Colonialism, Nationalism, and Colonized Women: The Contest in India. *American Ethnologist* 16(4): 622–633.

Chatty, Dawn. 1996. *Mobile Pastoralists: Development Planning and Change among the Harasiis Tribe in Oman*. New York: Columbia University Press.

Chittick, H. N., and R. I. Rotberg, eds. 1975. *East Africa and the Orient: Cultural Synthesis in Pre-Colonial Times*. New York: Africana Publishing.

Chittick, Neville. 1965. The "Shirazi" Colonization of East Africa. *The Journal of African History* 6(3): 275–294.

Clayton, Anthony. 1981. *The Zanzibar Revolution and its Aftermath*. Hamden, CT: Archon Books.

Cohn, Bernard S. 1967. Regions Subjective and Objective: Their Relation to the Study of Modern Indian History and Society. In *Regions and Regionalism in South Asian Studies: An Exploratory Study*, edited by Robert I. Crane. Durham: Duke University Program in Comparative Studies on Southern Asia, Monograph and Occasional Papers Series. Monograph Number 5.

Cohn, Bernard S. 1987. The Census, Social Structure and Objectification in South Asia. In *An Anthropologist among the Historians and Other Essays*, edited by B. S. Cohn. New Delhi: Oxford University Press.

Cooper, Frederick. 1980. *From Slaves to Squatters*. New Haven: Yale University Press.

Cooper, Frederick. 1994. Conflict and Connection: Rethinking Colonial African History. *American Historical Review* 99(5): 1516–1545.

Cooper, Frederick. 1997. *Plantation Slavery on the East Coast of Africa*. Portsmouth, NH: Heinemann.

Corbin, Henry. 1983. *Cyclical Time and Ismaili Gnosis*. London: Keegan Paul International.

Coronil, Fernando. 1997. *The Magical State: Nature, Money and Modernity in Venezeula*. Chicago: University of Chicago Press.

Coronil, Fernando. 2001. Smelling Like a Market. *American Historical Review* 106(1): 119–129.

Coulson, N. J. 1964. *A History of Islamic Law*. Edinburgh: Edinburgh University Press.

Coupland, Reginald. 1939. *The Exploitation of East Africa, 1856–1928*. London: Faber and Faber.

Crapanzano, Vincent. 2003. Reflections on Hope as a Category of Social and Psychological Analysis. *Cultural Anthropology* 18(1): 3–32.

Crone, Patricia, and Fritz Zimmerman. 2001. *The Epistle of Sālim ibn Dhakwān*. Oxford: Oxford University Press.

Crystal, Jill. 1990. *Oil and Politics in the Gulf: Rulers and Merchants in Kuwait and Qatar*. Cambridge: Cambridge University Press.

Cuperly, Pierre. 1972. Muhammad Atfayyas et sa Risala fi baʿd tawarih ahl wadi Mizab. *Institut des Belles Lettres Arabes* 130:261–303.

Curzon, George N. 1966 [1892]. *Persia and the Persian Question*. London: Frank Cass.

Daniel, E. Valentine. 1984. *Fluid Signs: Being a Person the Tamil Way*. Berkeley: University of California Press.

al-Darjini, Abu al-Abbas Ahmad bin Saʿid. n.d. *Kitāb Ṭabaqāt al-Mashāyikh*. Edited by I. Tallay. Constantine.

Davidson, Cathy N. 1998. Preface: No More Private Spheres! *American Literature* 70(3): 443–463.

Davin, Anna. 1978. Imperialism and Motherhood. *History Workshop* 5:9–65.

de Certeau, Michel. 1984. *The Practice of Everyday Life*. Berkeley: University of California Press.

Deeb, Lara. 2006. *An Enchanted Modern: Gender and Public Piety in Shi'I Lebanon*. Princeton: Princeton University Press.

al-Dhahab, Mohammed Hafied. 1987. The Historical Development of Education in Oman: From the First Modern School in 1893 to the First Modern University in 1986. PhD, Boston College, Boston.

Dirks, Nicholas B. 2001. *Castes of Mind*. Princeton: Princeton University Press.

Eickelman, Christine. 1984. *Women and Community in Oman*. New York: New York University Press.

Eickelman, Dale. 1978. The Art of Memory: Islamic Education and Its Social Reproduction. *Comparative Studies in Society and History* 20(4): 485–516.

Eickelman, Dale. 1983. Omani Village: The Meaning of Oil. *The Politics of Middle Eastern Oil*, edited by J. E. Peterson. Washington, DC: Middle East Institute.

Eickelman, Dale. 1985. *Knowledge and Power in Morocco*. Princeton: Princeton University Press.

Eickelman, Dale. 1989. National Identity and Religious Discourse in Contemporary Oman. *International Journal of Islamic and Arabic Studies* 6(1): 1–20.

Eickelman, Dale. 1991. Traditional Islamic Learning and Ideas of the Person in the Twentieth Century. In *Middle Eastern Lives: The Practice of Biography and Self-Narrative*, edited by Martin Kramer. Syracuse, NY: Syracuse University Press.

Eickelman, Dale. 1992. Mass Higher Education and the Religious Imagination in Contemporary Arab Societies. *American Ethnologist* 19:643–654.

Eiss, Paul. 2002. Redeption's Archive: Remembering the Future in a Revolutionary Past. *Comparative Studies in Society and History* 44(1): 106–136.

Ennami, Amr K. 1972. *Studies in Ibadism (al-Ibadiyah)*. Tripoli: University of Libya Press.

Escobar, Arturo. 1995. *Encountering Development: The Making and Unmaking of the Third World*. Princeton: Princeton University Press.

Fahy, Michael A. 1998. Marginalized Modernity: An Ethnographic Approach to Higher Education and Social Identity at a Moroccan University. PhD, University of Michigan, Ann Arbor.

Feld, Steven, and Keith H. Basso, eds. 1997. *Senses of Place*. Santa Fe: School of American Research Press.

Feldman, Allen. 1994. From Desert Storm to Rodney King via ex-Yugoslavia: On Cultural Anaesthesia. In *The Senses Still: Perception and Memory as Material Culture in Modernity*, edited by C. N. Seremetakis. Chicago: University of Chicago Press.

Ferguson, Ed. 1991. The Formation of a Colonial Economy, 1915–1945. In *Zanzibar under Colonial Rule*, edited by A. Sheriff and E. Ferguson. London: J. Currey.

Ferguson, James. 1990. *The Anti-Politics Machine: "Development," Depoliticization, and Bureaucratic Power in Lesotho*. Minneapolis: University of Minnesota Press.

Ferguson, James. 1999. *Expectations of Modernity: Myths and Meanings of Urban Life on the Zambian Copperbelt*. Berkeley: University of California Press.

Fischer, Michael. 1980. *Iran: From Religious Dispute to Revolution*. Cambridge: Harvard University Press.

Fischer, Michael, and Mehdi Abedi. 1990. *Debating Muslims*. Madison: University of Wisconsin Press.

Foucault, Michel. 1977. *Discipline and Punish: The Birth of the Prison*. Translated by Alan Sheridan. New York: Pantheon.

Foucault, Michel. 1978. *The History of Sexuality*. New York: Pantheon.

Frank, R. M. 1971. Several Fundamental Assumptions of the Basra School of the Mu'tazila. *Studia Islamica* 33:5–18.

Freeman-Grenville, G. S. P. 1962. *The East African Coast: Select Documents*. Oxford: Clarendon Press.

Galdieri, Eugenio. 1975. A Masterpiece of Omani 17th Century Architecture. *Journal of Oman Studies* 1:167–179.

Gaonkar, Dilip P., ed. 2001. *Alternative Modernities*. Durham: Duke University Press.

Geertz, Clifford. 1968. *Islam Observed: Religious Development in Morocco and Indonesia*. Chicago: University of Chicago Press.

Geertz, Clifford. 1972. The Wet and the Dry: Traditional Irrigation in Bali and Morocco. *Human Ecology* 1(1): 23–39.

Geertz, Clifford. 1973. *The Interpretation of Cultures*. New York: Basic Books.

Geertz, Hildred. 1979. The Meaning of Family Ties. In *Meaning and Order in Moroccan*

Society, edited by C. Geertz, H. Geertz, and L. Rosen. Cambridge: Cambridge University Press.

Ghassany, Harith. 1995. Kitman and Renaissance: Domination and the Limits of Development. PhD, Harvard University, Cambridge.

Ginsberg, Yona, and Arza Churchman. 1985. The Pattern and Meaning of Neighbor Relations in High-Rise Housing in Israel. *Human Ecology* 13(4): 467–484.

Glassman, Jonathon. 2000. Sorting out the Tribes: The Creation of Racial Identities in Colonial Zanzibar's Newspaper Wars. *Journal of African History* 41:395–428.

Gole, Nilufer. 1996. *The Forbidden Modern: Civilization and Veiling*. Ann Arbor: The University of Michigan Press.

Gray, John M. 1977. The Hadimu and Tumbatu of Zanzibar. *Tanzania Notes and Records* 81 and 82:135–153.

Grossman, Claude. 1976. Apercu sur l'Histoire Religieuse du Mzab en Algerie. 3eme Cycle, Université Paris Sorbonne—Paris IV, Paris.

Gupta, Akhil. 1998. *Postcolonial Developments*. Durham: Duke University Press.

Guyer, Jane I. 2007. Prophecy and the Near Future: Thoughts on Macroeconomic, Evangelical, and Punctuated Time. *American Ethnologist* 34(3): 409–421.

Habermas, Jürgen. 1991. *The Structural Transformation of the Public Sphere: An Inquiry into a Category of Bourgeois Society*. Cambridge: MIT Press.

Hacking, Ian. 1990. *The Taming of Chance*. Cambridge: Cambridge University Press.

Haddad, Yvonne Y., and John L. Esposito, eds. 1998. *Islam, Gender and Social Change*. Oxford: Oxford University Press.

Hagen, James. 1999. The Good Behind the Gift: Morality and Exchange among the Manco of Eastern Indonesia. *Journal of the Royal Anthropology Institute* 5:361–376.

Hakim, Bessim Selim. 1986. *Arabic-Islamic Cities: Building and Planning Principles*. New York: Routledge.

Hallaq, Wael B. 1997. *A History of Islamic Legal Theories*. Cambridge: Cambridge University Press.

Hallaq, Wael B. 2005. *The Origins and Evolution of Islamic Law*. Cambridge: Cambridge University Press.

Halliday, Fred. 1974. *Arabia without Sultans*. New York: Penguin

Hammoudi, Abdellah. 1985. Substance and Relation: Water Rights and Water Distribution in the Dra Valley. In *Property, Social Structure and Law in the Modern Middle East*, edited by A. E. Mayer. Albany: State University of New York Press.

Hansen, Thomas Blom, and Finn Stepputat, eds. 2001. *States of Imagination: Ethnographic Explorations of the Postcolonial State*. Durham: Duke University Press.

Harding, Susan, and Kathleen Stewart. 1999. Bad Endings: American Apocalypsis. *Annual Review of Anthropology* 28:285–310.

Hattox, Ralph S. 1985. *Coffee and Coffeehouses: The Origins of a Social Beverage in the Medieval Near East*. Seattle: University of Washington Press.

Heard-Bey, Frauke. 2004. *From Trucial States to United Arab Emirates: A Society in Transition*. Dubai: Motivate Publishing.

Herzfeld, Michael. 1991. *A Place in History: Social and Monumental Time in a Cretan Town*. Princeton: Princeton University Press.

Hirschkind, Charles. 2006. *The Ethical Soundscape: Cassette Sermons and Islamic Counterpublics*. New York: Columbia University Press.

Ho, Engseng. 2006. *The Graves of Tarim: Genealogy and Mobility Across the Indian Ocean*. Berkeley: University of California Press.

Hobsbawm, Eric, and Terence Ranger, eds. *The Invention of Tradition*. Cambridge: Cambridge University Press.

Hoffman, Valerie J. 2004. The Articulation of Ibādī Identity in Modern Oman and Zanzibar. *The Muslim World* 94(2): 201–216.

Hoodfar, Homa. 1997. *Between Marriage and the Market: Intimate Politics and Survival in Cairo*. Berkeley: University of California Press.

Hourani, George. 1951. *Arab Seafaring in the Indian Ocean in Ancient and Medieval Times*. Princeton: Princeton University Press.

Houtsonen, Jarmo. 1994. Traditional Quranic Education in a Southern Moroccan Village. *International Journal of Middle Eastern Studies* 26:489–500.

Hugh-Jones, Stephen. 1992. Yesterday's Luxuries, Tomorrow's Necessities: Business and Barter in Northwest Amazonia. In *Barter, Exchange and Value: An Anthropological Perspective*, edited by C. Humphrey and S. Hugh-Jones. Cambridge: Cambridge University Press.

Hughes, Francis. 1987. Oil in Oman: A Short Historical Note. In *Oman: Economic, Social and Strategic Developments*, edited by B. R. Pridham. London: Croom Helm.

Hunt, Robert C., and Eva Hunt. 1976. Canal Irrigation and Local Social Organization. *Current Anthropology* 17(3): 389–341.

Ibrahim, Abi al-Yaqzan al-Hajj. 1956. *Sulaimān al-Bārūni Bāshā*. Vol. 2. Algiers: Arabic Publishers.

Imbert, Alfred. 1903. *Le Droit Abadhite chez les Musulmans de Zanzibar et de l'Afrique Orientale*. Algiers: Typographie Adolphe Jourdan.

Ingrams, W. H. 1967 [1931]. *Zanzibar: Its History and Its People*. London: Frank Cass.

International Monetary Fund. 2000a. *Letters of Intent*. Washington, DC.

International Monetary Fund. 2000b. *Memoranda of Economic and Financial Policies*. Washington, DC.

Irvine, Judith. 1989. When Talk Isn't Cheap: Language and Political Economy. *American Ethnologist* 81:248–267.

Ivy, Marilyn. 1995. *Discourses of the Vanishing: Modernity, Phantasm, Japan*. Chicago: University of Chicago Press.

Jakobson, Roman. 1990. *On Language*. Cambridge: Harvard University Press.

Jameson, Fredric. 1984. Postmodernism, or the Cultural Logic of Late Capitalism. *New Left Review* 146:53–92.

Janzen, Jorg. 1986. *Nomads in the Sultanate of Oman*. Boulder: Westview Press.

Joseph, Suad. 1983. Working Class Women's Networks in a Sectarian State: A Political Paradox. *American Ethnologist* 10(1): 1–22.

Kamalkhani, Zahra. 1998. Reconstruction of Islamic Knowledge and Knowing: A Case of Islamic Practices among Women in Iran. In *Women and Islamization: Contemporary Dimensions of Discourse on Gender Relations*, edited by K. Ask and M. Tjomsland. Oxford: Berg.

Kandiyoti, Deniz, ed. 1991. *Women, Islam and the State*. London: Macmillan.

Kandiyoti, Deniz. 1998. Rural Livelihoods and Social Networks in Uzbekistan: Perspectives from Andijan. *Central Asian Survey* 17(4): 561–578.

Keane, Webb. 1997. *Signs of Recognition: Powers and Hazards of Representation in an Indonesian Society*. Berkeley: University of California Press.

Kelly, J. B. 1964. *Eastern Arabian Frontiers*. New York: Praeger.

Kelly, J. B. 1968. *Britain and the Persian Gulf, 1795–1880*. Oxford: Clarendon Press.

Kerber, Linda K. 1988. Separate Spheres, Female Worlds, Woman's Place: The Rhetoric of Women's History. *Journal of American History* 75(1): 9–39.

Kervran, Monique. 1996. *Miḥrāb*/s Omanais du 16e Siècle: Un Curieux Exemple de Conservatisms de l'Art du Stuc Iranien des Époques Seldjouqide et Mongole." *Archéologie Islamique* 6: 109–156.

al-Khalili, Ahmad. A.H. 1409. *al-Ḥaqq al-Dāmigh*. Muscat.

Khan, Naveeda. 2006. Flaws in the Flow: Roads and their Modernity in Pakistan. *Social Text 89* 24(4): 87–113.

al-Kindi, Ahmad bin Abdullah. n.d. *Kitāb al-Muṣannaf*. Muscat: Ministry of National Heritage and Culture.

al-Kindi, Muhammad bin Ibrahim. n.d. *Bayān al-Sharʿ*. Muscat: Ministry of National Heritage and Culture.

Kirkman, J. 1983. The Early History of Oman in East Africa. *Journal of Oman Studies* 61:41–59.

Kopytoff, Igor. 1986. The Cultural Biography of Things: Commoditization as Process. In *The Social Life of Things*, edited by A. Appadurai. Cambridge: Cambridge University Press.

Koselleck, Reinhart. 1985. *Futures Past: On the Semantics of Historical Time*. Cambridge: MIT Press.

Koselleck, Reinhart. 2002. *The Practice of Conceptual History: Timing History, Spacing Concept*. Palo Alto: Stanford University Press.

Lakoff, George, and Mark Johnson. 1980. *Metaphors We Live By*. Chicago: University of Chicago Press.

Lambek, Michael. 1996. The Past Imperfect: Remembering as a Moral Practice. In *Tense*

Past: Cultural essays in Trauma and Memory, edited by P. Antze and M. Lambek. London: Routledge.

Lamoreaux, John C. 2002. *The Early Muslim of Dream Interpretation*. Albany: State University of New York Press.

Landen, Robert Geran. 1967. *Oman Since 1856: Disruptive Modernization in a Traditional Arab Society*. Princeton: Princeton University Press.

Lane, Edward W. 1984 [1863–1893]. *Arabic-English Lexicon*. Cambridge: Islamic Texts Society.

Lansing, John Stephen. 1987. Balinese "Water Temples" and the Management of Irrigation. *American Anthropologist* 89(2): 326–341.

Lapidus, Ira M. 1984. Knowledge, Virtue, and Action: The Classical Muslim Conception of *Adab* and the Nature of Religious Fulfillment in Islam. In *Moral Conduct and Authority*, edited by Barbara Daly Metcalf. Berkeley: University of California Press.

Lawrence, Bruce. 1989. *Defenders of God: Fundamentalist Revolt Against the Modern Age*. San Francisco: Harper and Row.

Leaman, Oliver. 1980. 'Abd al-Jabbar and the Concept of Uselessness. *Journal of the History of Ideas* 41(1): 129–131.

Lévi-Strauss, Claude. 1969. *The Elementary Structures of Kinship*. Boston: Beacon Press.

Levinson, Stephen C. 1983. *Pragmatics*. Cambridge: Cambridge University Press.

Lewicki, Tadeusz. 1936. Notice sur la Chronique Ibadite d'ad-Dargini. *Rocznik Orjentalistyczny* 13:146–172.

Lewicki, Tadeusz. 1965. Halka. In *Encyclopedia of Islam*. Leiden: Brill.

Lewicki, Tadeusz. 1971. The Ibadites in Arabia and Africa. *Cahiers D'Histoire Mondiale* 13(1): 51–130.

Li, Tanya Murray. 2007. *The Will to Improve: Governmentality, Development, and the Practices of Politics*. Durham: Duke University Press.

Limbert, Mandana E. 2001. The Senses of Water in an Omani Town. *Social Text* 19(3): 35–55.

Limbert, Mandana E. 2005. Gender, Religious Knowledge and Education in an Omani Town. In *Monarchies and Nations: Globalization and Identity in the Arab States of the Gulf*, edited by P. Dresch and J. Piscatori. London: I. B. Taurus.

Limbert, Mandana E. 2008a. Depleted Futures: Anticipating the End of Oil in Oman. In *Timely Assets: The Politics of Resources and their Temporalities*, edited by E. Ferry and M. E. Limbert. Santa Fe: School for Advanced Research Press.

Limbert, Mandana E. 2008b. The Sacred Date: Gifts of God in an Omani Town. *Ethnos* 73(3): 361–376.

Limbert, Mandana E. 2008c. In the Ruins of Bahla: Reconstructed Forts and Crumbling Walls in an Omani Town. *Social Text 95* 26(2): 83–103.

Lofchie, Michael F. 1965. *Zanzibar: Background to Revolution*. Princeton: Princeton University Press.

Lorimer, John G. 1908–1915. *Gazetteer of the Persian Gulf, Oman and Central Arabia.* Calcutta, India: Superintendent Government Printing.

Ludden, David. 1992. India's Development Regime. In *Colonialism and Culture*, edited by Nicholas B. Dirks. Ann Arbor: University of Michigan Press.

Al-Maamiry, Ahmed Hamoud. 1989. *Oman and Ibadhism.* New Delhi: Lancers Books.

Mabry, Jonathan B. 1996. The Ethnology of Local Irrigation. In *Canals and Communities: Small-scale Irrigation Systems*, edited by J. B. Mabry. Tucson: University of Arizona Press.

Mahmood, Saba. 2001. Feminist Theory, Embodiment, and the Docile Agent: Some Reflections on the Egyptian Islamic Revival. *Cultural Anthropology* 16(2): 202–236.

Mahmood, Saba. 2005. *Politics of Piety: The Islamic Revival and the Feminist Subject.* Princeton: Princeton University Press.

Malinowski, Bronislaw. 1953. *Argonauts of the Western Pacific.* New York: E. P. Dutton.

Malti-Douglas, Fedwa. 1991. *Woman's Body, Woman's Word: Gender and Discourse in Arabo-Islamic Writing.* Princeton: Princeton University Press.

Manzo, Kate. 1991. Modernist Discourse and the Crisis of Development Theory. *Studies in Comparative International Development* 26(2): 3–36.

Marçais, W. 1928. L'Islamisme et la Vie Urbaine. *L'Academie des Inscriptions et Belles-Lettres Comptes Rendus*:86–100.

Martin, Emily. 1987. *The Woman in the Body: A Cultural Analysis of Reproduction.* Boston: Beacon Press.

Martin, Richard C., Mark R. Woodward, and Dwi S. Atmaja. 1997. *Defenders of Reason in Islam: Mu'tazilism from Medieval School to Modern Symbol.* Oxford: Oneworld Publications.

Mason, Arthur. 2007. The Rise of Consultant Forecasting in Liberalized Natural Gas Markets. *Public Culture* 19(2): 367–379.

Mauss, Marcel. 2000 [1924]. *The Gift: The Form and Reason for Exchange in Archaic Societies.* London: W.W. Norton.

al-Ma'wali, Abu Sulayman Muhammad. n.d. *Qiṣaṣ wa Akhbār.* Muscat: Ministry of National Heritage and Culture.

McCole, John. 1993. *Walter Benjamin and the Antinomies of Tradition.* Ithaca: Cornell University Press.

Meneley, Anne. 1996. *Tournaments of Value: Sociability and Hierarchy in a Yemeni Town.* Toronto: University of Toronto Press.

Mercier, Marcel. 1922. *La Civilisation Urbaine au Mzab.* Algiers: Imprimerie Administrative et Commerciale Emile Pfister.

Mercier, Marcel. 1927. *Etude sur le Waqf Abadhite et ses Applications au Mzab.* Jules Carbonel Imprimeur-editeur. Algiers: Ancienne Maison Bastide-Jourdan.

Messick, Brinkley. 1993. *The Calligraphic State: Textual Domination and History in a Muslim Society.* Berkeley: University of California Press.

Messick, Brinkley. 2001. Indexing the Self: Intent and Expression in Islamic Legal Acts. *Islamic Law and Society* 8(2): 151–178.

Metcalf, Barbara Daly, ed. 1984. *Moral Conduct and Authority: The Place of Adab in South Asian Islam*. Berkeley: University of California Press.

Middle East Economic Digest (MEED). 1960. Special report on Oman (July 20): ii–xxxi.

Middle East Economic Digest (MEED). 1973. Special Report on Oman (July 20).

Middleton, John, and Jane Campbell. 1965. *Zanzibar: Its Society and Its People*. Oxford: Oxford University Press.

Miles, Samuel B. 1910. On the Border of the Great Desert: A Journey in Oman. *Geographical Journal* 36:159–179, 405–425.

Miller, Daniel. 1994. *Modernity: An Ethnographic Approach*. Oxford: Berg.

Mintz, Sidney W. 1985. *Sweetness and Power: The Place of Sugar in Modern History*. New York: Penguin.

Mitchell, Timothy. 1988. *Colonising Egypt*. Berkeley: University of California Press.

Mitchell, Timothy, ed. 2000. *Questions of Modernity*. Minneapolis: University of Minnesota Press.

Mittermaier, Amira. 2007. The Book of Visions: Dreams, Poetry, and Prophecy in Contemporary Egypt. *International Journal of Middle East Studies* 39(2): 229–247.

Miyazaki, Hirokazu. 2003. The Temporalities of the Market. *American Anthropologist* 105(2): 255–265.

Miyazaki, Hirokazu. 2006. Economy of Dreams: Hope in Global Capitalism and Its Critiques. *Cultural Anthropology* 21(2): 147–172.

Mrázek, Rudolf. 2002. *Engineers of Happy Land: Technology and Nationalism in a Colony*. Princeton: Princeton University Press.

Mueggler, Erik. 2001. *The Age of Wild Ghosts: Memory, Violence and Place in Southwest China*. Berkeley: University of California Press.

al-Mufarji, Ali bin Nassir. 1995. *Abu Zayd al-Riyami: Humum wa Injazat*. Bahla.

al-Mughayri, Sa'id bin Ali. 1994 [1979]. *Juhaynat al-Akhbār fī Tārīkh Zinjibār*. Muscat: Ministry of National Heritage and Culture.

Muscat Trade Report for 1942–1943. 1946a. Simla: Government of India Press.

Muscat Trade Report for 1943–1944. 1946b. Simla: Government of India Press.

al-Naboodah, Hasan M. 1997. Banu Nabhan in the Omani Sources. *New Arabian Studies* 4:181–195.

Najmabadi, Afsaneh. 1998. Crafting an Educated Housewife in Iran. In *Remaking Women: Feminism and Modernity in the Middle East*, edited by L. Abu-Lughod. Princeton: Princeton University Press.

Nandy, Ashis. 1987. Reconstructing Childhood: A Critique of the Ideology of Adulthood. In *Traditions, Tyranny, and Utopias: Essays in the Politics of Awareness*. Delhi: Oxford University Press.

Nelson, Cynthia. 1974. Public and Private Politics: Women in the Middle Eastern World. *American Ethnologist* 3:551–563.

Nicholson, Linda. 1986. *Gender and History: The Limits of Social Theory in the Age of the Family*. New York: Columbia University Press.

Niebuhr, Carsten. 1792. *Travels through Arabia and Other Countries in the East*. 2 vols. Edinburgh: R. Morison and Son.

Norman, W. R., W. H. Shayya, A. S. al-Ghafri, and I. R. McCann. 1998. Aflaj Irrigation and On-Farm Water Management in Northern Oman. *Irrigation and Drainage Systems* 12:35–48.

Nwulia, Moses D. E. 1975. The Role of Missionaries in the Emancipation of Slaves in Zanzibar. *Journal of Negro History* 60(2): 268–287.

Oil and Gas Journal. 2007. Point of View: PDO Undertakes More Complex Production, Development Projects. *Oil and Gas Journal* 105(41).

Onley, James. 2008. *The Arabian Frontier of the British Raj: Merchants, Rulers, and the British in the Nineteenth-Century Gulf*. Oxford: Oxford University Press.

Ortiz, Fernando. 1995 [1947]. *Cuban Counterpoint: Tobacco and Sugar*. Durham: Duke University Press.

Pandolfo, Stefania. 1989. Detours of Life: Space and Bodies in a Moroccan Village. *American Ethnologist* 16(1): 3–23.

Pandolfo, Stefania. 1997. *Impasse of the Angels*. Chicago: University of Chicago Press.

Papailias, Penelope. 2005. *Genres of Recollection: Archival Poetics and Modern Greece*. New York: Palgrave Macmillan.

Peters, J. R. T. M. 1976. *God's Created Speech: A Study in the Speculative Theology of the Mu'taili Qadi l-Qudat Abu l-Hasan 'Abd al-Jabbar bn Ahmad al-Hamadani*. Leiden: Brill.

Peterson, John E. 1978. *Oman in the Twentieth Century*. London: Croom Helm.

Peterson, John E. 1987. Arab Nationalism and the Idealist Politician: The Career of Sulayman al-Baruni. In *Law, Personalities, and Politics of the Middle East: Essays in Honor of Majid Khadduri*, edited by J. Piscatori and George S. Harris. Boulder: Westview Press.

Peterson, John E. 2007. *Oman Insurgencies*. London: Saqi Books.

Pigg, Stacy Leigh. 1992. Inventing Social Categories through Place: Social Representations and Development in Nepal. *Comparative Studies in Society and History* 34(3): 491–513.

Poovey, Mary. 1988. *Uneven Developments: The Ideological Work of Gender in Mid-Victorian England*. Chicago: University of Chicago Press.

Pridham, B. R. 1986. Oman: Change or Continuity. In *Arabia and the Gulf: From Traditional Society to Modern States*, edited by I. R. Netton. London: Croom Helm.

Rassekh, Shapour. 2004. *Education as a Motor for Development*. Innodata Monographs 15. International Bureau of Education, UNESCO. Geneva: Switzerland.

Reinhard, Kenneth. 1997. Freud, My Neighbor. *American Imago* 54(2): 165–195.

Reinoehl, John H. 1959. Some Remarks on the American Trade: Jacob Crowinshield to James Madison 1806. *William and Mary Quarterly* 16(1): 83–118.

Reynolds, Gabriel Said. 2004. *A Muslim Theologian in a Sectarian Milieu*. Leiden: Brill.

Reynolds, Gabriel Said. 2005. The Rise and Fall of Qadi 'Abd al-Jabbar. *International Journal of Middle East Studies* 37(1): 3–18.

Ricks, T. M. 1988. Slaves and Slave Traders in the Persian Gulf, 18th and 19th Centuries. An Assessment. *Slavery and Abolition* 9(3): 60–70.

al-Riyami, Abdullah bin Muhammad. n.d. *Kitāb Ḥall al-Mushkilāt*. Muscat: Ministry of National Heritage and Culture.

Roald, Anne Sofie. 1994. *Tarbiya: Education and Politics in Islamic Movements in Jordan and Malaysia*. Lund, Sweden: Lunds Universitet.

Robertson, Jennifer. 1997. Empire of Nostalgia: Rethinking "Internationalization" in Japan Today. *Theory, Culture and Society* 14(4): 97–122.

Rodionov, Mikhail. 1999. Irrigation in Western Hadramawt: Khayyil as a Social Role. *Proceedings of the Seminar for Arabian Studies* 29:119–121.

Rofel, Lisa. 1999. *Other Modernities: Gendered Yearnings in China after Socialism*. Berkeley: University of California Press.

Rubinacci, Roberto. 1961. Un Antico Documento di Vita Cenobitica Musulmana. *Annali dell'Istituto Universale Orientale di Napoli* 10:37–78.

Sachau, Eduard. 1894. Muhammedanisches Erbrecht nach der Lehre der Ibaditischen Araber von Zanzibar und Ostafrika. *Sitzungsberichte der Koniglich Preussischen Akademie der Wissenshaften zu Berlin* 8.

al-Sadi, Jumayyil bin Khamis. n.d. *Qāmūs al-Sharī'a*. Muscat: Ministry of National Heritage and Culture.

Salameh, Nadim H. 1999. Customary Water-Rights in Mediaeval Wadi Zabid: Some Legal Cases on al-Adil bi'l-Qana'ah. *Proceedings of the Seminar for Arabian Studies* 29:137–142.

Salil ibn Razik. 1871. *Imams and Seyyids of Oman*. Translated by George Percy Badger. London: Darf Publishers Limited.

al-Salimi, Abdullah bin Humayd. 1989 [n.d.]. *Jawhar al-Niẓām*. Muscat: Ministry of National Heritage and Culture.

al-Salimi, Abdullah bin Humayd. n.d. *Talqīn al-Ṣibīyān*. Muscat.

al-Salimi, Abdullah bin Humayd. n.d. [1927]. *Tuḥfat al-A'yān bi Sīrat Ahl 'Umān*. Muscat: Ministry of National Heritage and Culture.

al-Salimi, Muhammad bin Abdullah. n.d. *Nahḍat al-A'yān bi Ḥurriyat 'Umān*. Cairo.

Sassen, Saskia. 1998. *Globalization and its Discontents*. New York: New Press.

Schacht, Joseph. 1964. *An Introduction to Islamic Law*. Oxford: Clarendon Press.

Schegloff, E. A., and H. Sacks. 1973. Opening up Closings. *Semiotica* 7(4): 289–327.

Scott, David, and Charles Hirschkind. 2006. *Powers of the Secular Modern: Talal Asad and His Interlocutors*. Palo Alto: Stanford University Press.

Scott, Joan. 1988. *Gender and the Politics of History*. New York: Columbia University Press.

Seigel, Jerrold. 2005. *The Idea of the Self: Thought and Experience in Western Europe since the Seventeenth Century*. Cambridge: Cambridge University Press.

Siegfried, Nikolaus A. 2000. Legislation and Legitimation in Oman: The Basic Law. *Islamic Law and Society* 7(2): 359–397.

Seremetakis, C. Nadia. 1994. Implications. In *The Senses Still: Perception and Memory as Material Culture in Modernity*, edited by C. N. Seremetakis. Chicago: University of Chicago Press.

Serjeant, R. B. 1963. *The Portuguese off the South Arabian Coast: Hadrami Chronicles*. Oxford: Oxford University Press.

Serjeant, R. B. 1983. Omani Naval Activities off the Southern Arabian Coast in the 11th/17th Century, from Yemeni Chronicles. *The Journal of Oman Studies* 6:77–90.

Shepherd, Anthony. 1961. *Arabian Adventure*. London: Collins.

Sheriff, Abdul. 1987. *Slaves, Spices and Ivory in Zanzibar*. Dar Es Salaam: Tanzania Publishing House.

Sheriff, Abdul, and Ed Ferguson, eds. 1991. *Zanzibar under Colonial Rule*. London: J. Currey.

El-Shibiny, Mohamed. 1997. Higher Education in Oman: Its Development and Prospects. In *Higher Education in the Gulf: Problems and Prospects*, edited by E. K. Shaw. Exeter, UK: University of Exeter Press.

Shryock, Andrew. 1997. *Nationalism and the Genealogical Imagination: Oral History and Textual Authority in Tribal Jordan*. Berkeley: University of California Press.

Silverman, Eric. 1997. Politics, Gender, and Time in Melanesia and Aboriginal Australia. *Ethnology* 36(2): 101–121.

Singerman, Diane. 1995. *Avenues of Participation: Family, Politics and Networks in Urban Quarters in Cairo*. Princeton: Princeton University Press.

Sirhan bin Saʿid. 1984. *Annals of Oman (Kashf al-Ghumma)*. Translated by E. C. Ross. London: The Oleander Press.

Skeet, Ian. 1992. *Oman: Politics and Development*. London: Macmillan.

Smiley, David. 1975. *Arabian Assignment*. London: Leo Cooper Press.

Smith, Simon C. 2004. *Britain's Revival and Fall in the Gulf: Kuwait, Bahrain, Qatar, and the Trucial States, 1950–1971*. London: RoutledgeCurzon.

Sonnier, A. 1933. *Le Regime Juridique des Eaux Maroc*. Paris: Librairie du Recueil Sirey.

Sowayan, Saad Abdullah. 1985. *Nabati Poetry: The Oral Poetry of Arabia*. Berkeley: University of California Press.

Spratt, Jennifer E., and Daniel A. Wagner. 1986. The Making of a Fqih: The Transformation of Traditional Islamic Teachers in Modern Cultural Adaptation. In *The Cultural*

Transition: Human Experience and Social Transformation in the Third World and Japan, edited by Merry I. White and Susan Pollak. London: Routledge and Kegan Paul.

Starrett, Gregory. 1998. *Putting Islam to Work: Education, Politics, and Religious Transformation in Egypt*. Berkeley: University of California Press.

Steedly, Mary Margaret. 2000. Modernity and the Memory Artist: The Work of Imagination in Highland Sumatra, 1947–1995. *Comparative Studies in Society and History* 42(4): 811–846.

Stewart, Kathleen. 1988. Nostalgia—A Polemic. *Cultural Anthropology* 3(3): 227–441.

Stewart, Susan. 1984. *On Longing: Narratives of the Miniature, the Gigantic, the Souvenir, the Collection*. Durham: Duke University Press.

Stoler, Ann L. 1992. Sexual Affronts and Racial Frontiers: European Identities and the Cultural Politics of Exclusion in Colonial Southeast Asia. *Comparative Studies in Society and History* 34(3): 514–551.

Stoler, Ann Laura, and Karen Strassler. 2000. Castings for the Colonial: Memory Work in 'New Order' Java. *Comparative Studies in Society and History (2000)* 42(1): 4–48.

Strathern, Marilyn. 1988. *The Gender of the Gift*. Berkeley: University of California Press.

Sultanate of Oman. 1992. *Statistical Year Book*. Muscat: Directorate General of National Statistics.

Sultanate of Oman. 1993. *General Census of Population, Housing and Establishments 1993*. Muscat: Ministry of Development.

Sultanate of Oman. 1995a. *The Royal Speeches of H.M. Sultan Qaboos bin Said, 1970–1995*. Muscat: Ministry of Information.

Sultanate of Oman. 1995b. *al-Dirāsāt al-Ijtimāʿiyya Lil-ṣaff al-Thānī al-Ibtidāʾī*. Muscat: Ministry of Education.

Sultanate of Oman. Ministry of Education. 2001 *National Report on the Development of Education in the Sultanate of Oman*. Muscat: Sultanate of Oman.

Taminian, Lucine. 2001. Playing with Words: The Ethnography of Poetic Genres in Yemen. PhD, University of Michigan, Ann Arbor.

Tannen, Deborah. 1989. *Talking Voices: Repetition, Dialogue and Imagery in Conversational Discourse*. Cambridge: Cambridge University Press.

Taylor, Charles. 1989. *Sources of the Self: The Making of Modern Identity*. Cambridge: Harvard University Press.

Taylor, Jean G. 1983. *The Social World of Batavia: European and Eurasian in Dutch Asia*. Madison: University of Wisconsin Press.

al-Thamini, Abd al-Aziz bin Ibrahim. n.d. *Kitāb al-Nīl*. Cairo: Baruni Press.

Thomas, Nicholas. 1991. *Entangled Objects*. Cambridge: Harvard University Press.

Thwaites, Peter. 1995. *Muscat Command*. South Yorks, UK: Leo Cooper Press.

Tonkin, Elizabeth. 1992. *Narrating our Pasts*. Cambridge: Cambridge University Press.

Torab, Azam. 1996. Piety as Gendered Agency: A Study of Jalaseh Ritual Discourse in an Urban Neighborhood in Iran. *The Journal of the Royal Anthropological Institute* 2(2): 235–252.

Townsend, John. 1977. *Oman: The Making of a Modern State*. New York: St. Martin's Press.

Trouillot, Michel-Rolph. 2001. The Anthropology of the State in the Age of Globalization. *Current Anthropology* 42(1): 125–138.

United Nations. 1997. *Irrigation in the Near East Region*. Rome: Food and Agricultural Organization of the United Nations.

United Nations. 1998. *Principles and Recommendations for Population and Housing Censuses*. New York: Department of Economic and Social Affairs, Statistical Division.

US Energy Information Administration. January 2005. Country Analysis Brief for Oman. *www.eia.doe.gov/emeu/cabs/oman.html*.

Van Arendonk, C. 1954. Kahwa. In *Encyclopedia of Islam*. Leiden: Brill.

Varisco, Daniel Martin. 1983. Sayl and Ghayl: The Ecology of Water Allocation in Yemen. *Human Ecology* 11(4): 365–383.

Varisco, Daniel Martin. 1996. Water Sources and Traditional Irrigation in Yemen. *New Arabian Studies* 3:238–257.

Veccia Vaglieri, Laura. 1934. Il Tripolitano Ibadita Suleiman el-Baruni e sue Notizie Sull' 'Oman. *Oriente Moderno* 14:392–6.

Vinogradov, Amal, ed. 1974. Visiting Patterns and Social Dynamics in Eastern Mediterranean Communities. Special issue, *Anthropology Quarterly* 47(1).

vom Bruck, Gabricle. 2005. *Islam, Memory, and Morality in Yemen: Ruling Families in Transition*. New York: Palgrave Macmillan.

von Grunebaum, Gustave. 1955. The Structure of the Muslim Town. In *Islam: Essays in the Nature and Growth of a Cultural Tradition*. Ann Arbor: American Anthropological Association.

Wagner, Daniel A. 1982. Quranic Pedagogy in Modern Morocco. In *Cross-Cultural Research at Issue*, edited by L. L. Adler. New York: Academic Press.

Wagner, Daniel A., and Abdelhamid Lotfi. 1980. Traditional Islamic Education in Morocco: Sociohistorical and Psychological Perspectives. *Comparative Education Review* 24(2): 238–251.

Ward, Philip. 1987. *Travels in Oman*. London: Oleander Press.

Warjalani, Yahya ibn Abi Bakr. 1878. *Chronique d'Abou Zakaria*. Translated by Émile Masqueray. Algiers.

Weber, Max. 1946. The Protestant Sects and the Spirit of Capitalism. In *From Max Weber: Essays in Sociology*. New York: Oxford University Press.

Weber, Max. 1958. *The Protestant Ethic and the Spirit of Capitalism*. New York: Charles Scriber's Sons.

Wedeen, Lisa. 1999. *Ambiguities of Domination: Politics, Rhetoric, and Symbols in Contemporary Syria*. Chicago: University of Chicago Press.

Weiner, Annette B. 1992. *Inalienable Possessions: The Paradox of Keeping-While-Giving*. Berkeley: University of California Press.

Weiss, Bernard G. 1998. *The Spirit of Islamic Law*. Athens, GA: University of Georgia Press.

Werner, Cynthia. 1998. Household Networks and the Security of Mutual Indebtedness in Rural Kazakstan. *Central Asian Survey* 17(4): 597–612.

Wheatley, Paul. 2000. *The Places Where Men Pray Together: Cities in Islamic Lands, Seventh through the Tenth Centuries*. Chicago: University of Chicago Press.

White, Hayden. 1973. *Metahistory: The Historical Imagination in Nineteenth-Century Europe*. Baltimore: Johns Hopkins University Press.

White, Jenny B. 2002. *Islamist Mobilization in Turkey: A Study in Vernacular Politics*. Seattle: University of Washington Press.

Wikan, Unni. 1982. *Behind the Veil in Arabia: Women in Oman*. Chicago: University of Chicago Press.

Wilkinson, John C. 1974. Bayasirah and Bayadir. *Arabian Studies* 1:75–85.

Wilkinson, John C. 1977. *Water and Tribal Settlement in South-East Arabia*. Oxford: Clarendon Press.

Wilkinson, John C. 1978. Islamic Water Law with Special Reference to Oasis Settlement. *Journal of Arid Environments* 1:87–96.

Wilkinson, John C. 1980. Changes in the Structure of Village Life in Oman. In *Social and Economic Development in the Arab Gulf*, edited by T. Niblock. London: Croom Helm.

Wilkinson, John C. 1982. The Early Development of the Ibadi Movement in Basra. In *Studies on the First Century of Islamic Society*, edited by G. H. A. Juynboll. Carbondale: Southern Illinois University Press.

Wilkinson, John C. 1983. The Origins of the Aflaj of Oman. *Journal of Oman Studies* 6:177–194.

Wilkinson, John C. 1985. Ibadi Hadith: An Essay on Normalization. *Der Islam* 62(2): 231–259.

Wilkinson, John C. 1987. *The Imamate Tradition of Oman*. Cambridge: Cambridge University Press.

Wilkinson, John C. 1990. Muslim Land and Water Law. *Journal of Islamic Studies* 1:54–72.

Williams, Raymond. 1977. *Marxism and Literature*. Oxford: Oxford University Press.

Winegar, Jessica. 2006. *Creative Reckonings: The Politics of Art and Culture in Contemporary Egypt*. Palo Alto: Stanford University Press.

Wittfogel, Karl August. 1957. *Oriental Despotism: A Comparative Study of Total Power*. New Haven: Yale University Press.

Woolard, Kathryn. 1992. Language Ideology: Issues and Approaches. *Pragmatics* 2(3): 235–249.

Yngvesson, Barbara. 1993. *Disruptive Citizens: Order and Complaint in a New England Court*. New York: Routledge.

Young, Iris M. 2000. House and Home: Feminist Variations on a Theme. In *Resistance, Flight, Creation: Feminist Enactments of French Philosophy*, edited by D. Olkowski. Ithaca: Cornell University Press.

Young, Robert. 1995. *Colonial Desire: Hybridity in Theory, Culture and Race*. New York: Routledge.

al-Yousef, Mohamed bin Musa. 1995. *Oil and the Transformation of Oman*. London: Stacey International.

Zimmermann, Wolfgang. 1989. Transformation of Rural Employment Structures—The Example of the Sultanate of Oman, South-East Arabia. *Applied Geography and Development* 33:7–26.

Index